MOTIVATED COGNITION IN RELATIONSHIPS

How can newlyweds believe they will be together forever, while knowing that the majority of marriages end in divorce? Why do people who desperately want to be loved end up alienating those who love them? How can partners that seem like complete opposites end up blissfully happy? This volume explores such fascinating questions. Murray and Holmes outline how basic motivations to be safe from being hurt and find value and meaning control how people feel, think, and behave in close relationships. Additionally, the authors highlight how these motivations infuse romantic life through succinct and accessible descriptions of cutting-edge empirical research and vivid evolving stories of four couples confronting different challenges in their relationship. Integrating ideas from the interdependence, goals, and embodiment literatures, this book puts a provocative new spin on seminal findings from two decades of collaborative research.

The book:

- provides a new, interdependence-based, perspective on motivated cognition in close relationships;
- advances a dyadic perspective that explores how motivation shapes perception and cognition in ways that result in motivation-consistent behavior;
- examines how "goal-driven" cognition translates a person's wishes, desires, and preferences into judgment and behavior, and ultimately, his or her romantic partner's relationship reality;
- offers a refreshing argument that the ultimate effects of motivated cognition on satisfaction and stability depend on whether the motivations which most frequently guide perception and cognition match the reality constraints imposed by the perceiver, the partner, and the characteristics of the relationship.

This book is essential for social and personality psychologists and will also be valuable to clinical psychologists and clinicians who work directly with couples to effect happier and more stable relationships. Advanced undergraduate and graduate students will find it a highly engaging compendium for understanding how motivation shapes affect, cognition, and behavior in close relationships.

MOTIVATED COGNITION IN RELATIONSHIPS

The Pursuit of Belonging

Sandra L. Murray
John G. Holmes

NEW YORK AND LONDON

First published 2017
by Routledge
711 Third Avenue, New York, NY 10017

and by Routledge
2 Park Square, Milton Park, Abingdon, Oxon, OX14 4RN

Routledge is an imprint of the Taylor & Francis Group, an informa business

© 2017 Taylor & Francis

The right of Sandra L. Murray and John G. Holmes to be identified as the authors of this work has been asserted by them in accordance with sections 77 and 78 of the Copyright, Designs and Patents Act 1988.

All rights reserved. No part of this book may be reprinted or reproduced or utilized in any form or by any electronic, mechanical, or other means, now known or hereafter invented, including photocopying and recording, or in any information storage or retrieval system, without permission in writing from the publishers.

Trademark notice: Product or corporate names may be trademarks or registered trademarks, and are used only for identification and explanation without intent to infringe.

Library of Congress Cataloging in Publication Data
A catalog record for this book has been requested

ISBN: 978-1-84871-519-6 (hbk)
ISBN: 978-1-84872-520-1 (pbk)
ISBN: 978-1-315-22548-7 (ebk)

Typeset in Bembo
by Swales & Willis, Exeter, Devon, UK

We dedicate this book to Colin, Derek, and Lynda.

CONTENTS

Acknowledgments viii
About the Authors ix

1 Introducing Motivated Cognition 1
2 Embodying Safety and Value Goals 16
3 Pursuing Safety 35
4 Pursuing Value 62
5 Why Safety Overrides Value 85
6 When Value Overrides Safety 107
7 Reality Constraints 124
8 Looking Forward 135

References 151
Author Index 171
Subject Index 173

ACKNOWLEDGMENTS

We are tremendously grateful to the many students and research colleagues who enriched the research we describe in this book. Their names populate the pages that follow. We also owe a special debt to Ziva Kunda, whose theorizing defined our thinking about motivated cognition. Memories of her as a mentor, colleague, and friend continue to inspire us today. We are also grateful to Monica Biernat for her astute editorial counsel. A National Science Foundation awarded to S. L. Murray (BCS-1143747) supported the preparation of this book.

ABOUT THE AUTHORS

Sandra L. Murray is a Professor of Psychology at the University at Buffalo, the State University of New York. Her research examines the automatic and controlled processes involved in the regulation of self-esteem, trust, and commitment in relationships. Her scholarship has received multiple awards, including Mid-Career Distinguished Contribution Awards from the International Association of Relationships Research (2016) and the Society of Experimental Social Psychology (2012), Early Career Distinguished Contribution Awards from the American Psychological Association (2003) and the International Society of Self and Identity (2001), and Best New Contribution Awards from the Society of Personality and Social Psychology (2007) and the International Society for the Study of Personal Relationships (1998, 2000). Her research has been supported by grants from the National Institute of Mental Health and the National Science Foundation. She has held Associate Editor positions at *Personality and Social Psychology Review, Journal of Personality and Social Psychology*, and *Journal of Experimental Social Psychology*.

John G. Holmes is a Professor of Psychology at the University of Waterloo, Ontario, Canada. His research focuses on the cognitive and motivational processes involved in perceiving another's motives. His teaching and scholarship have received multiple awards, including the Distinguished Career Award (2016) and Distinguished Mentoring Award (2004) from the International Association of Relationships Research, Best New Contribution Awards from the Society of Personality and Social Psychology (2007) and the International Society for the Study of Personal Relationships (1992, 1998, 2000), a commemorative page on the Heritage Wall of Fame (2014), and a University Research Chair from his home institution (2004–2012). His research has been supported by grants from the Social Sciences and Humanities Research Council of Canada and he served as an Associate Editor at *Journal of Personality and Social Psychology*.

1
INTRODUCING MOTIVATED COGNITION

Love is a canvas furnished by Nature and embroidered by imagination.
                                                                    Voltaire

There is always some madness in love. But there is also always some reason in madness.
                            Friedrich Nietzsche, "On Reading and Writing"

Love is not blind – it sees more, not less. But because it sees more, it is willing to see less.
                                                        Rabbi Julius Gordon

Love is an irresistible desire to be irresistibly desired.
                                                            Robert Frost

Nothing takes the taste out of peanut butter quite like unrequited love.
                                Charles M. Schulz, Charlie Brown in "Peanuts"

Social philosophers have long taken pen to paper to try to capture the essence of romantic love. Even the most haphazard samplings of their musings reveal the shared belief that love involves more than meets the eye. Falling in and out of love is thought to be transformative – turning what meets the eye into something that pleases or displeases the eye or even the taste buds (as in the case of the crestfallen Charlie Brown).

This process of transformation is the topic of this book. The idea that love transforms perception, cognition, and behavior is no stranger to anyone who has ever been in love or to anyone who has ever given advice to anyone who has ever been in love. It is certainly no stranger to social psychologists. Scholars of motivated cognition now take it as a given that personal wishes, desires, and preferences color the inferences people make about the social world (Balcetis & Dunning, 2010; Kunda, 1990).

What happens if we take the deceptively simple assumption that motivation biases social inference and apply it to romantic relationships? What would it buy us? Could it help explain why speed-daters forgo the very suitors who possess the qualities they say they want (Finkel & Eastwick, 2008)? Could it reveal how people come to believe that someone who is nothing like them is a perfect match to their personality (Lykken & Tellegen, 1993)? Might it help us understand how newlyweds' unconscious attitude toward one another can better forecast their marital fate than their conscious attitudes (McNulty, Olson, Meltzer, & Shaffer, 2013)? Could it explain why people with low self-esteem are happier in their relationships when they lose control over their thoughts (Murray, Derrick, Leder, & Holmes, 2008)? And might it also reveal why so many couples end up questioning why they ever got married in the first place, while others can be married 50 years and still be as happy together as they were when they first dated?

More than 20 years of studying adult close relationships as a collaborative team has convinced us that the answer to these questions is a resounding yes. We offer this book in the hope of explaining exactly how motivation infuses thought and behavior in romantic life. We do so with applied and conceptual objectives in mind.

On the applied side, we hope to dispel the popularized idea that happiness would reign in relationships if people were simply realistic and knew what they were getting in a partner. As perusing the self-help section in any bookstore reveals, there is no shortage of expert opinion attributing relationship fragility to partners' failure to accurately understand one another. This book will reveal why such unadulterated perceptions of reality are not all that likely and probably not even all that advisable.

On the conceptual side, we plan to identify a short-list of basic motivations that color how romantic partners think and control how they behave. Although our list might ultimately prove to be too short (or too long), we are happy to risk being proven wrong. By boiling romantic life down to its motivational essentials, we hope to integrate what we know about perception and behavior in relationships in ways that can clarify and enhance relationship science. Of course, no simple short-list is likely to be sufficient to explain how motivation infuses romantic life. Relationships involve two people interacting across different situations (e.g., grocery shopping, budgeting, sex, childcare, social support, self-disclosure). Given this interdependent reality, we cannot simply describe how the short-listed motivations shape *one* partner's thoughts and behaviors. We also need to consider how these motivations compete and change from one situation to the next and from one partner to the other. This book advances such an *interactionist* or *situated* perspective on how motivation infuses romantic life. By paying close attention to features of the situation and characteristics of the partner, we hope to reveal which of the perceiver's motivations *should* win the battle for control over thought and behavior, and whether they prevail or not.

In so doing, we hope to reveal the power of the motivational forces that bind and also break partners apart.

So where do we begin? In this chapter, we first introduce four hypothetical heterosexual couples, each of whom will help bring the theory and research we detail to life: Katy and Todd, Sylvia and Brian, Arya and Aaron, and Skyler and Walt. Next, we review the classic perspectives on motivated cognition that served as our starting point in developing an interactionist or situated perspective on motivated cognition in relationships. We conclude this chapter by introducing the four major themes that serve as the intellectual pillars for this book. We introduce these themes largely through examples and build their theoretical and empirical supports in subsequent chapters.

The Couples

No two relationships are exactly alike. Nonetheless, couples are more alike than different in one important respect. Each phase of a relationship's life cycle (e.g., first meeting, committing, becoming parents) poses similar adaptive dilemmas even if the details differ from one couple to the next. For instance, people who are about to meet a new romantic interest share a common problem – gauging this person's reciprocal interest in them. Discerning romantic interest will likely be easier for someone meeting a gregarious partner than someone meeting a reticent one, but the underlying problem that needs to be solved is the same. Couples who set up a shared household together also share a common challenge – adjusting to a precipitous increase in tedious responsibilities. Sustaining commitment in the face of chores and bills will be easier for couples with compatible preferences than incompatible ones, but again, the underlying problem to be solved is still the same. We created the couples that populate the pages of this book to highlight the common adaptive problems developing relationships create. In so doing, we hope to bring to life our contention that motivation infuses romantic life specifically to provide solutions for these problems.

Katy and Todd

Katy, a recent college graduate, has suffered more than her share of awkward first and last dates. Hearing her best friend gush about the "perfect" man she met on Tinder inspired Katy to give it a try. That's how she met Todd. Her first time on Tinder, she quickly dismissed dozens of possibilities before his photo and profile caught her eye. When they first met for coffee, she was drawn to him pretty immediately. The three-month anniversary of the first time they met for coffee is fast approaching and Katy wants to ask Todd to go away for the weekend with her. She was all set to ask him, but the last time they got together, Todd didn't seem like himself. Now she isn't sure what to do. She knows what she wants to do, but she's not sure it's wise.

Sylvia and Brian

Sylvia and Brian met because they were both taking the same electives during their first year of college. They have been dating for four years and recently decided to get engaged. Since graduation, they both found jobs and met new friends. Their relationship has had its growing pains as a result. They even considered breaking up once. Their differences are more salient to them now. Brian is an avid athlete and an adventurous spirit and his new friends tell him that Sylvia is too bookish and conventional for him. Sylvia's friends think that Brian has a few too many friends, especially female ones, and they tell Sylvia she should be more jealous. Despite these vocal naysayers, Brian and Sylvia are convinced they are meant to be together.

Arya and Aaron

Aaron finally persuaded Arya to marry him two years ago. She took a lot of convincing. Arya had always valued her independence and the idea of counting on Aaron to be there for her made her more than a little nervous. She had always had trouble trusting him, even though she did love him, and she just felt safer holding back. Their first year of marriage turned out much better than she had expected. Adjusting to life with Aaron certainly had its challenges. She was used to being in control of her own finances and now she had to explain her spending to Aaron. He also had to better mesh his tendency to be a night owl with her inclination to be an early bird. Even though she still caught herself wondering if she really deserved Aaron, she gradually discovered that Aaron really did seem to need her and she liked taking care of him, even if it was something as simple as making his lunch or picking out a book he'd like. Commitment did not seem as frightening to her now, much to her surprise.

Skyler and Walt

Skyler and Walt have been married for nearly a decade and they are beginning to wonder if they will make it through the next year, let alone the next 10 years. When they first got married, they were surprised by how compatible they were. They liked (a lot of) sex, agreed on finances, and enjoyed being out with friends as much as they enjoyed being home together. Walt's occasional brashness was the only thing that ever gave Skyler pause. He liked people to get to the point quickly in conversation and he pushed Skyler to be more forthright and concise. Because he always listened to her in the end, Skyler had no trouble seeing Walt's brashness as the downside of the intensity and passion she adored. But this changed after they had their first baby. Now his brashness makes Skyler feel unappreciated and dismissed. The financial stresses they experienced when she stayed home with Walt only made it even harder for her to see the best in Walt, even though she still wanted to see the best in him.[1]

What Is Motivated Cognition?

Scholars of motivated cognition assume that motivation biases attention, memory, and inference for a straightforward reason. People have needs and wants that must be fulfilled if they are to survive and be happy, healthy, and wise (Balcetis & Lassiter, 2010; Bruner & Goodman, 1947; Bruner & Postman, 1947; Maner et al., 2005). Someone who is thirsty needs to drink, someone who is cold needs shelter, someone who is lonely needs accepting friends, and someone who just married does *not* need to believe that she chose the wrong person and that the odds are better than even that she will one day divorce. The very fact that once-, twice-, and even thrice-divorced people marry again speaks to the power of the desire for optimism to triumph over experience in this regard.

Because people have needs and wants that must be met, it makes functional sense to perceive the world in ways that highlight opportunities for satiating those needs (Balcetis & Lassiter, 2010; Dunning & Balcetis, 2013; Radel & Clement-Guillotin, 2012). Someone who is thirsty should notice a water fountain, someone who is cold should spy an open window, and someone who is lonely should catch the first glimmer of a potential friend's smile. Visual perceptions of the environment are indeed powerfully biased by motivation. Balcetis and Dunning (2006) made this point in a series of elegant experiments. In one of these experiments, they first created the wish or motivation to obtain a specific, desirable outcome and avoid an undesirable one. They told participants they would be consuming a delicious, highly palatable glass of freshly squeezed orange juice or a green, sludge-like vegetable concoction. Next they learned that a computer would decide their culinary fate. Half of the participants learned that they would consume the delectable orange juice if a letter appeared on the screen and the vegetable sludge if a number appeared. The other half learned they would consume the delectable orange juice if a number appeared and the vegetable sludge if a letter appeared. Participants then saw a short flash of an ambiguous image that could be either the letter B or the number 13. The researchers then asked participants what they saw. Participants "saw" the image that afforded the outcome they desired. They saw a "B" when letters led to the coveted orange juice and they instead saw a "13" when numbers led to it.

A follow-up to this study revealed that motivation not only biases what people see, but motivation even biases *when* people see. When words are presented just below the threshold for conscious awareness, hungry people accurately identify food-related words that could satisfy their cravings (e.g., cake), though they cannot identify neutral words (that could do nothing to satisfy their hunger). Sated people are just as blind to these food-related words as they are to neutral words (Radel & Clement-Guillotin, 2012).

Motivation can also bias visual perception when the physical feature of the world to be judged is much less ambiguous. In another set of creative studies, Balcetis and Dunning (2007) activated the wish or motivation to protect one's self-image as a good person who makes sensible decisions for sound reasons. For most college students, choosing to traipse across the campus quad dressed in a grass skirt, coconut bra, and fruit-adorned hat challenges such a self-perception. So does volunteering to kneel on a skateboard and push oneself up a muddy hill. Balcetis and Dunning reasoned that people who freely committed themselves to such courses of action could satisfy the motivation to see themselves as good and sensible if they perceived the physical distance across the quad to be short and the slope of the hill to be gradual. That is exactly what they found. People who freely committed to traversing the quad while dressed outrageously saw a shorter physical distance from start to end point than people who had no choice in the matter. Similarly, people who freely committed to pushing the skateboard through the mud perceived a less steep hill than people who had no choice in the matter.

The Classic Conceptualization

In a now classic paper, Kunda (1990) made the case that motivation also has the power to bias higher-order categorization, inference, and evaluation processes. She defined motivation as a "wish, desire, or preference" concerning the outcome of a given reasoning task (p. 480). For instance, our newlywed Arya who wants to believe that she really did marry the "right" person in the end is motivated to see her new husband Aaron's behavior in ways that support this conclusion. Consequently, when he forgets her birthday, she is likely to evaluate this lapse with a particular conclusion already in mind. She wants to see it as inconsequential. However, she cannot just declare it inconsequential because she needs to believe that her husband prioritizes her needs. According to Kunda (1990), Arya needs to come up with a good and compelling reason to believe that this lapse truly is inconsequential. Attributing Aaron's forgetting her birthday to his lack of sleep during a busy week at work would serve just such a purpose.

This forgiving attribution probably seems perfectly logical, but it captures a motivated inference nonetheless. In grasping on to Aaron's fatigue as the explanation for his lapse in memory, Arya conveniently failed to notice that he did manage to remember all of his social engagements with friends on the days surrounding her birthday. Wanting to think the best of Aaron zeroed her attention on the exculpatory evidence (Voss, Ruthermond, & Brandtstädter, 2008). As this example illustrates, people have great flexibility to believe what they want because the desire to reach a particular conclusion biases which pieces of evidence capture attention, surface in memory, and appear credible to discerning eyes (Helzer & Dunning, 2012; Kunda, 1987, 1990). Consequently, people can think they are being objective because they do not realize how their wishes, desires, or preferences have already filtered which aspects of the social world they even notice or remember (Griffin & Ross, 1991).

For instance, people who have been led to believe that extraverts hold the secret to academic success are faster to access memories of themselves being the life of the party than people who have been led to believe that introverts hold the secret to academic success (Kunda & Sanitioso, 1989). People also seem to have no trouble maintaining the desired belief that they are smarter than average, or more cultured than average, or better drivers than average because they define the self-concept they desire in ways that suit their own idiosyncratic aptitudes (Dunning, Meyerowitz, & Holzberg, 1989). For instance, someone who excels in language arts, yet struggles mightily in math, is likely to regard writing skill as the marker of intelligence. Similarly, people can maintain the optimistic belief that they will stay fit and healthy in the future by impugning any suggestion that a steady diet of Doritos puts them at risk (Ditto & Lopez, 1992).

A Relationship Conceptualization

The research highlighted thus far illustrates how motivation can bias perceptions of the social world in ways that fulfill ego- or self-centered motivations. Thirst brings objects symbolizing water into focal attention (Balcetis & Ferguson, 2009) and wanting to be a good person makes embarrassing walks seem short (Balcetis & Dunning, 2007) and can even change how people define what it means to be kind, funny, or wise (Dunning et al., 1989). These fascinating phenomena are not our focus. Instead, we target the *other-oriented* motivations that must be fulfilled to sustain satisfying and stable romantic bonds. Shifting focus from the individual to the relationship necessitates making three further shifts in the conceptualization of motivation and how it operates.

First, Kunda (1990) defined motivation as a "wish, desire, or preference" concerning the outcome of a given reasoning task. We instead use the term motivation to refer to a specific *goal* on our short-list. Like a wish, desire, or preference, goals are cognitive representations of desired end states, such as a goal to be loved, successful, thin, rich, healthy, sexually satisfied, erudite, pampered, respected, or feared (Fishbach & Ferguson, 2007). Unlike a wish, desire, or preference that could be fleeting, goals are thought to monopolize attention, inference, and behavior until they are fulfilled (Fishbach & Ferguson, 2007; Huang & Bargh, 2014). As we proceed, we conceptualize our short-listed motivations as goals because these motivations have the monopolizing power of goals: They must be fulfilled for relationships to form and endure over the longer term.

Second, Kunda (1990) focused on wishes, desires, and preferences that people could probably consciously articulate if pressed. Her theorizing tacitly recognized that perceivers often choose what they want to believe or what they want to do. As an example, parents who refuse to vaccinate their children likely know they are on the lookout for "evidence" supporting their position. We instead assume that the goals on our short-list infuse romantic life in ways that are often automatic and unknown. Consequently, people can end up thinking thoughts and enacting behaviors that they did not realize they desired because subtle features of the situation primed goals without a perceiver's knowledge or intent (Bargh,

Gollwitzer, & Oettingen, 2010; Bargh, Schwader, Hailey, Dyer, & Boothby, 2012; Baumeister & Bargh, 2014). For instance, unconsciously activated goals can actually realign friendship bonds. Fitzsimons and Shah (2008) asked participants to nominate friends who helped them achieve their academic (or social or fitness) goals and friends who were no help in achieving each of these goals. Then they unconsciously primed the goal to achieve by asking experimental participants to form correct sentences from scrambled sentences containing achievement-related words. All participants then rated how close they felt to each friend. Participants unconsciously primed with the goal to achieve felt closer to friends who helped them achieve academic pursuits than friends who were no such help. No bias emerged for participants *not* primed with the goal to achieve.

Third, Kunda (1990) also imposed reality constraints on motivated cognition: People can only believe what they want *if* they can construct a rationale that would persuade a dispassionate observer. Think of our newlywed Arya. She has a number of psychological tools at her disposal to help her believe that Aaron really is the right person for her. For instance, she could come up with sensible excuses for his occasional lapses and transgressions that she could imagine might persuade her mother and friends (e.g., he was just distracted, I should have expressed myself more clearly). While we also believe that reality constrains the way in which motivation infuses romantic life, the interpersonal realities we target are much more limiting than the realities Kunda (1990) described. In a relationship, situations and partners play a major role in constraining what is reasonable to believe, essentially tying the perceiver's hands. Whether Arya's excuses can keep up with Aaron's antics depends on Aaron's response to having his transgression overlooked. If he takes her forgiveness as license to transgress again (McNulty, 2010a), such excuses are going to quickly lose any sense of reasonableness to Arya. Protecting her belief that Aaron really is the right person for her will then require an entirely different set of tactics. As we proceed, we assume that the way in which people fulfill our short-listed motivations can and should be responsive to the situation and partner's reality.

Our Central Themes

Understanding how motivation infuses romantic life might seem like an unsolvable problem. More than one skeptical politician has certainly argued that love is better left to poets and mystics. Nonetheless, we maintain that relationships can be readily understood by breaking them down into their most basic elements – namely, the situations partners face (Kelley & Thibaut, 1978; Thibaut & Kelley, 1959).

Katy is currently facing an especially delicate situation in her relationship with Todd. She wants to ask him to go away with her for the weekend to meet her parents, but she is not sure whether he really likes her enough to agree. Sylvia and Brian are facing newly challenging situations now that they are engaged and planning a wedding. They have less time for friends than they once did and Brian is getting more frustrated with Sylva's bookishness as a result. He wants her to go out rafting, biking, and hiking with him and she would rather stay put at home and read. This past weekend they had a pretty serious argument about it. For the first time, Arya and Aaron are finding it easier to rely on each other than it used to be. Arya is starting to believe that Aaron will be there when she needs him and she has started going to him whenever she needs support. Just the other day, Aaron gave her some advice that helped her solve a problem she was having at work. The only parents in the bunch, Skyler and Walt encounter a different set of situations. Skyler wants Walt to step up to the plate and take his son to soccer and they are trying to negotiate how they will manage financially if Walt cuts back on work.

The situations couples encounter in relationships vary along three dimensions: Content, interdependence, and compatibility (Kelley, 1979). Situations vary in *content* because partners do different things together. Partners interact across situations that involve allocating practical life tasks, like soccer practice and bills; situations that involve the expression of individual personalities, like Brian trying to mesh his preference for adventurous sports with Sylvia's need for calm; and situations that can meet or frustrate hopes for the relationship, such as Arya's increasing reliance on Aaron as her primary social support. Situations vary in *degree and mutuality of influence* because partners can have more or less control over one another's outcomes. Now that Sylvia and Brian are spending less time with their friends, Brian is more dependent on Sylvia's willingness to participate in weekend sports to feel like his most adventurous self. Situations vary in *compatibility* because partner interests and preferences can be more or less compatible. Skyler and Walt are having particular difficulty right now because Skyler has decided she wants Walt at home with his family more and Walt wants to focus on his career.

The Short-List: Safety and Value

Because relationships are lived through situations, the joys and frustrations partners experience interacting have tremendous adaptive significance (Kelley, 1979). These joys and frustrations control whether relationships are likely to satiate or frustrate the need to belong. Baumeister and Leary (1995) characterize the need to belong as a fundamental biological and psychological motivation to establish temporally persistent and consistently caring and responsive relationships with others. They maintain that people cannot be happy, healthy, wise, or even long-lived without establishing ties to others who persistently and consistently demonstrate their caring for them.

In adulthood, romantic relationships become especially important for fulfilling belongingness needs. Biologically, romantic partners need to stay together to secure the survival of offspring through early childhood (Hazan & Diamond, 2000). Culturally, they are supposed to be there for one another through thick and thin (Finkel, Cheong, Emery, Carswell, & Larson, 2015). Given these pressures, romantic partners limit time with other friends and family (Kalmijn, 2003; Milardo, 1982) and they become increasingly dependent on one another for a sense of belongingness (Finkel et al., 2015). Narrowing the social world in this way would be all well and good if romantic partners were unfailingly caring and responsive to one another's needs. The problem is that little about interdependent life makes it easy to be *consistently* caring and responsive (Kelley, 1979). As the situations our couples are facing illustrate, there are simply too many temptations to be selfish and too many temptations to stray. For romantic relationships to fulfill the need to belong, partners need considerable help behaving responsively – motivational bolstering, if you will (Murray & Holmes, 2011).

The goals on our short-list make it more automatic for romantic partners to be responsive, and thus, satisfy their fundamental need to experience a close and meaningful attachment to another person. Think about what needs to happen for Brian to get his weekend sports and adventure fix now that he and Sylvia are spending more time together. He has to gauge how much he can safely ask of Sylvia and she has to be willing to put down her books and join him in the activity he suggests. For weekend interactions to be fun-filled rather than conflict-ridden, Brian needs to coordinate his behavior with Sylvia's anticipated behavior (and vice versa). Concretely, Brian needs to be willing to ask Sylvia for what she is willing to provide. If Brian could read Sylvia's mind, it would be easy for him to know how much of a risk he'd be taking in asking her to spend the weekend on a white-water rafting trip, as he desires. But partners do not have direct access to the contents of one another's minds. Like everyone who has ever been in a relationship, Brian is all too often uncertain exactly what Sylvia will do. If Sylvia had no interest in life other than making Brian happy, it would also be straightforward for her to do whatever Brian wanted. Like everyone else, Sylvia has her own interests and desires independent of Brian. And they often tempt her to do the opposite of what Brian wants.

This example illustrates the crux of the adaptive problem people face in relationships. Like Brian and Sylvia, couples routinely face many situations where they do not want the same thing (or fear they might not want the same things, as in the case of Katy's worries about Todd). For ongoing interactions to be rewarding despite such differences, each partner needs to transform the reality of the situations they encounter in ways that makes responsiveness more natural for both. The motivations on our short-list do exactly that. Our perspective is a functionalist one akin to the approaches often taken by attachment and evolutionary theorists. The reality of relationships creates adaptive problems that motivation-infused attention, inference, and behavior can solve.

Two-plus decades of research convinced us that two core goals (aka motivations) monopolize attention, inference, and behavior in relationships. The short-listed goals are (drum roll, please): (1) The goal to be *safe* and protected from being let down and hurt by the partner and (2) the goal to see *value*, purpose, and meaning in nurturing and caring for the partner and relationship. For Brian to get the most out of his weekends with Sylvia, he needs to be safe from being hurt when he depends on her. In turn, Sylvia needs to value Brian enough to think he is worth putting aside the books she would rather read to tend to his desire for a more adventurous activity. In relationship terms, Brian needs to *trust* that Sylvia will not hurt him if he puts his welfare in her hands (Holmes & Rempel, 1989) and Sylvia needs to be *committed* enough to Brian to put meeting his needs above her own when he puts his welfare in her hands (Rusbult & Van Lange, 2003).

We explain why the goals for safety and value constitute our short-list in Chapters 2 through 4. Chapter 2 draws on research from the attachment (Mikulincer & Shaver, 2003), embodiment (Meier, Schnall, Schwarz, & Bargh, 2012), evolutionary (Kenrick, Neuberg, & White, 2013; Maner & Ackerman, 2013), and interdependence literatures (Arriaga, 2013; Rusbult & Van Lange, 2003) to argue that people are biologically and psychologically prepared to satisfy basic goals for safety and value.

Chapters 3 and 4 explore how the core goals to (1) be safe from harm and (2) perceive value and purpose in caring for the partner and relationship monopolize attention, perception, and behavior. In describing these dynamics, we explore one of the more paradoxical aspects of motivated cognition in relationships. The pursuit of safety and value does not always result in more positive relationship sentiments. Consider safety. On first reflection, it might seem people could simply satisfy the goal to be safe by exaggerating reasons to trust in their partner's caring. Pursuing safety can indeed involve becoming more trusting, as we will see. However, that is not always the case. Given Brian's taste for the extreme and Sylvia's risk aversion, Brian can better satisfy his goal to be safe by judiciously measuring and limiting his trust in Sylvia. At least when it comes to weekend activities, he's safer trusting and depending on her *less*. Even though Brian really wants to white-water raft, he better protects against the possibility of Sylvia's rejection by asking her to go for a more placid canoe trip because such smaller sacrifices demand less of her commitment. Subsequent chapters expand on such themes by examining how the situational context controls which particular goals are activated and how they are best pursued. In particular, these chapters describe how activated goals and means of goal pursuit vary as a function of the situation, partner, and perceiver.

Automaticity and Control

Imagine we asked Skyler to explain her behavior during her last, especially heated, discussion with Walt about soccer practice. She would probably focus on her conscious thoughts (e.g., "I thought he was being selfish and stubborn"). She likely wouldn't entertain the idea that thoughts and feelings she could *not* readily articulate had also guided her behavior. However, such a supposition on her part would be naïve. A longitudinal study of marriage conducted by McNulty and colleagues (2013) makes this point compellingly. They asked newly married couples to rate their relationship on evaluative dimensions (e.g., good versus bad). These ratings constituted a measure of self-report or conscious attitudes. Then, they had couples complete an association-based measure of unconscious attitudes. Each person sat in front of a computer screen and rated the valence of the words that appeared. On some trials, a picture of the partner flashed before the target word. If Skyler's unconscious attitude toward Walt is positive, his picture should activate positive affective associations, which should, in turn, make her faster to identify positive words and slower to identify negative words. The researchers tracked the marital satisfaction of these couples over a period of four years to see whether conscious or unconscious attitudes better predicted the fate of each marriage.

What people initially said on the self-report measure of attitudes had no bearing on later satisfaction. People who reported evaluating their marriage more *positively* were just as likely to be *un*happy later as people who initially reported more negative explicit attitudes. It was what people could *not* initially say that sealed marital fates. People who experienced more positive affective associations to a simple flash of their partner's photographs were happier after four years of marriage than people who experienced more negative associations. How could people have so little conscious insight into whether or not they really were in a relationship that could ultimately make them happy?

We spend much of the forthcoming chapters detailing exactly how thoughts and feelings people cannot readily articulate can nevertheless control the relationship's fate. In so doing, we borrow a metaphor Baumeister and Bargh (2014) used to describe goal-directed behavior. Unconscious processes typically drive the car (setting it in motion, shaping its speed and direction); conscious processes can step in to advise if there is a question whether an upcoming turn is the correct one to take. Consciousness thus functions as a navigational system, righting the course of action set by the unconscious if it needs to be righted. To translate the car metaphor into a relationship one, unconscious or automatic processes largely regulate interaction (directing attention, shaping the inferences drawn, and controlling the urgency and direction of behavior). Conscious or controlled processes can step in to advise on an as-needed basis whenever Skyler questions whether she (or Walt) has just gone off track. Once the path is reset, unconscious or automatic processes then take over to again guide interaction until the next bump or turn in the road (Baumeister & Bargh, 2014; Baumeister & Masicampo, 2010).

We argue that the core goals to feel safe and see value and meaning automatically drive attention, inference, and behavior in predictable ways (Murray & Holmes, 2009). However, consciousness may not always communicate the products of such automatic processes faithfully. As we will see, conscious representations of safety in feelings of trust and perceptions of partner value in feelings of commitment often belie their unconscious counterparts (Murray et al., 2011). Arya and Skyler present contrasting case studies on this point. Arya always had trouble convincing herself that the men she dated really could be trusted and Aaron was no exception. Despite the fact that she still finds herself wondering how much he *really* loves her, she learned to trust him nonetheless because she implicitly associates him with good experiences (Murray, Holmes, & Pinkus, 2010). Skyler, on the other hand, discounted her early unease about Walt's jealousy and decided she had to trust him nonetheless. Now she is wondering how she could have ever overlooked what he did.

Motivational Tension

Although positing two core goals might simplify romantic life to the extreme, satisfying both of these goals complicates it considerably. All too many situations put the goal to feel safe and protected from harm and the goal to see value and meaning in direct conflict (Murray, Holmes, & Collins, 2006). Imagine Walt promises Skyler to be a more involved father, but then dumps soccer practice on her at his first opportunity. To be safe from being hurt again, Skyler could tell herself that Walt is too selfish to ever count on. While such an attribution would satisfy a state goal to self-protect, it would completely defeat her chronic goal to see greater meaning and value in Walt as a father and husband.

As this example illustrates, people cannot successfully pursue two opposing goals at the same time (Orehek & Vazeou-Nieuwenhuis, 2013). In the case of conflicting goals, actions needed to satisfy one goal directly undermine actions needed to pursue an opposing goal. Imagine a dieter staring down a luscious and gooey piece of chocolate cake. He can diet and not eat the cake or indulge in the cake and not diet, but he cannot pursue both goals at the same time. To take some kind of definite action, he has to prioritize one goal over another. The same goal prioritization needs to happen in romantic life, often on a situation-by-situation basis. In Chapters 5 and 6, we explore how people resolve goal conflicts between safety and value (as well as between state and chronic goals, between partner goals, and between relationship-specific and -transcendent goals). As we will discuss, feeling safe from harm often takes priority over seeing value and meaning in the partner, but there are important exceptions to this rule. Especially powerful situations, influential partners, and relationship-transcendent goals can reprioritize relationship-specific goal pursuits and chart a new course for behavior.

Reality Constraints

Nothing would make Brian happier than believing that Sylvia is the kind of adventurous spirit who would be enthralled with the idea of spending her weekends white-water rafting with him. But the reality of his situation is that Sylvia is morbidly afraid of water, boats, river otters, and speed. To be safe when they negotiate weekend activities, Brian cannot just believe what he wants.

In this case, believing in Sylvia's intrepid spirit will likely only get him hurt. Instead, what Brian wants to believe about Sylvia and desires to do with her should be sensitive to the situational risks.

This brings us to our final theme. For safety and value goals to infuse romantic life in ways that fosters responsive interactions, the situational reality should help dictate which specific goal comes to monopolize attention, inference, and behavior in a given situation in the first place. The idea that motivation itself should be rooted in reality echoes an interdependence theory assumption: Situations open some opportunities and forgo others. For instance, situations afford personality (Kelley, 1979). Situations make it possible to be one kind of person over another kind of person. Situations where there can only be one clear winner and one clear loser make it easy to be a competitive person, whereas situations where everyone can win make it easy to be a cooperative person.

Situations in relationships also afford the pursuit of particular goals over others (Murray & Holmes, 2009). Imagine a typical week in the life of a long-married couple. Through the simple fact of living together, Skyler and Walter routinely, but unintentionally, interfere with one another's activities. To her great embarrassment, Skyler's snoring disrupts Walter's sleep. For morning interactions to be non-contentious nonetheless, losing sleep should motivate Walt to see value in Skyler that more than compensates for his disrupted night (Murray et al., 2009). Because Skyler and Walter place different priorities on family time, Walter can also be intentionally hurtful (as he was when he ditched the last soccer practice). For evening interactions to be non-contentious, being let down by Walter should motivate Skyler to back off and ask less of him until she's found some way to ensure he has little choice but to provide what she needs (Murray et al., 2008).

As we will explore, the specific goal that monopolizes attention, inference, and behavior should shift as situational affordances shift. The above examples illustrate such a dynamic. Just as situations vary within relationships, they also vary between relationships (Murray & Holmes, 2009). It's objectively harder for Skyler and Walt to be responsive to one another than it is for Sylvia and Brian to be responsive to one another because Skyler and Walt encounter so many more situations where they have opposite preferences (Kelley, 1979). Consequently, feeling safe should more often monopolize their attention, inference, and behavior because satisfying this goal has greater situational immediacy (and expediency). It's also harder for someone paired with a low self-esteem, anxiously attached, or neurotic person to satisfy the goal to see continued meaning and value in the partner because putting a positive spin on the negative behavior such partners perpetrate too often stretches credulity (Lemay & Dudley, 2011). Chapters 7 and 8 explore these and other reality constraints that underlie our situated perspective on motivated cognition in relationships. We argue the goals that infuse romantic life should to be attuned to the situational reality to effectively solve the adaptive problems that life in a given relationship creates.

Conclusion

In this first chapter, we undoubtedly raised more questions than we have answered. While we hope to address at least some of these questions in forthcoming chapters, we also hope we leave enough important questions unaddressed to spur further research and better thinking in a new generation of relationship scientists.

Note

1 We focus on heterosexual relationships because existing social psychological and personality research on relationships has focused primarily on opposite-sex romantic relationships. While we believe that the basic principles described in this book are equally applicable to same-sex relationships, verifying this claim awaits further research.

2
EMBODYING SAFETY AND VALUE GOALS

When Katy and Todd first met at that coffee shop, something she never understood drew her to him. Her chair was wobbly. Being physically unsettled, and feeling more than a little off-kilter, Katy found Todd's punctuality especially comforting. For some inexplicable reason, he just seemed like the kind of person she could trust.

In the experiment that inspired this example, David Kille and his colleagues randomly assigned romantically unattached participants to sit at a wobbly or stable table and chair (Kille, Forest, & Wood, 2013). Participants then rated the likelihood of famous couples, such as Barack and Michelle Obama, dissolving their marriage. They also described the traits they personally wanted in a romantic partner. The experience of being physically unstable made the romantic world seem inherently shakier. Those participants sitting at a wobbly table thought the Obamas would be more likely to divorce than those sitting at a stable table. Being physically, and feeling psychologically, shaken also changed what participants wanted in a romantic partner. Those sitting at a wobbly table indicated stronger preferences for a stable and steady partner (e.g., trustworthy, reliable, not adventurous) than those sitting at a stable table.

We raise the possibility that physically shaking could draw Katy's attention to Todd's punctuality to highlight our take on how safety and value goals infuse relationships. Namely, thinking is for doing. Therefore, the physicality of doing has to be bound up in the mentality of thinking to turn Katy's goal to avoid being hurt by Todd into the desired behavioral reality (Bargh, Schwader, Hailey, Dyer, & Boothby, 2012; Baumeister & Bargh, 2014). In fact, embodied cognition theorists assume that mental representations of the world incorporate physical experiences with the world to facilitate goal-directed action (Bargh et al., 2012; Barsalou, 2008; Meier, Moeller, Riemer-Peltz, & Robinson, 2012; Rueschemeyer, Lindemann, van Elk, & Bekkering, 2009). For instance, our mental representations of inanimate and animate objects, such as chocolates, flights of stairs, caregivers, and potential enemies, include our physical or bodily experience of such objects – as mouth-watering, steep, warm, or fearsome. When we imagine or perceive such objects, such bodily sensations are also activated and we automatically know how to behave. We indulge, climb, approach, or flee, as appropriate to the object, the next time it is encountered. To return to Katy, physically shaking cued her mental representations of harm and risk as well as a potential means to their alleviation – approaching a reliable other. By drawing her attention to Todd's punctuality, being physically shaken allowed her to restore her world to a psychologically, if not physically, more stable one.

This chapter builds on the "thinking is for doing" principle to make the first part of our case for safety and value goals occupying the top positions on our motivational short-list. In this chapter, we borrow the philosophy of embodied cognition theorists and look for the imprint of safety and value pursuits on relatively low-level or primitive perceptual, cognitive, and motivational processes. In the first section, we explain how safety and value goal pursuits serve the fundamental need to belong. Next, we argue that people are biologically and psychologically prepared to pursue safety and value goals as a means to belongingness. We argue these two goal pursuits can essentially co-opt more basic biological and psychological systems for (1) staying safe from physical harm and (2) perceiving value and purpose in action. We conclude the chapter by revealing the cognitive overlap between the general goals for staying safe from harm and perceiving value in action and motivated cognitive processes in relationships. Through varied empirical examples, we highlight the pervasive and powerful ways in which relationship perceptions affect physical sensations of the world as safe and meaningful and physical sensations of the world as safe and meaningful affect relationship perceptions.

What Thinking Needs to Do: The Belongingness Imperative

Baumeister and Leary (1995) define the need to belong as a fundamental biological and psychological motivation to establish temporally persistent and consistently responsive relationships with other people. But, even though romantic relationships are uniquely positioned to satisfy the need to belong in adulthood (see Chapter 1), the reality of interdependent life makes it difficult for partners to be persistently and consistently responsive to one another's needs.

Consider Katy's desire to ask Todd to take a weekend away to meet her parents. For Todd to be responsive, he first has to know that she wants him to take this leap forward in their relationship. However, Todd is not a mind reader; he does not have direct access to the contents of Katy's thoughts. She needs to tell him what she is thinking, so Katy's reticence could get in the way of his being responsive. Her tendency to assume the vague hints that she had been dropping were enough to alert Todd to her needs could also get in the way of his being responsive. In fact, people all too often assume hints and insinuations have effectively communicated their needs when their partner remains completely in the dark (Vorauer, Cameron, Holmes, & Pearce, 2003).

Even when Todd knows what Katy wants, incompatible preferences could get in the way of him being responsive to her needs (Kelley, 1979). As it happens, Todd is a busy law student and he had planned to spend the weekend camped out at the library preparing for his impending bar exams. All couples experience situations where they want different things; these incompatibilities make it difficult to be responsive (Kelley, 1979; Murray & Holmes, 2011). The nature of the incompatibilities partners face, and thus, the difficulties they are likely to face in being responsive, depend on the specifics of the *situation* they encounter (Murray & Holmes, 2009, 2011).

Partners generally interact across three broad classes of situations. They involve: (1) the management of daily life tasks; (2) the negotiation of similarities and differences in personality; and (3) the coordination of goals for the relationship (Kelley, 1979). The types of incompatibilities that arise in these domains differ from one stage of a relationship to the next and from one couple to the next. For instance, Katy and Todd just started dating so they have not had the dubious pleasure of allocating household chores. This means that Katy's half-hearted cleaning habits have not yet had the chance to rub Todd the wrong way. Katy's low self-esteem has come on to Todd's radar though. She over-interprets his slightest silences and Todd finds himself apologizing more than he wants, which has been difficult given his proud and impatient nature. Because they live together, Skyler and Walt no longer have the luxury of ignoring her more exacting standards for household cleanliness. They started having especially heated debates about who should take out the trash, vacuum, and shop for groceries once they had their son.

Katy and Todd and Skyler and Walt are like most couples. They have to find ways to coordinate incompatible interests, desires, and preferences so they can care for and support one another (Reis, Clark, & Holmes, 2004). Although this coordination process is crucial for responsiveness, it is not likely to be easy for anyone. Lykken and Tellegen (1993) made this point in a longitudinal study of twins and their spouses. They reasoned that the personalities of real couples should be more similar than the personalities of randomly paired couples *if* partners chose one another on the basis of personality fit. But that's not what they found. Real couples were no more similar in personality than random couples. This means that virtually all partners will encounter situations where they have at least some incompatible preferences, interests, and goals.

Incompatibilities make it difficult for partners to be responsive because of the "twin temptations of self-interest" (Murray & Holmes, 2011). Katy disclosing her desire for Todd to meet her parents is risky. Asking leaves her vulnerable to his rejection, especially if she knows that he already has plans to study.

Todd's temptation to meet his own needs and study thus gives Katy ample reason to succumb to her temptation to self-protect and keep her weekend desires to herself. For Katy and Todd's interactions to be mutually responsive, they each need to set aside self-interested concerns. Katy needs to set aside her temptation to self-protect and express her desires for Todd to meet her parents to him. In turn, Todd needs to set aside his temptation to be selfish and study and instead go home with Katy on the weekend to meet her parents.

We short-listed safety and value goals because these goal pursuits together manage these "twin temptations of self-interest" and make it easier for partners to be responsive to one another's needs. The pursuit of safety gives Katy the sense of assurance she needs to risk depending on Todd to meet her needs, which gives him behavioral opportunities to prove his caring. The pursuit of value gives Todd the sense of conviction in his commitment needed to do what is best for Katy and the relationship when she risks depending on him (Holmes & Rempel, 1989; Murray & Holmes, 2009; Murray, Holmes, & Collins, 2006; Murray, Holmes, & Griffin, 2000). Similarly, the pursuit of safety gives Todd the sense of assurance he needs to risk depending on Katy and the pursuit of value allows Katy to find enough to value in Todd to care for his needs when he depends on her (Rusbult, Drigotas, Arriaga, Witcher, & Cox, 1997).

Closing in on Belongingness: Marking Safety and Value Goal Progress

As these examples illustrate, relationship interactions are more likely to be responsive when partners are making sufficient progress in their pursuits of both safety and value. Indeed, we contend that safety and value goal pursuits are the sine qua non for satisfying the need to belong within romantic relationships. Unless Katy and Todd both feel safe and value one another enough, they are going to have inordinate difficulty behaving responsively and finding a sense of belonging in their relationship. This brings us to the logical question: How exactly do people mark progress toward these goals?

Like other goals, safety and value goals are cognitive representations of *desired* end-states (Fishbach & Ferguson, 2007). Katy wants to be safe; she wants to know that Todd loves and is not going to hurt her. She also wants to perceive value in action; she wants to believe that Todd really is worth her care and love (Mikulincer & Shaver, 2003; Murray & Holmes, 2009). Because thinking is for doing (Bargh et al., 2012), we venture a new claim: Safety and value goals are represented as *embodied* end-states. This means that progress in the pursuit of safety and value goals is marked by more than mentally accessible beliefs. Physical sensations of taste, touch, smell, sight, and sound and even imperceptible bodily movements also mark progress toward or away from these goals.

The way in which attitudes function to guide behavior illustrates embodied cognitive processes in action. Attitudes are cognitive representations that capture evaluative associations to given objects, places, and people (Fazio, 1986). They answer the question: Is this particular (object, place, or person) something that is good and to be approached or bad and to be avoided (Olson & Fazio, 2008)? Katy's positive automatic attitude toward chocolate captures her desire to consume this confection. Such an attitude can more effectively satiate her cravings if its activation compels her arm and then her hand to inch toward the chocolates in front of her. Growing evidence suggests that attitudes have just this function. Attitudes, once activated, elicit motor movements capable of satiating the desire to approach (or avoid) the object captured by the attitude (Fazio, 2007; Fazio, Ledbetter, & Towles-Schwen, 2000; Towles-Schwen & Fazio, 2006).

For instance, priming positively evaluated inanimate objects automatically elicits arm movements associated with moving coveted objects closer; priming negatively evaluated objects automatically elicits arm movements associated with pushing distained objects away (Chen & Bargh, 1999). For people with positive automatic attitudes toward the elderly, priming thoughts of being old automatically slows their walking speed to a leisurely pace commensurate with going for a stroll with a beloved grandmother. However, for those with more negative automatic attitudes toward the elderly, priming thoughts of being old accelerates their walking speed to a pace commensurate with beating a quick escape from a not-so-beloved grandmother (Cesario, Plaks, & Higgins, 2006). Similarly, imagining being approached by a close and desired friend elicits postural shifts needed to take a step forward, whereas imagining being approached by an undesired stranger activates postural shifts needed to take step back. Importantly, such anticipatory shifts in posture only occur when the possibility of interaction feels "real" to participants because they are imagining the event through their own eyes, just as they would experience it in real life (Miles, Christian, Masilamani, Volpi, & Macrae, 2014).

The Embodiment of Safety and Value

Traditionally, relationship scholars mark representations of safety and value through conscious beliefs. The state of Katy's trust in Todd's caring – from tenuous to confident – captures her progress toward her goal of feeling safe (Holmes & Rempel, 1989; Murray & Holmes, 2009). The state of Katy's commitment to Todd – from weak to strong – captures her progress toward her goal of perceiving meaning and value in Todd (Brickman, 1987; Rusbult & Van Lange, 2003). But, from an embodied perspective, Katy's representation of safety also includes the physical sensation of warmth or the visual perception of proximity. The physical warmth of preparing Todd's coffee thus could move Katy toward her goal of feeling safe (Williams & Bargh, 2008a) and the visual perception of distance could move her away (Williams & Bargh, 2008b). Todd's representation of value also includes his visual perception of attraction cues, his experience of scent, and the physical impetus to approach and move forward that comes from deciding how to implement difficult decisions. The allure of Katy's red top, charting his career goals, or bounding steps up his stairs thus could move Todd closer to his goal of seeing value and meaning in Katy.

The hypothesis that safety and value goals are embodied end-states invites myriad opportunities for these goals to infuse attention, inference, and behavior in relationships. For instance, Katy's physical experience of Todd's warm touch might activate automatic thoughts of his dependability even if her conscious thoughts urge caution. As we will see in subsequent chapters, such flexibility in goal pursuit has great functional utility in relationships. Safety and value goals are not static end-states that, once satiated, never need to be pursued again. In fact, we would hazard a guess that safety and value goals are rarely, if ever, fully satiated in relationships. Romantic goal pursuit is very much like weight control in this sense. The desire to remain at a perfect weight is constantly thwarted by the readings on the scale going above and below a desired end-state.

Without question, being safe from harm and perceiving sufficient value in a partner gets easier for some to approximate than others. We will see evidence on this point in Chapters 3 and 4. Nevertheless, even people who are highly trusting and committed encounter situations in their relationships that make them feel vulnerable and cause them to question their partner's value. Sylvia's unwillingness to even try any of the adventurous activities Brian relishes is one such sore spot for him (Murray & Holmes, 2011). Transitioning from one life stage of a relationship to the next can also thwart safety and value goal pursuits in unexpected ways (Kelley, 1979). Adjusting to the role of being parents created new conflict situations for Skyler and Walt that they never had to negotiate before (Doss, Rhoades, Stanley, & Markman, 2009). We view safety and value as ongoing goal pursuits because the complex adaptive challenges partners face in being consistently and mutually responsive to one another's needs never go away.

Preparedness for Safety and Value

If safety and value are goals that are elemental to the pursuit of belongingness, people should be biologically and psychologically prepared to satisfy them. Our review of the literature reveals telltale signs of such preparation. Indeed, humans actually carve the social world up perceptually in ways that serve basic goals for safety and value. For instance, infants develop a primitive sense of whether they are likely to receive care (i.e., safety) and whether others are willing to provide care (i.e., value) through early interactions with a primary caregiver (Bowlby, 1969; Mikulincer & Shaver, 2003). Across cultures, adults first judge others (individuals and groups) along the dimension of warmth, and then, on the dimension of competence (Fiske, Cuddy, & Glick, 2006). In a risky social world, judging warmth keeps people safe from harm by marking others likely to have more or less positive intentions toward the self. Judging competence keeps people pursuing meaningful actions by marking others capable of carrying out such positive intentions. To quote Fiske and colleagues: "Like all perception, social perception reflects evolutionary pressures . . . Social animals must determine, immediately, whether the 'other' is friend or foe (i.e., intends good or ill) and, then, whether the 'other' has the ability to act on those intentions" (p. 78). In other words, in navigating the social world, people must discern (1) who is safe to approach, and then, discern (2) whether those who are safe to approach are actually worth making a concerted effort to befriend.

Repurposing What's There

Neuroscientists believe that the human brain evolved so as not to reinvent the wheel. Rather than creating new biological and psychological systems to solve newly encountered adaptive problems from scratch, the brain instead repurposed what was already in place. Essentially, the brain evolved such that "modern human brain functions are built upon older, more primitive brain functions" (MacLean, 1990; Panskepp, 1998, as cited in Tritt, Inzlicht, & Harmon-Jones, 2012, p. 721). Conceivably, the capacity to co-opt more basic biological and psychological systems for (1) protecting against physical harm and (2) sustaining steadfast and purposeful action would make navigating an increasingly complex social world more manageable. As we will soon see, these general physical and psychological needs do seem to be represented as embodied goals. Further, the embodiment of these general goals likely favored safety and value goal pursuits as the means for satiating the belongingness imperative in romantic relationships.

So let's take a developmental step back. Attachment and evolutionary theorists contend that human minds and bodies developed in response to the adaptive problems posed by the necessity to survive and reproduce (Beckes & Coan, 2011; Kenrick, Neuberg, & White, 2013; Mikulincer & Shaver, 2003). For infants, the primary adaptive problem is to stay warm, comforted, and fed. For children and adolescents, it is to explore independently, gather kind and loyal friends and allies, and later find desirable mates. For adults, it is to retain a mate long enough to ensure the survival of offspring (Hazan & Diamond, 2000; Kenrick et al., 2013). As these examples illustrate, the adaptive problems people face change from one stage of life to the next. However, the solutions to these problems remain invariant. Whether the problem is an infant's need to escape the cold, an adolescent's need to discern friends from foes, or an adult's need to protect against disease, survival and reproduction require a mechanism for protecting against physical harm. Similarly, whether it is a child soliciting a caregiver's attention, an adolescent seeking a desirable mate, or an adult nurturing a child or partner, survival and reproduction require a mechanism for sustaining value and purpose in action.

The reason why human development would favor an integrated brain–body system for protecting against physical harm is obvious. Life is fragile and the world is fraught with dangers, such as brutal cold, biting hunger, contagious diseases, and fearsome foes that threaten physical survival. Those who avoid such threats are more likely to survive to reproduce than those who do not (Kenrick et al., 2013). The reason why human development would favor an integrated brain–body system for sustaining resolved, steadfast, and purposeful action may be less immediately obvious, but it is no less important. In colloquial terms, indecision kills. In psychological terms, effective behavior requires a certain and unconflicted course of action (Harmon-Jones, Amodio, & Harmon-Jones, 2009; Smith & Semin, 2007; Tritt et al., 2012). Those who can decisively choose to fight or flee, love or hate, and advance or retreat are more likely to survive to reproduce than those who remain in a state of uncertain behavioral paralysis (Tritt et al., 2012). For instance, people who see their own actions as full of clear purpose and meaning are more likely to attract friends and suitors than those who are less certain of the meaning and purpose underlying their actions (Stillman, Lambert, Fincham, & Baumeister, 2011). Even more striking, adults who see their lives as full of meaning and purpose are less likely to die over a 14-year period (Hill & Turiano, 2014). We now turn to the evidence that the general goals to (1) protect against harm and (2) sustain a steadfast sense of value and purpose in action are in fact embodied goals.

The Embodiment of Self-Protection

Because there is no shortage of physical dangers in the world, cognitively representing means for gauging such potential harms makes good evolutionary sense (Kenrick et al., 2013). Research from diverse theoretical perspectives suggests that protecting against harm is represented as an embodied goal. In fact, the goal to be safe from harm appears to be embodied through the biological immune system (Miller & Maner, 2011a, 2012). For instance, recently experiencing an illness activates the biological immune system and increases behavioral efforts to avoid potential sources of harm. People who have recently been ill are quicker to notice and push away potentially dangerous (i.e., disfigured) than normal faces (Miller & Maner, 2011a). The specific experiences of mind and body that cue progress toward (or away) from the goal to be safe and protected from harm vary depending on the situation. In familiar contexts, such as the relationship between a parent and child, the experience of physical warmth or closeness signals safety goal progress. In unfamiliar or potentially threatening contexts, such as an encounter with an out-group member or someone who is ill or diseased, the physical experience of distance and separation instead signal safety goal progress.

The Physicality of Warmth vs. Coldness

Imagining the world through the (blurry) eyes of an infant reveals one basic way in which progress toward the goal of being safe from harm is embodied. Humans are nearly helpless at birth. Survival depends on maintaining proximity to a caregiver, usually a mother, for nourishment, warmth, and protection from physical harm or predators (Hazan & Diamond, 2000; Mikulincer & Shaver, 2003).

In his seminal treatise, Bowlby (1969) posited a bio-behavioral system for maintaining such proximity – the attachment system. He reasoned that infants come into the world possessing innate behavioral systems for maintaining physical proximity to a caregiver. They include a herculean capacity to grasp an extended finger, a rooting response to suck in response to a breast (or hand) brushing against the cheek, and a double-decibel cry. In most circumstances, such behaviors are highly effective in eliciting a caregiver's physical proximity, and all the good that comes with it, such as warmth, nourishment, and an emotional sense of safety or felt security (Mikulincer & Shaver, 2003).

Through early experiences with a responsive caregiver, physical warmth comes to signal the proximity of safe and caring others (Bowlby, 1969; Mikulincer & Shaver, 2003). From an embodied goal perspective, such developmental experiences should result in warmth becoming part of the cognitive representation of the goal to be protected against harm (Fay & Maner, 2012; Ijzerman & Semin, 2009; Williams & Bargh, 2008a). If safety is embodied in this manner, coming into contact with something that is warm to the touch should signal progress toward this goal. Consequently, the world should appear safer and more inviting when people experience the physical sensation of warmth. The empirical evidence suggests that is the case. People perceive a target person to be interpersonally warmer after they have just held a cup of hot coffee than a cup of iced coffee. They are also more likely to reach out to a friend (by giving a gift they could have kept for themselves) after they just held a warm than a cold therapeutic pack (Williams & Bargh, 2008a). Similarly, people sitting on a heated pad report greater desire to get close to others than people sitting on an unheated pad (Fay & Maner, 2012). Conversely, people chilled from drinking an ice-cold glass of water feel less connected to others than people warmed by a heated glass of water (Chen, Poon, & DeWall, 2015).

Of course, physical warmth of touch is not the only cue that signals the proximity of safe and caring others. The physical sight and sound of such others should also signal progress in the pursuit of safety. It does. Having friends within sight and earshot makes the social world seem safer and less threatening. For instance, men in the company of friends perceive a potential foe as less physically intimidating. Fessler and Holbrook (2013) approached men walking with their friends. The participant then rated the height and muscularity of the headshot photograph of a convicted terrorist. They did so within sight and earshot of their friends (i.e., the safety condition) or isolated from their friends. Men who could neither see nor hear their friends perceived the terrorist to be significantly taller, more muscular, and more physically intimidating than men who could see and hear their friends. The simple presence of friends effectively shrank this foe down to size.

The Physicality of Distance

The social world that greets an infant is narrower and more familiar than the social worlds that children, adolescents, and adults inhabit. In these ambiguous social worlds, people encounter those who might befriend *and* those who might betray them and survival depends on the capacity to detect the difference (Kenrick et al., 2013). Therefore, just as the physical warmth (vs. coldness) cues progress toward the goal to be protected against harm in familiar social circumstances, the perception of physical distance may cue progress in less familiar ones.

The idea is an intuitive one. Physically close threats pose a greater risk to survival than physically distant threats. A bear that is two feet away poses an imminent safety hazard, but one that is 200 feet away does not. Because people feel safer when physically removed from a threat, Williams and Bargh (2008b) reasoned that priming physical distance would be enough to make threats appear innocuous. In one study, they first had participants plot near or far points on a Cartesian plane. They then read a story about someone who was horribly disfigured, and suicidal, in the aftermath of a car accident. Participants primed with distance (by plotting far points on the Cartesian plane) reported significantly less negative affect after reading the story than participants primed with closeness (by plotting near points). In a further study, participants primed with distance (by plotting far points) perceived fatty foods to possess fewer (dangerous) calories than participants primed with closeness (Williams & Bargh, 2008b).

The equation of distance with progress toward self-protection goals is so firmly engrained in the mind and body that activating the goal to be safe elicits the *psychological* perception of social distance and separation (Maner et al., 2005). People effectively keep themselves safe by perceiving the social world in a way that justifies fear and gives them reason to avoid unfamiliar and potentially threatening others. For instance, Maner and his colleagues (2005) primed the goal to self-protect against harm through fear. They exposed White participants to a clip from the film *Silence of the Lambs*, which featured a psychopath stalking a woman through a basement. Control participants watched a neutral film. Participants then rated the emotions they perceived in the neutral facial expressions of potentially threatening (Black men) and non-threatening targets (Black women and White men and women). Priming the goal to self-protect resulted in these White participants perceiving anger in the faces of Black men. Fearful participants restored safety to their social worlds by perceiving reason to avoid the very targets (given cultural stereotypes) that might pose a threat to them (Maner et al., 2005). Similarly, priming self-protection goals (through fear) also makes people more likely to notice and later remember the distinguishing features of out-group members (Becker et al., 2010).

The Physicality of Pain

For humans, like other social animals, there is perhaps no greater physical danger than exclusion by others. Social isolates suffer greater illness and live shorter lives than people who are socially included (Baumeister & Leary, 1995). Because the companionship of others signals progress toward safety goals (Kenrick et al., 2013; Maner,

DeWall, Baumeister, & Schaller, 2007), social rejection and exclusion should *hurt*. It does. Even logically inconsequential rejections – such as being excluded from a ball-tossing game by computer-generated players – cause both physical (Eisenberger, 2012) and psychological pain (Leary, Tambor, Terdal, & Downs, 1995).

As it turns out, the metaphor of a broken heart is an enormously apt one. MacDonald and Leary (2005) argued that the evolution of social pain co-opted the biological system already in place to regulate physical pain (Panksepp, 1998). Indeed, the experience of interpersonal rejection activates the exact same neural regions (i.e., the dorsal anterior cingulated cortex and the anterior insula) implicated in physical pain (Eisenberger, 2012). Because being rejected is embodied as physical pain, taking a daily pain reliever such as Tylenol actually takes away the pain of the daily social hurts. When people are so medicated, interpersonal slights that would normally hurt, such as a stranger's rebuff or a friend's criticism, simply lose any sting (DeWall et al., 2010).

There is a straightforward reason why losing the companionship of others is represented as an embodied threat to safety. Pain is adaptive. Pain draws attention to potential threats (e.g., "Ouch, this stove is hot!") and motivates pain-alleviating behavior (e.g., pulling a hand away from a hot stove). Social pain is also adaptive. Being hurt by rejection draws attention to potential threats to safety (e.g., "Ouch, this person is nasty") and motivates safety-restoring behaviors, such as forging new social bonds (Maner et al., 2007) or avoiding damaged ones (Twenge, Baumeister, Tice, & Stucke, 2001).

The Embodiment of Purposeful Action

Because uncertainty inhibits action, cognitively representing a behavioral means for effecting a resolved and steadfast sense of value and purpose in action also makes evolutionary sense. As we saw in the last chapter, the unconscious is usually in the behavioral driver seat (Baumeister & Bargh, 2014). Subtle features of the situation activate unconscious goals, not all of which have consistent implications for behavior (Harmon-Jones et al., 2009). For people to pursue a steadfast, purposeful course of action in the face of competing action tendencies, they need to (1) monitor the unexpected and (2) accommodate to it (Jonas et al., 2014). Think of what it takes to maintain a commitment to diet in the face of a sea of opportunities to eat. People need to be able to monitor when they are tempted and quickly enact a contingency plan to keep them on the straight and narrow (Gollwitzer, 1990). Diverse theoretical perspectives suggest that maintaining a resolved sense of value and purpose in action is represented as an embodied goal (Harmon-Jones et al., 2009; Proulx et al., Smith & Semin, 2004; Tritt et al., 2012). The goal to pursue purposeful action appears to be embodied through biological systems for monitoring response conflicts and motivating approach behavior (Harmon-Jones et al., 2009).

Let's back up a bit. Before social psychologists had neuropsychological and psychophysiological methods at their disposal, they long had argued that behavioral action requires an unequivocal state of mind (Brickman, 1987; Festinger, 1957; Jones & Gerard, 1967). To understand why certainty or a clear sense of purpose is a requisite for effective action, just consider the phrase, "I don't know what to do." Its invocation conjures up the uncomfortable image of someone, uncertain and agitated, perhaps teetering on a precipice, not sure whether to take a step forward or a step back.

Dissonance theorists were among the first to argue that maintaining clarity and purpose in action is represented as an embodied goal (Festinger, 1957). Rather than using this particular term, they instead argued that people experience an aversive state of physiological arousal (namely, dissonance) when their behavior does not follow from their thoughts. The sole purpose of this state of aversive physiological arousal is to make the direction behavior is taking feel "right" again by motivating people to reduce the inconsistency between their thoughts and behavior (Zanna & Cooper, 1974).

Consider someone making a difficult choice between two romantic partners, who each have significant pluses and minuses (Festinger, 1957). Choosing Partner A over Partner B creates dissonance arousal because it invites uncertainty. Partner A's negative qualities and Partner B's positive qualities provide reason to doubt the choice of Partner A – putting one's happy and efficacious pursuit of a relationship with Partner A in jeopardy. People resolve the dissonance that results from difficult choices by justifying the choice made. They make pursuing Partner A feel "right" by minimizing A's negative qualities and Partner B's positive qualities. In doing so, they imbue purpose to the decision to be with Partner A and make a chosen pursuit behaviorally unconflicted. Research on decision making under uncertainty suggests that the need to see one's choices as meaningful might even create a belief in fate. Tang and his colleagues reasoned that difficult choices, such as voting for a candidate in a contentious presidential race, evoke uncertainty. But, believing that fate was guiding one's vote could restore a sense of meaning in one's choice. Consistent with this logic, people who were faced with a difficult choice between two similar candidates believed fate would guide their hands (and votes) to the right choice (Tang, Shepherd, & Kay, 2014).

The Physicality of Uncertainty

The modern instantiation of these ideas is captured in the action-based model of dissonance. Its underlying premise is that "dissonance between cognitions evokes a negative affective state because it has the potential to interfere with effective and unconflicted action" (Harmon-Jones et al., 2009, p. 128). In this instantiation, people experience dissonance when unexpected or inconsistent thoughts interfere with goal-directed behavior. For instance, the inconsistent or unexpected thought, "I am eating chocolate cake," interferes with the goal-directed behavior to diet.

To continue to see dieting as a meaningful goal pursuit in the face of chocolate cake consumption, the inconsistent or unexpected needs to be made expected. This might involve changing perceptions of the calorie content of the cake (e.g., "It was low-fat") or the significance of the lapse (e.g., "Everyone breaks diets now and again").

Dissonance is thought to provide the energy or impetus for effective and goal-driven behavior by transforming the *un*expected into the expected. The experience of dissonance has this effect because of the way in which effective action or goal-directed behavior is embodied in the brain (Harmon-Jones et al., 2009; Harmon-Jones, Harmon-Jones, Serra, & Gable, 2014). The area of the brain responsible for monitoring response conflicts (i.e., the anterior cingulate cortex) intersects with the area of the brain responsible for motivating approach-oriented behavior (i.e., the left prefrontal cortex). Through this neural circuitry, the detection of something inconsistent or unexpected (i.e., "What am I doing eating this cake?") can provide the compensatory approach-oriented motivational state needed to keep behavior moving forward (e.g., "This cake just isn't so bad for me"). In a study testing this hypothesis, participants wrote a counter-attitudinal essay under either high-choice (i.e., high dissonance) or low-choice (i.e., low dissonance) conditions while their EEG activity was recorded (Harmon-Jones, Gerdjikov, & Harmon-Jones, 2008). Participants who behaved unexpectedly (i.e., volunteered to write an essay they did not believe) evidenced greater left prefrontal activation (indicating an approach-motivated state) and they also changed their attitudes to match their behavior (making their behavior meaningful again).

The neural imprint of dissonance in the brain areas generally related to approach motivation supports the evolutionary basis of the goal for purposeful action. So does evidence from studies of non-human primates and young children. Capuchin monkeys and four-year-old children both justify difficult choices by favoring hard-chosen stickers or M&M candies over easily forgone ones (Egan, Santos, & Bloom, 2007). Dissonance is also evident across cultures, although its behavioral manifestation is culturally specific. People from Western cultures justify choices that threaten a sense of "rightness" or purpose in the choices they make for themselves. People from Eastern cultures instead justify the choices that threaten a sense of "rightness" or purpose in choices they make for others (Hoshino-Browne et al., 2005).

The Physicality of Approach

Because the goal for purposeful action is embodied in approach motivation, activating approach intentions (through physical movement) should engender more unequivocal and purposeful behavior. The existing evidence on this point is suggestive. When people want something or want to do something, they usually need to behave in some way that moves them physically closer to their goals. For instance, bringing a delectable piece of chocolate to the lips involves flexing one's upper-arm muscles. So does picking up a small child. Through repeated experiencing picking up what we want or walking toward what we want, such bodily approach movements should be part of the embodied representation of what it means to be engaged in purposeful and valued behavior. Consequently, engaging in the bodily approach movement should make the target of the movement more desirable as a pursuit.

Making the physical arm movements associated with approach (i.e., upper-arm flexion) increases liking for neutral-attitude objects (Cacioppo et al., 1993). Training people to approach what they would otherwise avoid even creates new incipient behavioral commitments. Math-apprehensive women trained to approach math (by pulling a joystick toward them whenever a math-related symbol appears) reported greater identification with math and attempted to solve more math problems than women trained to avoid math (Kawakami, Steele, Cifa, Phills, & Dovidio, 2008). People trained to approach members of a negatively stereotyped group (by pulling a joystick toward them in response to the subliminal presentation of Black faces) engaged in more positive non-verbal behavior toward a Black confederate (Kawakami, Phills, Steele, & Dovidio, 2007). The real-world act of physically approaching a speed date by moving from one table to the next (vs. sitting at the same table) even heightens romantic desire and increases willingness to accept an invitation for a date (Finkel & Eastwick, 2008)!

The Psychology of the Expected

The idea that sustaining steadfast and purposeful action is an embodied goal is also evident in uncertainty reduction models (Heine, Proulx, & Vohs, 2006; Jonas et al., 2014). Like the action-based dissonance model, these models assume that uncertainty invites behavioral paralysis. Consequently, experiencing the unexpected provokes anxiety and motivates compensatory behavior that reduces anxiety by restoring meaning and purpose to action. What is so fascinating about the uncertainty models is how trivial a violation of expectancy it takes to elicit compensatory processes. Simply being exposed to incongruent word pairings (like "quickly–blueberry") is sufficient. In such an experiment, Randles and his colleagues subliminally exposed participants in the expectancy-violation condition to incongruent word pairings and participants in the control condition to congruent word pairings. They then asked their participants to set the bond for a hypothetical prostitute. Because prostitutes violate social convention, setting a higher bond provides a means of restoring the sense that the world is good and right (because bad behaviors are appropriately punished). Participants exposed to incongruent word pairings actually set a higher bond for the prostitute than control participants (Randles, Proulx, & Heine, 2011).

Embodied Safety and Value Goals in Action

The previously reviewed evidence suggests people are biologically and psychologically prepared to satisfy the belongingness imperative. Therefore, the systems already in place for pursuing the general goals to (1) protect against harm and (2) sustain unequivocal action could be co-opted to pursue the relational goals to (1) protect against being let down and hurt by close partners and (2) see value and meaning in caring for close partners. If such co-option has occurred, the representations regulating the pursuit of general and relational goals for safety and value should be cognitively overlapping. This means that activating the general goal for safety or value should bias perceptions of specific actual or potential relationship partners in ways that satisfy the more general goals. Conversely, activating the specific relational goals for safety or value should also bias more general perceptions of the self and the physical world in ways that satisfy these relational goals. The evidence reviewed next provides promising evidence that general and relational pursuits of safety and value are indeed cognitively overlapping.

The Embodied Pursuit of Safety

If safety functions as an embodied goal, the threat of physical harm should sensitize people to safety-restoring features of the social world. In *A Streetcar Named Desire*, Blanche Dubois memorably opined, "I've always depended on the kindness of strangers." Core to this confession is the idea that the trustworthiness and good will of others can protect one from harm. If people do indeed rely on the "kindness of strangers" (as well as friends) to satisfy the basic goal to be safe, posing a threat to safety should heighten sensitivity to social cues that reveal the kindness (or duplicity) of strangers.

Young, Slepian, and Sacco (2015) made this point in two experiments we wish we had designed. In each study, they primed the goal to be safe from physical harm by subjecting participants to a frightening clip from the *Silence of the Lambs*. Control participants viewed a neutral film clip. Study 1 participants then viewed digital images of strangers, tasked with the goal of discriminating trustworthy faces from those who could not be trusted. Study 2 participants also viewed the faces of strangers, but they discriminated genuine (i.e., Duchenne) from forced smiles. Activating the goal to self-protect effectively armed people with the perceptual sensitivity to make their social worlds physically safer. Experimental participants better discriminated trustworthy from untrustworthy faces and genuine from faked smiles than controls. The goal to be safe from physical harm essentially made features of the social world that diagnosed the potential for such harm more visible, restoring safety (Young et al., 2015).

Although others in the social world can pose direct threats of bodily harm, they can also threaten safety in more indirect ways. As we discussed earlier, the proximity and companionship of others powerfully signal safety (Leary & Baumeister, 2000). Because safety depends on the proximity of caring others, even the potential of being excluded or rejected by another person threatens progress in the pursuit of this goal. Because rejection is such a powerful threat to safety, researchers can use the threat of rejection to reveal the embodied means through which safety is pursued. As we will see next, the experience of interpersonal rejection changes perceptions of the physical and social world in ways that best afford renewed progress in the pursuit of safety (DeWall, Maner, & Rouby, 2009; Oishi, Schiller, & Gross, 2012; Pitts, Wilson, & Hugenberg, 2014).

In a fascinating set of experiments, Oishi and colleagues (2012) activated the relational goal to be safe from harm. They created a palpable rejection experience by leading experimental participants to feel misunderstood by someone they had just met. To do this, they first had participants select two personality characteristics that described them most well and two personality characteristics that described them least well (from a list of 10). Then participants had a conversation with a confederate who either understood them (because the confederate described them as they described themselves) or misunderstood them (because the confederate described them opposite to the way they described themselves). They then assessed how safe and inviting participants perceived the world to be. They asked participants to submerge their hand in an icy bucket of water (to measure pain tolerance) and to estimate the walking distance between specific geographical locations and the steepness of a hill. Participants who felt misunderstood by their interaction partner perceived a less physically safe and inviting world. They perceived the icy water to be more painful, the distance to be longer, and the hill to be steeper. Magnifying the level of threat in the physical world might seem like a paradoxical means of satisfying safety goals, but it is actually quite functional. Aspects of the physical world that seem less safe and inviting, like painful ice buckets and arduous travails, are more likely to be avoided. Thus, being more likely to see the physical world as intimidating furthers the pursuit of safety goals because it motivates perceivers to avoid physically risky or dangerous situations that could pose an even greater threat to physical safety (Pietrzak, Downey, & Ayduk, 2005).

Not everything should seem foreboding when safety goals are thwarted. Features of the social world that could afford a sense of safety should seem more physically and psychologically inviting when the goal to be safe from being hurt is activated.

First, rejection should make accepting others appear physically closer in space if physical proximity is part of the embodied representation of safety. Pitts and colleagues (2014) primed interpersonal rejection by asking experimental participants to spend five minutes writing about a time when they had been rejected or excluded by someone. Control participants wrote about what they had done when they first got up in the morning. Participants were then asked to toss a beanbag to a confederate (to provide a surreptitious measure of how close participants perceived the confederate to be). Participants primed with rejection perceived the confederate to be physically closer to them; their beanbag tosses typically fell several inches short of reaching the confederate! In a second study, they created a live rejection experiencing by having a confederate refuse to work with the participant. Participants then estimated the physical distance between them and a real-live new interaction partner or a cardboard cutout of the same interaction partner. Rejected participants perceived the actual person to be physically closer to them, but not the cardboard cutout. In fact, people who have just been rejected not only perceive amiable and potentially accepting others to be physically closer; they also intend to work harder to win over physically distant others (Knowles, Green, & Weidel, 2014). Activating the goal to protect against hurt thus makes actual social connections that could restore safety seem physically closer in space and more reachable.

Second, the comfort of physical touch should also make others seem more socially inviting if physical warmth is part of the embodied representation of safety. Indeed, being physically touched by a romantic partner makes psychologically stressful situations feel appreciably safer (Robinson, Hoplock, & Cameron, 2015). Even touching a teddy bear – an inanimate object physically associated with warmth and closeness – is enough to restore a sense of safety and embolden social connection. When people have been excluded, touching a teddy bear makes the world feel interpersonally safe again. Specifically, excluded participants who touched and cuddled a bear behaved much more generously than those who only gazed at the bear (Tai, Zheng, & Narayanan, 2011).

The Embodied Pursuit of Value

Because unequivocal and directed action is signaled through the bodily activation of approach motivations (Harmon-Jones et al., 2009), the activation of the approach motivational system should signal progress in the pursuit of value goals. Specifically, activating the specific desire to approach another should motivate people to see others as *worth* approaching. Enhancing the value of who (or what) is approached essentially imbues greater meaning and purpose to the behavior of approaching them (Brickman, 1987; Cacioppo, Priester, & Berntson, 1993; Rim, Min, Uleman, Chartrand, & Carlston, 2013).

Activating approach intentions does seem to result in people seeing positive qualities in others that make them more sensible and desirable to approach. For instance, when people enact the bodily movements associated with approach (i.e., flexing arm muscles toward the body), they automatically make more positive dispositional inferences about desirable others (Crawford, McCarthy, Kjaerstad, & Skowronski, 2013). Priming the goal to approach another also automatically elicits greater valuing of others. People primed with affiliation words automatically make more positive, but not negative, dispositional inferences about others (Rim et al., 2013). Priming the more specific approach goal to mate also results in men seeing greater value (in the form of heightened sexual arousal) in the neutral facial expressions of attractive women (Maner et al., 2005).

People primed with the hope of making a new friend or romantic connection even remake their own self-concepts in this person's image. They imbue the desire to approach this person with greater value and meaning by making the person part of something most people already value highly – themselves! Slotter and Gardner (2009) explored this process of motivated self–other integration in a series of inventive experiments. In one, participants first identified characteristics as "me" or "not me" (e.g., athletic, artistic, musical, studious, creative, agreeable). This allowed the researchers to identify characteristics that participants thought were highly characteristic (and uncharacteristic) of themselves. Weeks later, participants came to the laboratory. Those in the romantic approach goal condition learned they would be evaluating the profile of a potential partner placed on a dating website. Those in the control condition learned they would be evaluating a profile on a professional website. These profiles indicated that the target possessed one of the traits the participant had described as "not me." Slotter and Gardner reasoned that participants would claim the trait they had once disavowed as part of their self-concept when someone who offered the hope of a romantic relationship possessed this trait. That is exactly what they found. In fact, people primed with the hope of a romantic connection even incorporate a potential partner's negative qualities as part of their own self-concepts (Slotter & Gardner, 2012).

Approach has such a powerful effect in imbuing behavior with value and meaning that priming physical cues associated with past approach behaviors is itself enough to activate greater valuing of others. Sweet tastes are culturally and biologically associated with desire. Simply tasting a sweet bit of chocolate is enough to make people value the company of others more and sacrifice more on their behalf (Meier et al., 2012). The color red is culturally and biologically associated with love and sex. Simply exposing men to pictures of women on red backgrounds is enough to make these women appear more attractive and sexually desirable (Elliot & Niesta, 2008; Elliot, Tracy, Pazda, & Beall, 2013). However, this valuing effect only emerges when these women are within child-bearing years, and thus, desirable targets to approach (Schwarz & Singer, 2013). Physically attractive facial features are also culturally (and biologically) associated with love and sex. Men and women both direct their attention toward physically attractive others (Maner et al., 2003). Just the thought of a physically attractive partner also automatically elicits positive evaluative responses to such attractive others (Eastwick, Eagly, Finkel, & Johnson, 2011). The scent of a woman ovulating is even enough to make men imbue women with greater inherent value. Men who first detect the scent of ovulation in an item of clothing perceive the next woman they encounter as more sexually interested and they take greater risks in pursuing her (Miller & Maner, 2011b). In sum, priming the desire to approach another, whether directly by priming the thought of a relationship, or indirectly, by priming cues to approach, automatically elicits the tendency to see greater value in another, giving meaning to the desire to approach him or her.

Conclusion

This chapter made our preliminary case for ascribing safety and value goals the number 1 and 2 positions on our motivational short-list. The pursuit of safety and value goals is essential in the pursuit of belongingness. For relationships like Katy and Todd's to progress from a fledgling to a fully committed and satisfying one, they need to find ways to be responsive to each other's needs (Murray & Holmes, 2009, 2011; Reis et al., 2004). The pursuit of safety and value goals does just that by giving Katy reason to feel safe when she puts herself in Todd's hands and by motivating Todd to be responsive to her needs when she does. The evidence reviewed suggests that safety and value are represented as embodied goals whose pursuit co-opts more general motivational systems for (1) protecting against harm (safety) and (2) sustaining unequivocal action (value).

In the next two chapters, we describe exactly how progress in the pursuit of safety and value in romantic relationships is represented cognitively. In so doing, we return to the "thinking is for doing" principle that opened this one. We will argue that safety and value are contingent and flexible goal pursuits because different situations, partners, and relationships call for different goal priorities and behavioral responses. Thinking is so much for doing that changing the situation automatically shifts how particular goals are even pursued (Cesario, Plaks, Hagiwara, Navarrete, & Higgins, 2010). For instance, activating the general goal to be safe from harm automatically elicits the safety-restoring response the *situation* best affords. When people are trapped in a small room, priming Black men (and the stereotypic expectation of aggressiveness and hostility) automatically elicits the inclination to "fight," but when people are in an open space, priming Black men (and this same stereotypic expectation) automatically elicits the inclination to "flee" (Cesario et al., 2010). Because situations better afford some goals and some means of goal pursuit than others, we will begin to explore our situated or contextual take on how safety and value goals can and should bias attention, inference, and behavior in the different types of situations that emerge at each stage of a relationship's development.

3
PURSUING SAFETY

As Katy and Todd sat across from one another at that coffee shop table, they both had a lot to think about. On first meeting, Katy noticed that Todd was heavier than his (apparently none too recent) Tinder picture and Todd noticed Katy's deep blue eyes and what seemed like self-deprecating wit. Katy wondered whether she was speaking too much or too loudly and Todd wondered whether he was leaving too little time to get across town on time for his bar exam prep class. They also shared one vexing obsession – trying to figure out what the other was thinking. When Katy noticed Todd checking his watch, she couldn't help but wonder whether he was laughing at her jokes just to be polite. Todd couldn't escape his self-conscious preoccupation that Katy was staring disapprovingly at his midriff. Hoping for the best, but feeling anxious and unsettled, they both wanted to feel safe in the knowledge that hurt and rejection were unlikely.

The reason why Katy and Todd felt so vulnerable to rejection at first meeting comes up time again in interdependent relationships: Partners cannot read each other's minds (Griffin & Ross, 1991). That's why, months later, Katy is now experiencing such trepidation at the thought of asking Todd to take a weekend away to meet her parents. She has no way to know the precise priority he will put on her needs as opposed to studying for his bar exam (Murray & Holmes, 2011). If she could read his mind, her vulnerability would disappear because knowledge of his goal priorities would tell her exactly what to do to be safe (i.e., ask him to go vs. keep silent).

In this chapter, we argue that the experience of safety functions as an embodied goal because its control over perception and inference gives people the power to believe they actually *are* reading their partner's mind. Moving closer to the goal of being safe makes Katy believe that Todd depends on her and will not hurt her if she depends on him, whereas moving further away sends a warning that rejection might be imminent. The pursuit of safety disambiguates risky and unfamiliar situations by making the unknowable contents of a partner's mind manifest.

What marks progress toward the goal of being safe from being hurt? Which specific affective sensations, physical perceptions, situational assessments, and reasoned beliefs signal progress toward this goal and which thwart it? Is satisfying the goal to be safe a more preoccupying concern in some situations than others? Is it a more preoccupying concern for some people than others? How do people restore safety when ongoing events threaten progress toward this goal? This chapter tackles such questions as we explore in depth how the goal to be safe from being hurt and let down by the partner infuses attention, inference, and behavior.

In the first section of the chapter, we introduce the desired end-state: To be safe and protected from the potential for physical or psychological harm by a partner. We argue that safety comes from partners' equal and mutual dependence on the relationship. We then describe how progress toward mutual dependence, and thus safety, is signaled through mental representations and bodily states associated with the experience of trust in the partner. In describing how trust signals safety, we advance three interrelated arguments.

One. Trust is *not* equivalent to safety. Being more trusting does not necessarily move people closer to the goal of being safe and being less trusting does not necessarily move people further away. In making this point, we hope to set the imprecision in our past writing on this topic right. Attachment and interdependence theorists (like us) usually equate trust and safety by defining trust as a state of felt security in the partner's presence (Holmes & Rempel, 1989; Murray, Holmes, & Collins, 2006; Simpson, 2007). Feeling more trusting involves the secure and comforting anticipation of good things to come through dependence on the partner, whereas feeling less trusting involves the anticipation of bad things to come (Deutsch, 1973). However, *feeling* safe is not the same as *being* safe. Todd may feel quite safe and secure in situations where Katy is actually highly likely to hurt him and Katy may feel quite unsafe and insecure in situations where Todd is actually highly *un*likely to hurt her. As we will see, trust provides a *means* for Katy to gauge how she might best make herself physically and psychologically safe from harm, but being more trusting itself does not guarantee progress toward the goal of actually being safe.

Two. Trust involves more than people typically think it does. The term "trust" usually invokes beliefs that can be readily articulated (e.g., "I don't know if she really cares about me" or "I don't think I can trust him to do what is best for us"). Such reasoned beliefs capture a crucial part of trust (Holmes & Rempel, 1989), but they do not tell the whole story. We will argue that the automatic affective or evaluative associations and bodily movements that merely thinking of the partner provokes are also crucial to the experience of trust.

Three. Trust varies more than people think. The term "trust" usually refers to a chronic state denoting a perceiver who is more or less trusting across situations.

We will use this individual difference sense of the term when we describe how automatic evaluative associations and deliberative beliefs provide bases for trust. However, we also maintain that trust is as much a reactive and dynamic sentiment as it is static. It must vary from one situation to the next to sensitively signal progress toward the goal of being safe from the potential for hurt. This dynamic property to trust means that becoming less trusting in a given situation or relationship context can actually move people closer to the goal of being safe from the potential for harm. Although this assertion might seem paradoxical, it is central to our contextual take on motivated cognition. Think of Katy's predicament. She wants Todd to spend the weekend meeting her parents, but as devoted as he is to her, this weekend he is actually more devoted to his need to study for his bar exam. Given Todd's strong incentive to disappoint her, Katy can better keep herself safe from harm by being more hesitant to trust and depend on Todd than usual.

In the second section of the chapter, we describe exactly how people satisfy the goal to be safe. That is, we focus on the means of goal pursuit. We detail how the goal to be safe from hurt and rejection at the partner's hands biases perception and inference in situations that create inequality in dependence (Overall & Sibley, 2008, 2009a). We argue that people have two basic means for restoring safety in such situations: Increasing their partner's dependence on them and decreasing their own dependence on their partner. As we will see, the specific motivational machinations needed to restore safety depend on the (1) specific situation and (2) overall progress in pursuit of the goal to be safe as signaled by trust. Katy feeling vulnerable because she feels inferior to Todd elicits different tactics for restoring mutual dependence than feeling vulnerable because he has been intentionally hurtful. Further, people who are more chronically trusting restore safety in different ways than people who are less trusting (Murray et al., 2011). Such flexibility in goal pursuit echoes a point raised in the last chapter. Goal pursuit depends on situational affordances (Cesario, Plaks, Hagiwara, Navarrete, & Higgins, 2010). Consequently, fighting to preserve trust is a more viable means of restoring safety in some situations and for some people than others.

We conclude the chapter by explaining when being safe from harm is a more preoccupying goal. We highlight the role that relationship transitions, difficult partners, and personal dispositions play in making the pursuit of safety goals a more (or less) chronic preoccupation, a topic we take up again in later chapters.

The Desired End-State: Safety

What does it actually mean to be safe from the potential to be hurt by a partner? Katy could keep herself safe from being hurt by Todd by never venturing into that coffee shop for a first date – but taking such extreme protective measures would also forgo the possibility of the relationship even existing. To satisfy fundamental needs to belong (Baumeister & Leary, 1995), and to reap the rewards gained from interdependence (Murray & Holmes, 2011), people need to risk some level of dependence on a partner. However, risking such dependence invites the possibility of being hurt and rejected by a partner (Murray et al., 2006).

Interdependence theorists believe that the "principle of least interest" holds the key to safety (Drigotas, Rusbult, & Verette, 1999; Thibaut & Kelley, 1959; Waller, 1938; Wieselquist, Rusbult, Foster, & Agnew, 1999). Succinctly stated, this principle is: Whoever needs a relationship the least, holds the most power within it. If Katy is completely enamored with Todd, but Todd could take or leave Katy, Todd holds the power in the relationship. In such an unequal relationship, Katy would have no choice but to cater to Todd's needs in order to keep him, but Todd would have little incentive to take care of Katy's needs when it costs him. He simply would not have anything to lose by being selfish and uncaring. Indeed, in relationships where one partner is markedly less committed than the other, the less committed or "weak link" partner is more likely to behave in rejecting and hostile ways in conflict situations (Orina et al., 2011). To keep safe from being hurt, Katy needs to avoid being caught in such a position of vulnerability. She can do this by ensuring that Todd generally needs her at least as much as she needs him. That is, she needs to ensure they have equal interests in the relationship. In an equal relationship, Katy and Todd both stand to lose the other's good will by being uncaring. Therefore, both have strong incentive to take care of the other's needs. Equal and mutual dependence essentially keeps them both safe from being hurt.

To best satisfy the goal of being safe from harm, Katy should track Todd's dependence on her as she navigates situations within her relationship and use his dependence to decide how much dependence she should risk herself. That is, she should only allow herself to depend on Todd in a given situation when she knows he is motivated to be caring because he needs *her*. The problem is that Todd's commitment to Katy controls his dependence on her (Drigotas & Rusbult, 1992) and Katy does not have unfettered access to the contents of Todd's consciousness. She cannot know exactly how committed he is at any point in time. The best Katy can do to satisfy the goal to be safe and protected against harm is guess at the contents of Todd's consciousness. Katy's uses her trust in Todd to measure just that (Murray et al., 2006).

Trust: Marking the Best Means of Goal Pursuit

The experience of trust marks progress toward the goal of being safe because trust provides a means for mindreading a partner's likely dependence and motivations in a given situation (Deutsch, 1973; Holmes & Rempel, 1989; Murray et al., 2006; Simpson, 2007). Figure 3.1 depicts the conceptual model of trust that underlies our thinking.

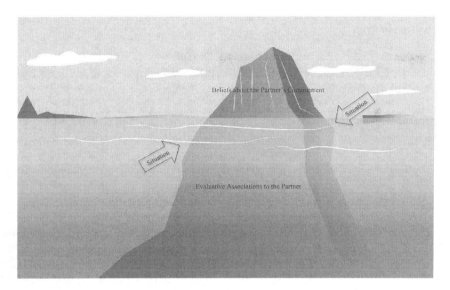

FIGURE 3.1 The Iceberg Model of Trust

This model conceptualizes trust as a metaphoric iceberg because trust has two main characteristics in common with icebergs. Both are deceptive in appearance. Just as the tip of an iceberg conceals its mass and depth beneath the ocean waves, trust captures considerably more than the beliefs that come to the tip of a person's tongue. Both are also dynamic in impact. Just as toppling an iceberg can trigger climatic changes, including tsunamis (!), threatening or upending trust can also create profound changes in the partners' interaction patterns.

Figure 3.1 uses these points of similarity to illustrate how Katy's sense of trust in Todd's availability and responsiveness dynamically shifts with three markers of his dependence. In this figure, the visible "tip" of trust corresponds to readily articulated beliefs about the partner's commitment (Holmes & Rempel, 1989). The invisible "undercurrent" of trust corresponds to automatic evaluative attitudes toward the partner (Murray et al., 2011; Murray, Gomillion, Holmes, Harris, & Lamarche, 2013). The "portability" of trust corresponds to changes in situation risk that alter the threshold for what it takes to be safe in ways that can make the goal to restore safety more or less acutely pressing (Overall & Sibley, 2008, 2009a). Just as much of an iceberg's power lies beneath the surface, this model conceptualizes automatic partner attitudes as having disproportionate power over trust because these attitudes are especially diagnostic of the partner's actual trustworthiness, activated without awareness in most trust-relevant situations, and require both motivation and cognitive resources to overrule (Murray et al., 2011).[1] We go into more detail about each of these three markers of partner dependence and trust next.

Below the Surface: Automatic Evaluative Associations to the Partner

For the experience of trust to accurately diagnose the partner's dependence, it should be sensitive to the overall quality of such past experiences with the partner (Holmes & Rempel, 1989). Safer, more dependent and committed partners behave differently than riskier, less dependent and committed partners. More dependent and committed partners are more likely to forgive transgressions, make sacrifices, and provide instrumental and emotional support (Rusbult & Van Lange, 2003). Therefore, receiving a partner's support, sacrifices, and forgiveness should signal equality of dependence and move people closer to the goal of being objectively safe. Conversely, being targeted by a partner's selfish and rejecting behavior should signal inequality of dependence and move people farther from the goal of being objectively safe.

Close relationships scholars have always assumed that explicit reports of trust adequately track such diagnostic behavioral experiences (Holmes & Rempel, 1989). But there is now evidence to suggest that automatic or unconscious attitudes toward the partner might track such diagnostic behavioral experiences much more faithfully (McNulty, Olson, Meltzer, & Shaffer, 2013). The idea that people can know things implicitly that they cannot explicitly articulate is central to social psychology (Zajonc, 1980). In a classic study on introspection, Wilson and Schooler (1991) asked participants to taste-test jams and identify their favorites. Participants in the "reasons" condition first listed the reasons why they liked and disliked each jam before they rated their preferences for each jam. Participants in the "intuition" condition went with their gut and rated the jams without thinking about it. The experimenters then compared the ratings of the participant jam tasters to the ratings of expert jam tasters. The participants who went with their gut chose the jams favored by the expert jam tasters. However, participants who explained why they liked each jam made suboptimal choices that diverged from the expert jam tasters.

So what do the results of this taste-test study have to do with trust? They suggest that people can reason themselves right out of knowing who is safe to approach and who is best avoided. Research on the detection of deception makes this point dramatically. People do no better than chance when they rely on conscious thoughts to discriminate liars from truth tellers. However, people's automatic associations to liars are more negative than their automatic associations to truth tellers (Brinke, Stimson, & Carney, 2014). Just as people intuitively know which jams are best, they also seem to intuitively know the truth when they see and hear it.

Given the diagnostic superiority of intuition over reason (at least for jams and lies), we reasoned that people probably also know more about their partner's trustworthiness than they can reliably profess. Indeed, attitude theorists believe that people implicitly learn whether specific objects are good or bad through experience interacting with the attitude object (Fazio, 1986; Gawronski & Bodenhausen, 2006; Gregg, Seibt, & Banaji, 2006; Olson & Fazio, 2008; Wilson, Lindsey, & Schooler, 2000). Consequently, interacting with a more dependent (and reliably responsive) partner should condition more positive automatic evaluative associations to the partner than interacting with a less dependent (and reliably responsive partner).

We first tested the hypothesis that automatic partner attitudes capture past behavioral experiences with the partner in a longitudinal study of newlywed couples (Murray, Holmes, & Pinkus, 2010). In this study, each partner completed daily interaction diaries for 14 days within six months of marriage. These daily reports allowed us to assess how much caring and responsive behavior the partner engaged in on a daily basis (e.g., "My partner listened to and comforted me"; "My partner was physically affectionate toward me") and rejecting and non-responsive (e.g., "My partner criticized or insulted me"; "My partner put his/her tastes ahead of mine"; "My partner did something I did not want him/her to do"). Four *years* later we then measured automatic attitudes toward the partner using the Implicit Association Test (IAT) (Zayas & Shoda, 2005).[2]

People's automatic attitudes toward their partner uniquely diagnosed the prior likelihood of a partner being rejecting and non-responsive! When people perceived their partner as engaging in more non-responsive behavior in the initial months of marriage, they evidenced less positive (or more negative) automatic associations to their partner on the IAT four *years* later. The time span of this effect might seem inexplicable. Pavlov's dogs could never have learned to salivate at the sound of a bell if dinner arrived four years after the bell. We doubt that the behaviors we picked up early on in these marriages were the very behaviors that predicted automatic partner attitudes four years later. It's much more likely that similarly non-responsive behaviors recurred over the next four years and this ongoing *pattern* of behavior conditioned later automatic partner attitudes. Incidentally, the partner's non-responsive behavior early in marriage did not predict later explicit evaluations of the partner, which suggests that automatic partner attitudes do indeed pick up on things explicit attitudes miss (McNulty et al., 2013).

People can more readily distort and deny unpleasant realities when they have executive resources available to support motivated reinterpretations of the evidence (Gawronski & Bodenhausen, 2006; Olson & Fazio, 2008). For instance, high self-esteem people can better fend off threats to self-esteem when their executive resources are intact than depleted (Cavallo, Holmes, Fitzsimons, Murray, & Wood, 2012). If taxing executive resources also makes it harder to distort a partner's behavior, automatic partner attitudes should be especially diagnostic of past experience with the partner for people who chronically experience diminished executive resources. People with chronically impaired executive resources should be more likely to take their partner's behavior at face value than creatively distort and deny such behavior. Consequently, their automatic attitudes should be especially diagnostic of their partner's trustworthiness, conditioned by largely unvarnished perceptions of their partner's behavior.

We tested this hypothesis in a community sample of married couples (Murray et al., 2013). Each participant first completed the IAT (described above) to index automatic partner attitudes. We also assessed individual differences in cognitive resources through working-memory capacity (Hofmann, Gschwendner, Friese, Wiers, & Schmitt, 2008, p. 966). Working-memory capacity is the capacity to allocate control and attention in ways that effectively manage incoming demands and inhibit unwanted thoughts and impulses. Greater working memory makes it easier for people to creatively distort a partner's behavior (Cavallo et al., 2012).

Each participant then completed 14 days of daily diary assessments to index how much caring and responsive and rejecting and non-responsive behavior their partner engaged in each day. At the end of the diary period, each participant again completed the IAT to index automatic partner attitudes. This study design allowed us to predict changes in automatic partner attitudes from partner behavior in the preceding two weeks. For people who were low in working-memory capacity (e.g., low in cognitive resources), the partner's behavior conditioned changes in automatic partner attitudes. Those who identified more responsive (and less non-responsive) partner behavior later evidenced more positive automatic affective associations to their partner than those who perceived more non-responsive (and less responsive) partner behavior. However, the partner's behavior did not condition later automatic attitudes for people who were high in working-memory capacity. In reflecting on the meaning of their partner's behavior, these people were presumably more likely to selectively interpret, construe, and distort in ways that made their perceptions a less than perfectly reliable barometer of their partner's actual behavior. As we noted earlier with the jam study, people can reason themselves right out of knowing what is good and safe to approach or bad and best to be avoided; when it comes to automatic partner attitudes, people high in working-memory capacity appeared to do just that.

Truly a Marker of Trust?

Although the longitudinal studies suggest that immediate evaluative associations to the partner accurately gauge the safety of interacting with the partner, they fall short of demonstrating that these attitudes instill trust in a partner. To make this point, we subliminally conditioned automatic attitudes toward the partner and then measured trust (Murray et al., 2011). In the first experiment, we conditioned more *positive* automatic attitudes toward the partner by subliminally pairing the partner's name with positive words, like warm, sweet, attractive, strong, and funny. We conditioned more *neutral* automatic attitudes toward the partner by subliminally pairing the partner's name with neutral words, like bike. In the second experiment, we added a further control condition where we subliminally paired an X with positive words (e.g., warm, sweet, etc.). This latter condition allowed us to show trust depends on *associating* the partner with positivity, not just on activating positive thoughts. We then measured trust in the partner's caring and commitment (e.g., "I am confident my partner will always want to stay in our relationship") and perceptions of the partner (e.g., "attractive," "intelligent," "warm") in both experiments.

Participants subliminally conditioned to associate their partner with positivity felt safer. They reported greater trust in their partner's caring and commitment than participants in the neutral conditioning condition in both experiments, suggesting that experiencing a more positive automatic evaluative association to the partner gave them an inarticulate reason to feel safe. In the second experiment, participants subliminally conditioned to associate their partner with positivity also reported greater trust than participants simply primed with positivity. However, participants subliminally conditioned to associate their partner with positive words did *not* report more positive evaluations of their partner relative to control participants. These divergent effects suggest that immediate affective associations to the partner provide an implicit means of assessing whether the partner is *safe* to approach, not necessarily whether the partner is *desirable* to approach. Although this might seem counter-intuitive, it echoes the point of Fiske et al. (2006) when they identified safety (i.e., "Is this person a friend or foe?") and value (i.e., "Is this person worth befriending?") as fundamental and separable dimensions of social perception. The fact that automatic attitudes signal partner safety, not simply partner value, also makes functional sense given the embodied nature of attitudes.

In sum, the physicality of doing is bound up in the mentality of thinking because thinking is ultimately for doing. Trust is ultimately for doing too. People are motivated to gauge their partner's trustworthiness so they "know" what actions to take to satisfy the goal to keep safe and protected from harm (Murray & Holmes, 2009). Because automatic attitudes translate past experience with an attitude object into future action, automatic partner attitudes are an efficient means of embodying trust. As we have seen, behavioral experience interacting with a partner conditions more or less positive automatic evaluative associations to the partner. Like any other automatic attitude, such associations function to keep us safe (Alexopoulos & Ric, 2007; Banaji & Heiphetz, 2010; Chen & Bargh, 1999). For instance, priming positively evaluated objects automatically activates the behavioral tendency to draw objects in one's environment closer to oneself, whereas priming negatively evaluated objects automatically activates the behavioral tendency to push objects away (Chen & Bargh, 1999). Subliminally priming positive-affect words (e.g., happy) also automatically activates the behavioral tendency (i.e., arm flexion) to draw closer; subliminally priming negative-affect words (e.g., angry) activates the behavioral tendency (i.e., arm extension) to push away (Alexopoulos & Ric, 2007). Automatic partner attitudes thus signal trust and mark progress toward the goal of being safe precisely because the safety-promoting inclinations to approach accepting and responsive and avoid rejecting and non-responsive partners are embodied in the attitude itself.

Above the Surface: Reasoned Beliefs

Although reasoning can lead people astray in the choice of jams (Wilson & Schooler, 1991), and romantic partners (Wilson & Kraft, 1993), people still need to explain their beliefs to themselves and others (Kunda, 1990). Consequently, the capacity to articulate and explain why trust in a partner is rational and well reasoned also provides an important marker of trust.

Tooby and Cosmides (1996) used the logic of the bankers' paradox to delineate the beliefs most likely to afford reason to trust. The bankers' paradox refers to the fact that people most need "loans" of interpersonal sacrifice and good will when they are bad credit risks. When people are sick, distressed, or fearful, they need the aid afforded by close interpersonal ties. But, when something is wrong, people are least able to repay any help they receive. For people to survive to reproduce, they need to discriminate committed and loyal friends they can trust to sacrifice for them from fair-weather friends who will reject them as soon as the going gets tough.

Culturally, people see being irreplaceable as the key to securing another's commitment and loyalty (Tooby & Cosmides, 1996). Possessing qualities that make one indispensable to select friends guarantees they have reason to stick around when it is costly (Eastwick & Hunt, 2014). Given such cultural constraints, people need to be able to make their partner's commitment to them "add up" in light of everything they know about the social economics of relationships. They need to be able to offer evidence and reasons why their partner would see them as special and want to be loyal to them over other, potentially less costly, partners (Murray & Holmes, 2011). Our research suggests that these reasons to trust are represented cognitively as "if-then" rules linking evidence of special value (IF) to the tendency to trust (THEN).

What Reasons Matter?

Table 3.1 lists four trust contingencies we identified (Murray & Holmes, 2009, 2011). Over time in relationships, people report greater trust in their partner's commitment when they witness their partner's forgiveness and personal sacrifices on their behalf (Wieselquist et al., 1999). The "partner sacrifices" rule thus specifies Katy has greater reason to trust in Todd when he is willing to act against his own self-interest for her betterment. In ongoing relationships, people who believe their partner regards them as more warm, understanding, intelligent, and attractive (etc.) also report greater trust in their partner's commitment (Murray, Holmes, & Griffin, 2000; Murray, Holmes, Griffin, Bellavia, & Rose, 2001). The "values traits" rule thus specifies that Katy should trust more in Todd when he sees more positive qualities in her (Murray, Holmes, & Griffin, 2000; Murray et al., 2001; Murray, Rose, Bellavia, Holmes, & Kusche, 2002).

TABLE 3.1 The Reasons to Trust

Contingency Rule	Interpretation
Partner sacrifices	If partner acts against his/her self-interest, then trust
Values traits	If partner sees special qualities in oneself, then trust
Equal match	If partner equal to oneself, then trust
Better than alternatives	If partner's alternatives inferior to oneself, then trust

The "equal match" rule specifies that Katy further has reason to trust in Todd if she is at least as good a person as he (Derrick & Murray, 2007; Murray et al., 2005). This reason to trust recognizes the power of fairness norms in limiting one's romantic options (Berscheid & Walster, 1969). In tacit observation of this rule, people use their sense of their own value in the interpersonal marketplace to set their sights on attainable romantic prospects (Leary & Baumeister, 2000; Lee, Loewenstein, Ariely, Hong, & Young, 2008). For instance, people who perceive themselves less positively on interpersonal traits, such as warm, intelligent, attractive, and sociable, set lower aspirations for an ideal partner (Campbell, Simpson, Kashy, & Fletcher, 2001; Murray, Holmes, & Griffin, 1996a, 1996b). People thus make it easier to believe that a partner is likely to be trustworthy by pursuing partners who are equal to them and more likely to value them.

Finally, the "better than alternatives" rule specifies that being superior to a partner's alternatives gives Katy still more reason to believe she can trust in Todd. Such comparisons cue the partner's trustworthiness because fair-trade norms also constrain the partner's romantic options (Thibaut & Kelley, 1959). Todd's commitment can waver when the life that he might have with an alternative partner looks better than his life with Katy (Rusbult & Van Lange, 2003; Thibaut & Kelley, 1959). Because the entreaties of available and better-matched alternatives can pose real temptation, Katy's sense of her value to Todd also requires tracking how she stacks up against his best options. In this social comparative metric, believing her worth exceeds Todd's most viable alternatives signals trust because her relative superiority makes her harder to replace (Murray et al., 2009).

Dynamic Changes: The Nature of the Situational Risks

> *You may be deceived if you trust too much,*
> *But you will live in torment if you do not trust enough.*

Crane's sage words about the dangers of trusting either too much or too little highlight the situational specificity of safety. If Katy trusts too much, and asks Todd for a sacrifice he is not willing to give, she might be setting herself up for disappointment. But if she doesn't trust Todd enough, and keeps her desires to herself, she could never benefit from his willingness to sacrifice on her behalf, which sets her up for even more enduring hurt. Because Katy needs to anticipate Todd's actions across a variety of situations, trust needs to be sensitive to situational risk to be a functional signal of progress toward safety and the state of mutual dependence.

The arrows impinging on the trust iceberg in Figure 3.1 capture such situational influences. Situations vary in risk because some situations are more likely to tempt partners to be rejecting and non-responsive (Kelley, 1979; Murray & Holmes, 2011). Consider the difference between Katy wanting Todd to meet her parents on a weekend when he is itching for an out-of-town trip (a low-risk situation) to wanting him to sacrifice a study weekend right before his bar exam (a high-risk situation). In the high-risk case, Todd has a much stronger incentive to refuse her request because his personal goals more strongly oppose her goals. High-risk situations essentially threaten or unsettle trust, functioning to tip or submerge the iceberg, because they raise the stakes. These situations raise the functional threshold for the *level* of trust it takes to feel safe because Katy has to put herself much further out on a psychological limb when she asks Todd for a major than a minor sacrifice. Consequently, such high-risk situations stir feelings of unease and distrust in Katy to ensure that she is not taking any unnecessary risks.

Overall and Sibley (2008) used a daily diary methodology to better understand the situational parameters that cue reason to trust versus distrust the partner. Participants completed interaction diaries whenever they interacted with their romantic partner for 10 minutes or longer. In each interaction, participants rated how accepted they felt by their partner as a marker of trust. They also quantified risk by rating how much personal influence or control they had in the interaction (i.e., less control = more risk, like Katy in the bar exam scenario). In those situations where people felt especially vulnerable and powerless, they expected their partner to be much more rejecting. Situations where people feel especially vulnerable and powerless are ones that involve inequality in dependence because one person is more in need of the other's cooperation. In the weekend scenario, Katy cannot get her wish for Todd to meet her parents unless Todd give her his full cooperation, but Todd can study as he planned without any cooperation from Katy at all. To sum up, Overall and Sibley (2008) make two important points. The first is that trust can vary from one situation to the next (see also Simpson, Rholes, & Phillips, 1996). The second is that situations that involve significant physical, emotional, or psychological unilateral vulnerability to the partner's potentially hurtful actions move people further from the goal of being safe. These situations have a distinct signature: Needing something from a partner, but feeling relatively powerless to compel it. Being at a partner's mercy, literally and figuratively.

Restoring Goal Progress: Motivated Perceptual and Behavioral Tactics

Mutual dependence is the requisite condition for safety (Drigotas & Rusbult, 1992). Consequently, situations that impose the perception of relative powerlessness and vulnerability – such as Katy wanting Todd to sacrifice his plans for her – threaten safety goal pursuits because they amplify the risk of harm. People can restore safety in such risky situations by restoring mutual dependence, either in perception or actual fact. As we see next, Katy can restore safety by (1) increasing Todd's dependence on her or (2) decreasing her dependence on Todd (Murray & Holmes, 2009). Such motivated machinations can be perceptual or behavioral in nature.

Increasing Partner Dependence

As we have said, people do not have direct access to the contents of their partner's consciousness. They instead use a mindreading proxy – trust – to gauge the strength of their partner's dependence and commitment to them (Murray & Holmes, 2009). This peculiarity in the perception of partner dependence means that motivated perceptual biases could afford Katy one ready means of increasing Todd's perceived dependence on her (Balcetis & Lassiter, 2010). Namely, she could make herself feel safer simply by "seeing" testament to Todd's commitment to her in his behavior (Murray et al., 2002). For instance, she might engage in a biased search through memory for evidence, such as the especially thoughtful gift Todd gave her on her last birthday, to convince herself that he really does depend on her and care about making her happy (Kunda, 1990). She might also flexibly change her criteria for dependence and trustworthiness to exclude any time he went to someone else for support (Dunning, Meyerowitz, & Holzberg, 1989). For such biased perceptions to effectively restore safety, they should function relatively automatically – that is, without intention or awareness (Bargh, Schwader, Hailey, Dyer, & Boothby, 2012). After all, Katy would probably take little comfort in a newfound sense of safety if she knew that wanting to see Todd as caring for her had systematically biased what she saw in him.

Feeling powerless and vulnerable to hurt and rejection by a romantic partner can indeed elicit an automatic tendency to "see" greater evidence of trustworthiness. This perceptual bias is so powerful that priming vulnerability to a specific romantic partner elicits a *general* tendency to see novel others as dependent and trustworthy. Koranyi and Rothermund (2012a) made this point in a series of inventive experiments. In one study, experimental participants imagined stressors that could seriously threaten the stability of their relationship (e.g., long period of physical separation). Controls imagined stressors that could threaten their satisfaction at work. Participants then judged the trustworthiness of 12 faces. Participants primed with thoughts of interpersonal vulnerability actually perceived greater evidence of trustworthiness in the faces of strangers than control participants. Being interpersonally unsafe made them see what they needed to see – "evidence" that others are unlikely to hurt them. In a further study, experimental participants imagined their romantic partner wanted to study abroad. Controls imagined they were suffering from an intense toothache. Participants then played a one-shot trust game with an anonymous stranger. In this game, the participant chooses how much of his/her financial endowment to send to a co-player, knowing that the amount he/she sends will be tripled and the co-player will then choose how much money to return. Greater outlays of money on the participant's part require trusting the co-player to reciprocate and share his/her gains. Being vulnerable resulted in people seeing the trustworthiness they needed to see in their partner in the person they just happened to be depending on at that particular moment. Participants primed with the thought of their partner abroad donated more money than control participants.

Of course, the powers of such perceptual biases are limited. In the context of an actual relationship, wishing does not make it so. Believing a partner is dependent is one thing, but actually making the individual more dependent and thus trustworthy is even better. This practical constraint suggests that a certain kind of motivated behavioral intention could afford Katy a further means of increasing Todd's dependence on her. In situations where Katy feels inferior to Todd, she might make herself safer and less vulnerable by finding quick concrete ways to make herself especially useful and valuable to Todd. However, cooking Todd's favorite meals or getting his favorite books from the library probably wouldn't be all that effective in making Katy feel safe if she realized she was doing all of these things just to make him depend on her. Conceivably, such tacit awareness might even undermine her trust in Todd. Such motivated behavioral intentions should instead guide Katy's behavior without her awareness.

An ongoing study of newlywed couples provided initial evidence that working models of relationships do indeed contain implicit procedural knowledge for restoring mutuality in dependence (Murray, Aloni, et al., 2009). Just after they married, the newlyweds in this study completed a 14-day daily diary. These daily reports allowed us to pinpoint the safety-restoring behaviors that feeling inferior to a partner elicits. On days after these newlyweds felt especially concerned about measuring up to their partner, they took action to restore mutuality in dependence. They made sure their partner depended on them by doing practical and tangible favors for them, like packing lunches and finding lost keys. This motivated safety-restoring behavior also seemed to occur automatically. Feeling acutely inferior to the partner on Monday elicited dependence-eliciting behavior on Tuesday controlling for Tuesday's feelings of inferiority to the partner. Thus, feelings of inferiority that people could no longer consciously report nonetheless motivated compensatory efforts to secure the partner's dependence. Still more impressive, this remedial response worked. On days after people did more practical and tangible favors, their partner reported being more committed!

To study this safety-restoring dynamic in the lab, we had to find a way to induce worries about the partner's dependence on the relationship without participants really being aware of the source of their worries. We took advantage of people's knowledge of the exchange script to do this. This cultural script specifies that partners need to make equitable contributions to the relationship to avoid being replaced (Thibaut & Kelley, 1959). Consequently, priming this cultural script should activate concerns about measuring up to the partner. In one experiment, we asked participants to evaluate how appealing personal ads would be to other people (Murray, Aloni, et al., 2009, Experiment 2). In the exchange priming condition, these ads emphasized the romantic hopeful's expectation of making an equitable or matched trade. In the control condition, the ads invoked no such expectation. In the second experiment, we superimposed pictures of U.S. coins on the computer screen to prime the economic metaphor that quantities are bought and sold. In the control condition, we superimposed pictures of circles (Murray, Aloni, et al., 2009, Experiment 3). Then we measured concerns about measuring up to the partner and consequent intentions to engage in behaviors that could increase the partner's dependence (e.g., "cooking for my partner," "keeping track of my partner's school schedule," "remembering my partner's important appointments"). In both experiments, participants primed with the exchange script reported greater concerns about measuring up to their partner. They also reported much stronger intentions to do concrete things to make their partner depend on them.

Decreasing Own Dependence

The research just reviewed suggests that people can restore safety by perceiving (Koranyi & Rothermund, 2012) and even physically creating evidence that their partner really does depend on them (Murray, Aloni et al., 2009). Because safety depends on *mutuality* in dependence, motivated manipulations of Todd's dependence are not Katy's only option for restoring safety. People can also restore safety through motivated manipulations of their *own* dependence. In situations where she is feeling relatively vulnerable and powerless, Katy can regain safety by trusting and relying *less* on Todd. Todd simply cannot hurt Katy if she won't let him get close enough to her to do so (Murray et al., 2006). Rather than pulling the partner in, people can restore mutual dependence by withdrawing themselves. As we see next, people can reduce their own dependence and pull away from their partner through complementary motivated perceptual biases and distance-producing behavioral intentions.

We realize this might seem paradoxical, but for someone who is feeling vulnerable and powerless, there is safety to be gained through greater distrust and suspiciousness. People who are highly anxious and fearful provide a case in point. Even though one might expect a spider phobic to be motivated *not* to see spiders, people who experience such anxieties are especially disposed to see the target of their fear. Being quick to perceive a tangled ball of thread on the floor as a spider is actually functional for people who fear spiders because such vigilance better equips them to *avoid* the targets of their fears (Lang, Bradley, & Cuthbert, 1990; Mineka & Sutton, 1992). For instance, threatening words, such as "injury" or "criticized," automatically capture attention for people high in generalized anxiety (MacLeod, Mathews, & Tata, 1986).

Being suspicious and vigilant in a relationship context similarly appears to function to ensure safety from both physical and psychological harm. Distrust and suspicion can promote safety for a very fundamental reason. People generally only let themselves risk closeness to another when they are sure another's acceptance will be forthcoming (Murray et al., 2006).[3] Perceiving reason to distrust thus motivates people to distance themselves from a potential source of harm – just like physical pain motivates people to remove their hand from a hot stove (MacDonald & Leary, 2005). If Katy is quick to perceive the potential for rejection on Todd's part, she is less likely to let herself be caught up in a situation where she could be hurt (Murray, Bellavia, Rose, & Griffin, 2003; Pietrzak, Downey, & Ayduk, 2005). Ironically, in some situations, feeling less trusting can thus signal greater safety than feeling more trusting.

For instance, people who chronically worry about being vulnerable to a partner are quick to interpret their partner's negative mood as anger directed toward them (Bellavia & Murray, 2003). Such a motivated perceptual bias on Katy's part restores safety by motivating her *not* to depend on Todd in situations where she might get hurt. Consistent with this logic, directly priming reasons to distrust others automatically activates the motivated behavioral intentions to impose greater physical distance between oneself and the source of such hurts. As one example, people subliminally primed with the name of a consistently rejecting significant other were quicker to identify synonyms of social distance, such as "distance," "dismiss," "withdraw," and "detach" in a lexical decision task (Gillath et al., 2006). Similarly, people who vividly recounted a time when their dating partner had hurt them were quicker to identify distancing words, such as "oppose," "condemn," "angry," "blame," "hate," "annoy," and "accuse," in a lexical decision task (Murray, Derrick, Leder, & Holmes, 2008).

Being quicker to respond to distancing words does not necessarily mean that people would actually choose to avoid others when they are feeling vulnerable, but such behavioral evidence also exists. Feeling suspicious and distrustful motivates people to distance themselves from diagnostic social situations where they could learn how others feel about them (Beck & Clark, 2009). For instance, people who had just thought of someone they distrusted chose not to learn what a new interaction partner thought of them. Unlike control participants who welcomed this opportunity, distrust-primed participants effectively closed off the opportunity for a relationship before it even had the chance to begin. People who were chronically distrustful and suspicious of others also preferred teachers to assign them to work partners rather than risk finding out which of their classmates actually wanted to work with them (Beck & Clark, 2009).

Fitting Motivation to Context: Situation Calibration

To return to Crane's observations, people face a dilemma between trusting too much and trusting too little because they cannot both trust and not trust a partner in any one situation. Motivated perceptual biases that highlight the partner's worthiness of trust foreclose the possibility of pursuing safety through suspicion, vigilance, and distance. Because some means of precluding safety preclude others, we now turn to the next logical question: What factors determine whether people restore mutuality in dependence through automatic perceptual biases and behavioral intentions that either *increase the partner's* dependence or *reduce their own* dependence? These automatic machinations depend on the (1) nature of the situational threat and (2) overall progress toward the goal of being safe from harm as marked by trust.

The Situation

In the preceding pages, we described studies that reveal two opposite effects of priming interpersonal vulnerability. Vulnerability can increase both trust *and* distrust! Priming thoughts of a partner studying abroad motivates people to see trustworthiness in others (Koranyi & Rothermund, 2012), and priming inferiority motivates people to engage communally toward their partner (Murray, Aloni et al., 2009), but priming thoughts of a partner being overtly untrustworthy and rejecting motivates people to be suspicious and hostile (Murray et al., 2008).

These seemingly conflicting findings echo the third theme of this book. For motivation to infuse romantic life in ways that facilitate the pursuit of belongingness, the specific goal (whether safety or value) that monopolizes attention, inference, and behavior needs to be sensitive to situational affordances. In situations that favor the pursuit of safety over value goals (or vice versa), the specific *means* of goal pursuit also needs to be flexible and sensitive to situational affordances. Katy can make progress toward her goal to be safe by (1) pulling away from Todd or (2) drawing Todd closer to her. Which particular means of safety goal pursuit she favors in any given situation needs to adjust to the affordances of that situation.

Not all situations that involve vulnerability and powerlessness have the same affordances. Some situations simply highlight the *possibility* for a partner to be hurtful, an eventuality that may or may not unfold. Imagining a partner going abroad highlights the possibility that a partner might not be available, but it does not guarantee it. Similarly, feeling inferior to the partner highlights the possibility that a partner's eye might wander, but it does not guarantee it. However, thinking of a concrete time when a partner actually did something very hurtful makes partner rejection a hard, cold *actuality*. In our thinking, situations that prime the *possibility* of partner rejection better afford the opportunity to prevent hurt by increasing the partner's dependence – essentially going on the motivational offense. In contrast, situations that prime the *actuality* of partner rejection better afford the opportunity to blunt hurt by distancing oneself from the source of the pain – essentially going on the motivational defense. Consistent with this affordance logic, people respond differently to the experience of being rejected than being ignored (where rejection is a possibility, not an actuality). Specifically, people reminded of a time when others rejected them withdraw from others to avoid another hurtful interpersonal loss. In contrast, people reminded of a time when others ignored them draw closer to others in the hopes of gaining acceptance (Molden, Lucas, Gardner, Dean, & Knowles, 2009). Similarly, being rejected by a spouse has a palpably different effect on daily marital interactions than feeling inferior to a spouse. Feeling rejected motivates people to engage in selfish and hurtful behavior that decreases their dependence on their partner. Feeling inferior instead motivates people to engage in kind and communal behaviors that increase their partner's dependence on them (Murray, Aloni et al., 2009; Murray, Bellavia et al., 2003).

Fitting Motivation to Context: Trust Calibration

As we have just seen, some situations better afford one means of restoring safety over another. In our theoretical writing on interdependence, we argue that specific situations have the power to compel behavior because diagnostic features of situations are included within the behavioral representations used to navigate such situations (Murray & Holmes, 2009). For instance, feeling inferior to Todd automatically primes Katy's intention to increase his dependence on her because her mental representations of relationships contain procedural knowledge that links threatening situation features (IF) to threat-mitigating behaviors (THEN).

The power such IF-THEN rules have to compel behavior is limited though. To return to the car-driving metaphor Baumeister and Bargh (2014) introduced, the unconscious may be responsible for most of the mechanics of driving the car, but the driver can still decide whether the car is veering off in the wrong direction. Therefore, Katy might only act on an automatically activated perceptual bias or behavioral intention if such inclinations feel "right" to her (Murray & Holmes, 2009). Whether such intentions feel "right" depends on how much *overall* progress people have made toward the goal of being safe as marked by trust.

According to our iceberg model, the overall experience of trust marks the best means of making progress toward safety goals. It does so through automatic evaluative associations to the partner and reasoned beliefs (Figure 3.1). More positive evaluative associations or more optimistic reasoned beliefs generally afford increased trust, which creates a cross-situational sense of being closer to the goal of being safe. Less positive evaluative associations or less optimistic reasoned beliefs afford decreased trust, which creates a cross-situational sense of being further away from the goal of being safe. More readily attainable goals surely have different psychological effects than less readily attainable goals. Therefore, Katy and Todd's subjective experience of insufficient (or sufficient) progress toward the goal of being safe should affect how vigilantly each responds to situational setbacks in this goal pursuit.

In specific situations that move him further from the goal of being safe, a more trusting Todd likely still feels closer to the desired goal of being safe than a less trusting Katy (Murray, Griffin, Rose, & Bellavia, 2003). Greater *overall* goal progress gives a more trusting Todd a greater psychological cushion in the pursuit of safety than a less trusting Katy. Any misstep is not going to hurt a more trusting Todd as much as a less trusting Katy because he is already closer to the desired goal of being relatively safe from hurt. The metaphor of a foot race is an apt one here. A faster runner can better afford to run a riskier race with more potential for misstep than a slower runner because the faster runner is already closer to the finish line and can more readily recoup lost ground. The same principle appears to apply to trust and the pursuit of safety.

Being able to afford missteps in the pursuit of safety goals gives a more trusting Todd the luxury to pursue a riskier motivational course. In situations that highlight his vulnerability to Katy's actions, he can better afford to simply believe in Katy's dependence and trustworthiness while discounting automatic inclinations to take quick behavioral steps to restore mutual dependence. However, a less trusting Katy cannot afford any missteps in her pursuit of safety in specific situations because she cannot afford to fall even further short of this goal. This leaves her with little choice but to pursue a more cautious motivational course that prioritizes taking quick and immediate perceptual and behavioral action to guard against any further threats to safety. The empirical examples we highlight next illustrate exactly how chronic implicit and explicit markers of trust can control the actions people take to restore safety.

Automatic Evaluative Associations

Imagine that Todd has just handed Katy an itemized list of every last one of her personal qualities that annoy him. Such a vulnerability-inducing situation automatically activates behavioral inclinations associated with the situation itself. In this particular case, being rebuked by the partner activates the inclination to withdraw (Murray et al., 2008). However, such situations also activate automatic attitudes toward the partner because this marker of trust allows people to read their partner's mind. Just as automatic attitudes embody bodily intentions to approach safe and avoid unsafe objects (Chen & Bargh, 1999), automatic partner attitudes also embody representations of partner proximity and availability (Mikulincer & Shaver, 2003; Williams & Bargh, 2008b). Experiencing more negative automatic evaluative associations to the partner signals the partner's physical and psychological *un*availability, marking insufficient progress toward safety. However, experiencing more positive automatic evaluative associations to the partner signals the partner's physical and psychological availability, marking greater overall progress toward the goal of being safe.

Consequently, in vulnerability-inducing situations, a less trusting Katy is more likely to act on the automatic inclination to reduce dependence. Katy's more negative automatic attitude should motivate her to guard against any further threats to safety and reinforce the situational impetus to withdraw and reduce her dependence on Todd. However, Todd's more positive automatic attitude toward Katy marks greater progress toward the goal of being safe. Being closer to this goal should strengthen Todd's goal to connect to Katy, making it easier for him to suppress the competing inclination to withdraw (Fishbach, Friedman, & Kruglanski, 2003).

We created an experimental analogue to this scenario to examine just these possibilities. We brought dating couples into the lab and measured their automatic attitudes toward one another using the IAT. We then led one member of the couple to believe that his or her partner had a laundry list of complaints about that individual's personal qualities. We first told couples that they would each be completing the same measures in tandem throughout the study. We then sat partners back to back at two separate tables. In the experimental condition, we gave the target participant (let's say, Katy) a one-page questionnaire asking her to list important qualities in Todd that she disliked. The instructions also stipulated, in bold type, that Katy did not need to list any more than *one* quality. So, typically, Katy listed one of Todd's faults, stopped, and sealed her questionnaire in an envelope. Then she had to wait for Todd to finish before she could start the next experimental task. But as she sat, Todd kept writing and writing! Todd wrote so copiously because, unbeknownst to Katy, he was asked to list at least 25 items in his residence. Almost invariably Todd took much longer to complete the writing task than Katy – which gave Katy considerable time to worry that Todd was being hurtful and rejecting. In the control condition, both partners completed the one-fault listing task and neither had any reason to think the other had a long list of complaints.

Next we measured the dependent variable – automatic inclinations to increase (vs. decrease) dependence on the partner. Under the guise of doing a categorization task, participants had to decide (yes/no) whether words appearing on the computer screen could ever possibly be used to describe their partner. These words were either trait words, like warm or stubborn, or object words, like truck. If the automatic inclination to reduce dependence on Todd is controlling Katy's behavior, we reasoned that she should be slower to identify positive traits in Todd on this task. Why? Questioning his value should make her less dependent on Todd and his approval, thereby restoring safety in a situation where she is feeling rejected.

Figure 3.2 presents the results. We plotted reaction times to positive-trait words as a function of experimental condition (partner rejection vs. control) and automatic partner attitudes. People with less positive automatic partner attitudes (on the right) automatically reduced dependence; they were markedly slower to identify positive traits in their partner in the partner rejection than in the control condition. However, participants with more positive automatic partner attitudes (on the left) sustained dependence; they were just as quick to identify positive traits in their partner in the partner rejection condition as they were in the control condition. To return to Katy and Todd, these results suggest that people who are less trusting restore safety in ways that minimize the potential for further harm. Questioning a partner's value, and thus reducing dependence

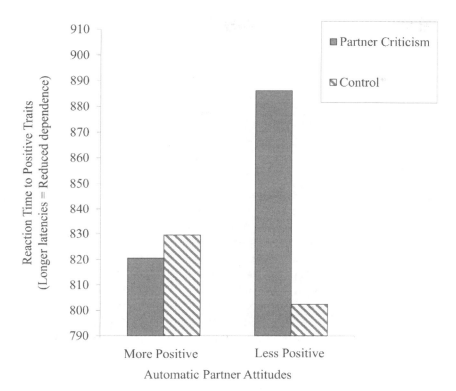

FIGURE 3.2 More Positive Automatic Partner Attitudes Protect Against Partner Criticism. (Adapted from Murray, S. L., Pinkus, R. T., Holmes, J. G., Harris, B., Gomillion, S., Aloni, M., Derrick, J., & Leder, S. (2011). Signaling when (and when not) to be cautious and self-protective: Impulsive and reflective trust in close relationships. *Journal of Personality and Social Psychology, 101*, 485–502. Copyright American Psychological Association; adapted with permission.)

on the partner, does just that. However, people who are more trusting take a riskier motivational course and suppress automatic intentions to reduce their own dependence that may not feel "right" given their greater progress toward safety.

Reasoned Beliefs

Katy's automatic evaluative association to Todd is not the only marker of trust activated in situations that highlight her vulnerability and powerlessness. The reasons she can articulate for trusting in Todd are also activated (Simpson, 2007). Believing that Todd sees her as both funny and warm and overly sensitive and demanding gives her reason to question whether he truly values her (Murray, Holmes, & Griffin, 2000). Consequently, in risky situations, a less trusting Katy may have greater difficulty explaining Todd's commitment. This difficulty articulating reasons to trust marks insufficient progress toward the goal of being safe and should motivate Katy to cautiously guard against further threats to safety. Therefore, being less trusting should reinforce Katy's situationally provoked temptation to reduce dependence and minimize her vulnerability. In contrast, Todd's greater ease explaining why Katy stays with him gives him the luxury to pursue a riskier motivational course because the prospect of rejection is less likely and hurtful. Therefore, being more trusting should motivate Todd to override the temptation to withdraw and instead restore safety in ways that preserve his trust and dependence on Katy.

A daily diary study provided one of our first tests of these hypotheses (Murray, Bellavia, et al., 2003). In this study, we indexed reasons to trust in the partner through people's beliefs about their partner's regard for them. To do this, we asked participants to describe how they believed their partner saw them on 20 or so interpersonal traits. Believing that Katy sees him as warm, responsive, and not at all stubborn gives Todd greater reason to trust in Katy. We then asked both partners to complete a standardized diary each day for 21 days. Each partner recorded what had happened each day (e.g., "we had a fight"); reported confidence in the other's caring (e.g., "I felt rejected or hurt by my partner"); and indicated whether they engaged in behaviors that could increase/decrease dependence (e.g., "I insulted or criticized my partner").

People who could readily point to qualities their partner valued in them restored safety through perceptual biases that increased their own dependence. They even "saw" greater evidence of trustworthiness in negative than positive partner behavior. They reported greater confidence in their partner's caring on days after they had serious conflicts or witnessed their partner engaging in manifestly hurtful behavior (relative to better days). In contrast, people who could *not* as readily point to qualities their partner valued in them restored safety through motivated perceptual biases and behavioral intentions that reduced their own dependence. They interpreted events as potentially innocuous as their partner simply being in a bad mood as testament to rejection. On days after they felt acutely rejected, they also engaged in rejecting behavior that communicated how little they needed their partner (Murray, Bellavia et al., 2003).

Differences in the safety-restoring tactics of more or less trusting people also emerged in an observational study of couples negotiating sacrifices (Shallcross & Simpson, 2012). Each partner in this study first completed a pre-interaction measure of trust tapping chronic perceptions of their partner's caring and reliability. Next, they tasked one member of the couple (e.g., Katy) to initiate a discussion with the other (e.g., Todd) about something that she personally wanted to do that required a major sacrifice on his part. In a subsequent discussion, Todd was similarly tasked to discuss a major sacrifice he wanted from Katy. Each partner then completed a post-interaction measure of state trust and objective raters coded the videotaped interactions for how responsively and accommodatingly partners behaved toward one another.

These ratings allowed the researchers to index both the objective threat to safety evident in the interaction and the safety-restoring tactics partners implemented. For instance, Todd's behavioral responsiveness to Katy's sacrifice request indexed the level of threat Katy experienced when she made herself vulnerable to Todd (with less responsive behavior indicating greater threat). Katy's behavioral responsiveness to Todd after she requested her sacrifice in turn indexed how she restored mutuality in dependence, and thus, her own state of safety (with less responsiveness behavior indicating her inclination to reduce her dependence). People who initially reported greater trust in their partner took greater psychological leaps of faith to restore safety than people who were less trusting. When highly trusting people requested a sacrifice, they saw greater "evidence" of accommodation and responsiveness in their partner's behavior than objective observers. In fact, highly trusting requestors reported *increases* in trust over the interaction when their partner engaged in *less* accommodative and responsive behavior. They essentially saw the evidence of responsiveness they needed to see to stay safe. In contrast, the motivation to restore safety had an opposite effect on the perceptions and behavior of less trusting people. When less trusting people requested a sacrifice, they behaviorally withdrew from partners even when their partner tried to be responsive and accommodate them.

Because relationships extend in time, a partner's hurtful behaviors are not locked in the past. The memory of these behaviors can intrude on the present to remind people of the risks of depending on their partner. When this happens, the motivated perceptual biases that color perceptions of the present also need to color perceptions of the past to restore safety (Luchies et al., 2013). Luchies and her colleagues (2013) studied such reconstructive memory biases in a series of diary studies. They asked participants to record their partner's every transgression daily, to rate every transgression's severity and hurtfulness, and to report whether or not they had forgiven each misdeed. Several weeks later, the researchers reminded participants of each transgression and they asked them to recall how they had felt about the transgression when it happened. People who initially reported greater reason to trust in their partner restored safety in the face of this threat through motivated reconstructive biases that whitewashed the past. More trusting people remembered partner transgressions as being less frequent and hurtful, and more forgivable than they had originally perceived them to be. However, less trusting people remembered their partner's transgressions as being even more frequent, hurtful, and unforgivable than they had originally perceived them to be. Less trusting people essentially restored safety in the face of this threat by reminding themselves exactly why they should keep a safe distance from their partner.

The Two Sources Will Not Always Agree

Our running examples of a less trusting Katy and more trusting Todd make the implicit assumption that each uniformly trusts or distrusts the other. That is not always going to be the case. Automatic partner attitudes and reasoned beliefs can send different messages about a partner's trustworthiness because they draw on different sources of information (Gawronski & Bodenhausen, 2006; LeBel & Campbell, 2009; Lee, Rogge, & Reis, 2010; Scinta & Gable, 2007). Automatic partner attitudes usually develop "bottom-up" – subliminally conditioned through behavioral interaction. Beliefs about a partner's trustworthiness usually develop "top-down" – informed by introspection and abstract reasoning (Fazio, 1986; Gregg et al., 2006; Wilson et al., 2000). Consequently, Katy could develop positive automatic attitudes toward Todd because he has always treated her well, but still question whether she can really trust him because she cannot readily explain why she should feel safe in his presence. We return to this complication in Chapters 5 and 6 when we discuss motivational conflicts between the goals to be safe from harm and perceive meaning and value.

When Safety Becomes a Preoccupation

We began this chapter arguing that automatic partner attitudes and reasoned beliefs mark the best means of making progress in the pursuit of safety by giving people the means to mindread their partner's dependence and commitment. We then transitioned to discuss how situations that highlight one partner's relative vulnerability and powerlessness make safety an acutely pressing concern. Next, we described how the goal to restore mutual dependence, and thus safety, activates different perceptual biases and behavioral intentions as a function of trust. For a less trusting Katy, safety comes in motivated perceptual biases and behavioral intentions that reduce her dependence on Todd. But, for a more trusting Todd, safety comes in motivated perceptual biases and behavioral intentions that increase Katy's dependence on him. Before moving on to the pursuit of value goals, we need to make one final point about safety pursuits: Safety is more likely to become a chronic and preoccupying goal in some relationships than others. By preoccupying, we mean that the goal to be safe is both more readily activated and less readily satiated. We develop this theme in Chapter 5 and just foreshadow these arguments here.

The first reason why safety can become a preoccupying goal comes from the power the life stage of the relationship has to put partners in vulnerable situations. Certain transitions in relationships, such as moving in together (Kelley, 1979) or the birth of a first child (Doss et al., 2009), dramatically increase interdependence. Caring for a newly arrived infant would unilaterally increase the number of ways in which Katy had no choice but to rely on Todd; even her capacity to eat, sleep, and bathe would require his cooperation. Such "enforced" interdependence is going to create more situations where partners have unequal dependence. Frequent exposure to such situations could turn safety into a chronically accessible goal through basic principles of priming and spreading activation. Each new situation of vulnerability activates the goal to be safe, which then makes the subsequent activation of this goal more likely in any situation that bears close enough resemblance to the original one (Higgins, 1996).

The second reason why safety can become a preoccupying goal rests in the power that *partners* have to behave in ways that make it *objectively* more or less difficult to trust them across situations. Partners differ in interaction risk because they differ in the dispositions they bring to the relationship (Murray & Holmes, 2011). For instance, low self-esteem partners present a greater interaction risk because they resist self-disclosure (Forest & Wood, 2011), push partners away when they feel hurt (Ford & Collins, 2010), and demand unrelenting affection and support (Lemay & Dudley, 2011; Marigold, Cavallo, Holmes, & Wood, 2014). Anxiously attached partners provide inconsistent support (Collins & Feeney, 2004) and try to exact guilt in their partners to hold sway over them (Overall, Lemay, Girme, & Hammond, 2014). Partners who are more neurotic are also quicker to cast accusations and blame for mistakes (Karney & Bradbury, 1997). Because difficult partners often behave in uncaring ways, people paired with such partners will more often find themselves questioning whether their partner really needs and depends on them. Consequently, safety is likely to become a chronically preoccupying goal because it stands to be activated in almost any situation that involves the partner (Higgins, 1996).

The third reason why safety can become a preoccupying goal rests in the perceiver and the power personal motivations have to infuse attention, inference, and behavior in relationships. The motivated cognitive processes that allow people to believe that they are smarter or more attractive than they are can also be harnessed to make people believe their partner merits far less trust than they actually do. For Katy to believe that she has good reason to trust in Todd, she has to pretend to know something that is essentially unknowable. She has to look into an uncertain future and simply have faith that Todd will always need and depend on her and want to be there for her, no matter what happens (Holmes & Rempel, 1989). Unfortunately, some people are poorly equipped to find resounding support for this conclusion in the evidence.

Low self-esteem people are a case in point. They are notorious for questioning their value to others (Leary, Tambor, Terdal, & Downs, 1995). They underestimate how much their partner loves and values them even though they are loved just as much as high self-esteem people (Murray et al., 2001). Low self-esteem people cannot quite explain why they should trust their partner for one basic reason: They are unsure of themselves and hesitant to believe anything truly good about themselves or other people for fear they might be wrong (Baumeister, 1993; Heimpel, Elliot, & Wood, 2006). Rather than believe their partner sees them as good and valuable, low self-esteem people self-verify and assume that their partner sees them in the same negative light as they see themselves (Murray, Holmes, & Griffin, 2000). The subversive personal agendas that come with low self-esteem thus make safety a more chronically preoccupying goal. Because low self-esteem people cannot quite convince themselves they have reason to be safe, they see threats to safety at every corner. Vulnerable perceivers essentially learn to associate safety and its pursuit with any situation involving the hint of vulnerability, making its pursuit a habit.

Conclusion

Shaken by a work-weary Todd's apparent lack of interest in spending time with her in the past week, Katy decided against asking Todd to go to see her parents for the weekend. Consequently, Todd lost an opportunity to prove his willingness to be trustworthy and responsive to Katy's needs. The unfortunate outcome to this tale reiterates two important themes to carry forward.

The first is that the outcomes of safety goal pursuits are not necessarily good ones. Through her reticence, Katy lost the hope of getting what she really wanted – Todd meeting her parents. Nonetheless, her actions did keep her safe from being hurt in that particular situation, satisfying the goal to be safe. Though this point might seem paradoxical, it bears emphasis. Satisfying the goal to be safe does not always result in people finding safety and comfort in their partner's hands. Sometimes people can also find the safety and comfort they seek by taking their outcomes *out* of their partner's hands. The second theme to carry forward is that safety goals are not static. Safety is never achieved in some absolute sense, freeing a person from the need to ever again protect against the possibility of hurt. Even though Katy backed away from Todd for this weekend trip, she will still face new situations in her relationship that make her feel vulnerable and uncertain – renewing the need to take some kind of psychological and behavioral precaution to restore safety. With these points in mind about the pursuit of safety, we now turn to consider the second fundamental goal – value.

Notes

1 This conceptualization of trust makes explicit what is usually implicit in measurement. Any construct is more than the sum of its measured parts. In our case, the construct of trust captures "something more" than any method of measurement captures. This "something more" is intangible and intrinsic to the person, an essential property of subjective experience. In this chapter, we use the term "experience of trust" to remind the reader that Katy's trust in Todd captures something intrinsic to her experience that cannot just be boiled down to responses on a trust scale. Katy's experience of trust in Todd is dynamic and changing, a complex interplay of automatic evaluative associations, reasoned beliefs, and situational influences. Much as researchers might want to capture lightning in a bottle, collectively we have only begun to understand the complex algorithm involving the different sources of measured influences that create Katy's experience of trust in Todd and Todd's experience of trust in Katy.
2 Participants categorized words belonging to four categories: (1) pleasant words (e.g., vacation, pleasure); (2) unpleasant words (e.g., bomb, poison); (3) words associated with the partner (e.g., partner's first name, partner's birthday); and (4) words not associated with the partner (Zayas & Shoda, 2005). We contrasted reaction times on two sets of trials to diagnose partners' automatic attitude toward their partner. In one set of trials,

participants used the same response key to respond to pleasant words and partner words (i.e., compatible pairings). In the other set of trials, participants used the same response key to respond to unpleasant words and partner words (i.e., incompatible pairings). The logic of the IAT says reaction times should be faster when the nature of the task matches the nature of one's automatic associations to the partner. In particular, people who possess more positive automatic attitudes should be faster when categorizing words using the same motion for "partner" and "pleasant" than when using the same motion for "partner" and "unpleasant."

3 We explore this risk regulation principle fully in Chapter 5.

4
PURSUING VALUE

When Sylvia and Brian started dating, they never imagined taking a circuitous path to the altar. Those first semesters at college, it seemed like they were perfect for one another. They took the same classes, spent every day and night together, and enjoyed an overlapping circle of friends. They graduated convinced they would spend the rest of their lives together. Recently, the future has not seemed quite as clear. Brian got a job before Sylvia did and met a new circle of friends. Spending time with his engineering colleagues reminded Brian how much he loves high-adrenaline sports and adventure – pursuits he had largely put aside so he could share in Sylvia's tamer interests. The prospect of an endless string of quiet movie nights alone with Sylvia does not feel quite as enticing as it once did. Watching Brian explore his new circle of friends, Sylvia is having some second thoughts too. On the odd occasion, she even catches herself daydreaming about one of her more refined and bookish male colleagues. Despite spending a short time apart as they settled into new jobs, Sylvia and Brian still want a future together. They just moved in together and they both feel like they have invested too much of themselves in their relationship to let it go, but they need to be sure that they really are right for one other and their future will be a rosy one.

The growing pains that Sylvia and Brian are experiencing naturally occur as interdependence increases. As encountered situations expand in breadth, partners discover new ways in which their needs and goals are less compatible than they thought (Kelley, 1979). Such expectancy violations can take many shapes and sizes. Partner qualities that first appeared charming may prove grating with time. The first time Brian was late for an appointment, it was easy for Sylvia to embrace it as part of his easy-going attitude. Now that they are both working and time is tight, his punctuality problems are a little harder to dismiss. At transition points in relationships, taking a new job, or having a baby, partners can also discover things they never knew, and do not particularly like, about one another. Sylvia seems a little too tame to Brian now that he sees her love for peace, quiet, and calm through the eyes of his new friends. Even familiar situations can violate expectations if one partner decides the status quo is no longer acceptable.

When reality disappoints, and partners violate one another's expectations, doubt and ambivalence can start to creep in (Brickman, 1987). Rather than setting the stage for a relationship's demise, doubt can actually sow the seeds for its resilience. This chapter takes us back to the functional imperative for purposeful and directed action introduced in Chapter 2. Decisive action requires certainty (Harmon-Jones, Amodio, & Harmon-Jones, 2009; Smith & Semin, 2004; Tritt, Inzlicht, & Harmon-Jones, 2012). Therefore, the experience of doubt is aversive and unpleasant because it interferes with directed and purposeful action. Doubt and ambivalence are even embodied as conflicted or stymied action. People instructed to physically sway side to side feel more doubtful, indecisive, and uncertain than people instructed to move up and down or stand still (Schneider et al., 2013). People exposed to two sides of an attitude issue also physically teeter side to side, conflicted both physically and mentally, unable to take a decisive step, either forward or backward (Schneider et al., 2013).

This chapter argues that seeing value and meaning in caring for the partner and relationship functions as an embodied goal because its ongoing pursuit neutralizes the doubts that could otherwise paralyze action. To care for Sylvia with a clear heart and mind, Brian needs to turn her distaste for his adventurous pursuits into something that he values in her. Such a capacity to defensively *create* value and meaning in action is crucial in relationships because perceiving value in the partner fosters steadfast intentions to be responsive and meet a partner's needs when it is difficult to do so.

In the first section of this chapter, we introduce the desired end-state: To perceive *unequivocal* value in relationship-promotive action. "Relationship-promotive action" refers to behaviors that are personally costly, but nurture the partner and relationship, such as forgiveness, support, and sacrifice. We argue that people experience such actions as inherently valuable when they are convinced they are right; that is, when they are not ambivalent or uncertain (Brickman, 1987). We then describe how progress toward the goal of perceiving unequivocal value in relationship-promotive action is signaled through mental representations and bodily states associated with the experience of clear-minded conviction. We argue dissonance-related affective and bodily states capture *incipient* threats to conviction and signal when the basis for relationship-promotive action *could* become questionable (Harmon-Jones, Harmon-Jones, & Levy, 2015; van Harreveld, van der Pligt, & de Liver, 2009). We also argue that conscious thoughts of commitment capture the history of *realized* threats to commitment and signals when the basis for relationship-promotive action has *already* become questionable (Brickman, 1987).

In the second section of the chapter, we explain how people make progress towards the goal of perceiving unequivocal value and meaning in caring for the partner and relationship. That is, we focus on the means of goal pursuit. We examine how the goal to perceive value in relationship-promotive action biases attention, perception, and inference in situations that threaten conviction. We argue that the motivational machinations that restore value and meaning in action depend on (1) the decision context, that is, whether it is an initial versus ongoing choice and (2) overall progress in pursuit of value as represented by chronic commitment.

In describing goal pursuit, we first focus on the uncertainties provoked by initial romantic choice. As we will explore, deciding which partner to pursue selectively biases attention toward diagnostic cues to partner value that support decisive and confident choices. We then turn to the uncertainties that arise as people live with the choice they made. Because no partner is as perfect as he or she initially seemed, people inevitably encounter situations that cause them to question their choices (even if it is just for a moment). In such situations, evidence of a partner's faults, the lure of a tempting alternative, the frustration of losing autonomy, or the necessity of making a sacrifice automatically activate biases in attention, perception, and memory that defuse doubt and restore certainty to relationship-promotive action. We will also see that people who are more committed are more likely to evidence the automatic biases that protect conviction.

In the final section, we explore the effects that perceiving (or failing to perceive) sufficient meaning and value in the partner have on ongoing relationships. We specifically focus on the role that possessing positive illusions about the partner plays in suppressing doubt and strengthening conviction and commitment. We conclude by acknowledging an unacknowledged reality. Although this chapter focuses on the motivational machinations that *create and sustain* a sense of value in action, such a sense of conviction is much more difficult to sustain for some people and in some relationship contexts than others (Baumeister & Leary, 1995). We return to the situational and motivational pressures that compete with value goal pursuits in the remaining chapters.

The Desired End-State: An Unconflicted Basis for Relationship-Promotive Action

Even decisions that seem incontrovertible – like parenting – still require ongoing rationalization. Eibach and Mock (2011) confronted parents with the exorbitant financial costs of raising children, but varied how much existential angst such costs could provoke. They let parents in the "uncertainty" condition ruminate about these costs. But they mitigated these costs for parents in the "certainty" condition by telling them that their children would take care of them in old age. Then they gave parents the opportunity to justify their parenting behavior by proselytizing for pronatalism (e.g., "Parents experience a lot more happiness and satisfaction in their lives compared to people who have never had children"). The findings spoke to the power of the need to construct value in action: Parents in the "uncertainty" condition were much more pronatal in their proselytizing than parents in the "certain" basis for action condition.

Ambivalence Is the Relationship Reality

Unlike parenting, the decision to commit to one particular partner over others has much less built-in justification. In fact, living with someone is bound to make the reasons *not* to commit especially salient, as Sylvia and Brian discovered once they moved in together (Kelley, 1979). Because greater interdependence reveals the good, the bad, and the ugly, Zayas and Shoda (2015) reasoned that significant-other representations should be inherently ambivalent. Thinking of a valued significant other should automatically and simultaneously activate positive and negative associations.

To test this hypothesis, they had participants generate four names: (1) the significant other they liked the most; (2) the significant other they liked the least; (3) the significant object they liked the most (e.g., sunset); and (4) the significant object they liked the least (e.g., spider). These names then served as primes in a sequential priming task. The experimental prime (e.g., Sylvia, sunset) or control prime (i.e., random-letter string) first flashed imperceptibly on the computer screen. A target word then appeared (e.g., chocolate, cockroach). This target word remained on the screen until participants decided whether this target word was "pleasant" or "unpleasant" (Zayas & Shoda, 2015).

Sequential priming tasks such as this one use basic principles of spreading activation to uncover how people really think and feel about particular attitude objects (Fazio, Sanbonmatsu, Powell, & Kardes, 1986). If priming Sylvia only activates positive associations, Brian should be faster to identify chocolate as "pleasant" and slower to identify cockroach as "unpleasant" when Sylvia is primed (as compared to a random-letter string). But, if priming Sylvia activates both positive *and* negative associations, Brian should be faster to identify chocolate as "pleasant" and cockroach as "unpleasant" when Sylvia is primed (as compared to a random-letter string).

Priming most-liked significant others automatically activated both positive and negative associations. Participants were faster to identify positive targets as pleasant and negative targets as unpleasant when thinking of the significant other they valued most. In contrast, priming the significant *object* participants liked the most automatically activated primarily positive associations and priming the significant others and objects participants liked the least generated primarily negative associations. Representations of beloved significant others are unique in this important respect: They are inherently conflicted. Significant others automatically bring positive *and* negative associations to mind.

But Ambivalent Realities Are Behaviorally Untenable

In most situations, people are not troubled by the internal contradictions in their beliefs because their attitudes do not have any immediate implications for action. During the work week, when Brian has no time to go on a sports adventure, the fact that he loves and hates Sylvia's caution never really enters his mind. However, when people *do* need to act, the internal contradictions in ambivalent attitudes can become accessible (Newby-Clark, McGregor, & Zanna, 2002). Such conflicted attitudes, feelings, or beliefs point people in two opposite directions, making these conflicted or internally contradictory representations behaviorally untenable (Harmon-Jones et al., 2015).

Therein lies the problem people face in relationships (and elsewhere in life). People want and need to act with a clear-minded sense of purpose, but the conflicted nature of many attitudes, beliefs, and feelings thwarts that sense of purpose. Everything Brian likes about Sylvia's caution motivates him to sacrifice his weekends freely, but everything he dislikes motivates him to go off with his friends. Because Brian cannot pursue both courses of action simultaneously, he needs to turn his behavioral indecision into the "right" decision (Elliot & Devine, 1994; Harmon-Jones et al., 2015).

The participants in the Zayas and Shoda (2015) studies did exactly this. Even though significant others automatically activated both positive and negative associations, people were not wracked by conscious doubts and uncertainties about those dearest to them. Instead, they reported uniformly positive feelings about their most liked significant others. The discrepancy between conflicted automatic associations and *un*conflicted conscious feelings makes perfect sense from our perspective. Conflicted feelings and beliefs stymie action (Schneider et al., 2013). To actually move forward, people need to turn such incipient conflicts into clear-minded resolve (van Harreveld, van der Pligt, et al., 2009).

Van Harreveld and Bullens and colleagues report fascinating illustrations of these basic dynamics in related programs of research on (1) ambivalent attitudes and (2) reversible versus irreversible decisions (Bullens, van Harreveld, Higgins, & Forster, 2014; Nordgren, van Harreveld, & van der Pligt, 2006; van Harreveld, Rutjens, Rotteveel, Nordgren, & van der Pligt, 2009; van Harreveld, Rutjens, Schneider, Nohlen, & Keskinis, 2014; van Harreveld, van der Pligt, et al., 2009). Their research warrants recapping here because it aptly illustrates how the basic need to perceive an unconflicted, unequivocal, and meaningful basis for action commandeers more specific goal pursuits in its service.

The ambivalence studies tested two related hypotheses. The first: Acting on the basis of an internally inconsistent attitude elicits angst and discomfort. Consistent with this hypothesis, people experience stress-related physiological arousal, conscious feelings of uncertainty, and generalized negative affect when they need to take a decided behavioral stand (either pro or con) on a conflicted attitude (van Harreveld, Rutjens, et al., 2009).

The second: Experiencing ambivalence motivates people to make actions "right." What makes this hypothesis provocative is the flexibility with which people can make their decisions "right." People can actually make their questionable actions seem sensible by perceiving greater order, consistency, and meaning in the world in *general*. For instance, people who feel ambivalent and uncertain because they just read about the pros *and* cons of enacting controversial abortion legislation restore perceptual order. They are more likely to perceive meaningful pictures in random dots than people who feel unconflicted (van Harreveld et al., 2014, Study 1). Similarly, people who feel anxious and uncertain because they just thought about something they feel personally conflicted about restore psychological order. They are more likely to grasp on to implausible conspiracy theories to explain the inexplicable than people thinking of a personal topic they feel unconflicted about (Study 2). Restoring physical order by straightening a messy lab room even inoculates people against the disorder in their personal lives. When people had to sit in a messy lab room, those who had just thought about a personal conflict restored order and consistency to their worlds by perceiving meaningful pictures in random dots. But this psychological meaning-restorative response disappeared when people first had the opportunity to straighten a messy lab room, and thus restore physical order to their worlds (van Harreveld et al., 2014, Study 3).

Research comparing the psychological effects of reversible versus irreversible decisions further suggests that constructing consistency, order, and value in choice actually fosters unconflicted behavior. In their experiments, Bullens and colleagues instructed participants to decide between two equally desirable options (Bullens et al., 2014; Bullens, van Harreveld, & Forster, 2011; Bullens, van Harreveld, Forster, & van der Pligt, 2013). They manipulated the pressure to make the decision orderly and meaningful by telling participants the decision was either irreversible (i.e., they could not take it back) or reversible (i.e., they could take it back).

When decisions are *irreversible*, people need to *act* on the basis of the choices they made. But, when decisions are reversible, people do not need to live with the choice they made; they can bail at any point in time. Because irreversible decisions need to be acted upon immediately, irreversible decisions should motivate people to make their decision the "right" one. That is, people making irreversible decisions should justify and come to see greater value in their choices than people making reversible decisions (Gilbert & Ebert, 2002). Such a clear-minded sense of purpose should free people to move forward, productively acting on the basis of the decision. Consistent with this logic, people who had just made an irreversible decision showed greater promotion or approach-oriented motivation than people who had just made a reversible choice (Bullens et al., 2014). However, people who had just made a reversible decision were left stuck in ambivalence; they exhausted themselves cognitively, continually revisiting their choice, which left them unable to move forward (Bullens et al., 2013).

Conviction: Marking Goal Pursuit

The reviewed research suggests that the motivation to perceive an unconflicted and unequivocal basis for action commandeers goal pursuits in its service. The necessity of acting in the face of uncertainty compels people to perceive the actions they ultimately take as meaningful, purposeful, and "right." Such clarity of mind can then afford effective and vigorous behavior (van Harreveld, van der Pligt, et al., 2009). In relationships, the need to perceive an unconflicted and unequivocal basis for relationship-promotive action manifests itself in the pursuit of value and meaning in the partner. Perceiving Sylvia as valuable and meaningful – as the "right" partner for him – takes any internal contradiction out of Brian's inherently ambivalent or conflicted actions. His resistance to his coworker's flirtations, his weekend sacrifices of adventure time, and his efforts to bite his tongue when she criticizes him all make sense. These actions are meaningful and rational rather than purposeless and foolish because seeing incontrovertible value and meaning in Sylvia makes her worth it.

Brian's strength of conviction marks his progress in the pursuit of value goals, and thus, his current state of clarity in mind and action. Figure 4.1 depicts our conceptual model of conviction. It resembles a third-class lever because conviction is the psychological and bodily force applied to drive caring, communal, and responsive behavior in the face of resistance. In this model, "conviction strength" refers to a state of mind internal to the person. Conviction boils down to Brian's resolute belief that he is in the "right" relationship with the "right" partner. Unless shaken, conviction gives clear value and meaning to caring, communal, and responsive behavior because it elevates it to a higher calling (Brickman, 1987). "Resistance" refers to situations that test conviction by making the unexpected

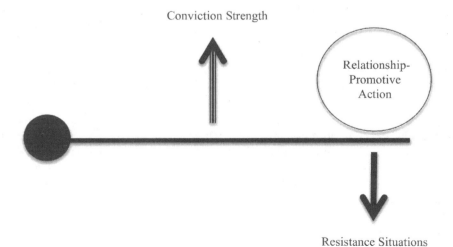

FIGURE 4.1 The Lever Model of Conviction

costs of interdependence salient. Such unwelcome surprises might involve temptations of the flesh, such as Sylvia's attraction to a colleague, weaknesses of the spirit, such as Sylvia's reluctance to share in Brian's outdoor activities, and impulses of emotion, such as Brian's desire to snap at Sylvia in retaliation.

The psychological lever depicted in Figure 4.1 functions straightforwardly: The greater the situational "resistance," the greater the "force" of conviction that needs to be applied to drive and energize unconflicted relationship-promotive behavior. Stronger convictions stabilize motivations to behave responsively because conviction necessitates a belief structure that puts doubt in context. For instance, people who put doubts in context by mentally linking their partner's faults to their greater, compensatory virtues are involved in more rewarding and more stable relationships (Murray & Holmes, 1999).

For conviction to leverage unconflicted relationship-promotive behavior, perceivers need to "know" when situations necessitate applying more force. In our conceptual model, the intangible strength of conviction has two tangible experiential markers: (1) the affective state of dissonance arousal and uncertainty and (2) the cognitive state of commitment. These markers signal progress in the pursuit of value goals and motivate people to apply more force and solidify conviction when it is in question *by adding compensatory value and meaning to the partner and relationship itself.*

The experience of dissonance serves as an immediate or impulsive bodily signal that the value and purpose of relationship-promotive behavior might be in question. Brian's experience of affective uncertainty and bodily discomfort in a threatening situation – such as when he has to choose between spending a quiet weekend with Sylvia or going off with his adventurous friends – functions as a first line of defense; a proverbial warning shot that Sylvia might not be worth the sacrifice of staying. The experience of commitment serves as a less immediate, more reflective, and more persistently pressing signal of whether the value of engaging in relationship-promotive behavior is already in question. Brian coming to consciously question his commitment functions as a second line of defense – a last-call warning that Sylvia might not be worth the sacrifices he has made in the past or might make in the future.

The Affective Marker of Conviction: Dissonance

In the action-based model, dissonance motivates people to make conflicted actions *un*conflicted (Harmon-Jones et al., 2015; Harmon-Jones, Schmeichel, Inzlicht, & Harmon-Jones, 2011). In signaling disquiet, dissonance motivates people to make their actions meaningful, valuable, and "right." Dissonance-worthy internal contradictions between thought and behavior happen routinely in relationships. Now that Brian and Sylvia are living together, he consistently challenges her ideals for the division of domestic labor. She wants a 50/50 division, but she is the only who notices the need to dust, vacuum, and do the dishes. She is starting to think that Brian is a lot more stubborn and selfish than she ever realized. The secret delight she takes in talking to her bookish and impeccably neat workmate has also caught her by surprise. She never expected to be attracted to anyone else. Now that Sylvia takes up more and more of his weekends, Brian spends more time wondering what it would be like to be single than he thinks he should. Sylvia's new hours at work also precipitated his unhappy discovery that she is a lot more irritable than he ever thought. Even though they are generally happy and eager to move their relationship forward, reality is not always turning out exactly as they expected.

Left unchecked, such expectancy violations put the basis for being kind, loyal, and responsive to the partner into question. In our conceptualization of conviction, expectancy violations such as these elicit feelings of disquiet and discomfort to motivate constructing clear-minded and unconflicted intentions to engage in caring, communal, and committed behavior. When ongoing events violate expectations, experiencing dissonance provides a "first-line of defense" signal that motivates partners to construct new and better justifications for the kindnesses they bestow on one another.

Research using misattribution paradigms suggests that the affective discomfort underlying dissonance indeed motivates people to create a clear and unconflicted basis for action. Nordgren and colleagues (2006) activated ambivalent attitudes by exposing participants to the pros and cons of genetically modified foods. Then they gave some participants an alternate explanation for their discomfort (by telling them a pill they had just taken would make them feel tense). When participants did *not* expect to feel tense, the internal contradiction in their attitudes elicited angst and discomfort. Such aversive feelings in turn motivated them to clarify their thoughts by favoring one side of the issue. The experience of dissonance thus motivated them to create value in decisions to eat (or not eat) genetically modified foods (Nordgren et al., 2006).

In sum, the activation and alleviation of dissonance provide situation-sensitive markers of incipient threats to conviction that signal when Sylvia's value to Brian might be in jeopardy. In expectancy-violating situations, the activation of dissonance signals insufficient progress toward value goals, motivating Brian to reclarify Sylvia's value to him, solidifying the value of behaving with her best interest in mind (van Harreveld et al., 2014). In turn, the alleviation of dissonance then signals renewed progress toward the goal of perceiving value in action, remotivating decisive and steadfast relationship-promotive action (Harmon-Jones et al., 2009, 2011).

The Cognitive Marker of Conviction: Commitment

In the investment model, commitment motivates people to behave with the long-term interests of the relationship at heart (Rusbult & Van Lange, 2003). Commitment captures intentions for the future that are based in the history of dependence, a structural property of the relationship (Rusbult & Van Lange, 2003). Brian is more dependent on Sylvia when she satisfies more of his needs, when he has invested more time, energy, and resources in the relationship, and when he cannot imagine being happier living his life alone or with another partner (Rusbult, Martz, & Agnew, 1998). However, commitment also captures something more than just the history of dependence.

Interdependence theorists use the term "commitment" to capture psychological attachment to the partner and relationship that essentially goes beyond logic (Rusbult & Van Lange, 2003). Brian's commitment to Sylvia is not something that can simply be reduced to his reliance on her for need satisfaction, his concrete investment of time and energy, or his lack of other viable dating options. His commitment is intrinsic to his experience; it transcends practicalities and gives being with Sylvia meaning and purpose all on its own. In fact, commitment predicts greater relationship stability even controlling for its basis in dependence (Le & Agnew, 2003). Commitment supplies intrinsic meaning to action because it absolves the need to explain oneself (Brickman, 1987). Committed people do not need to think; they act. It is this clear-minded, resolute sense of purpose that gives rise to Brian's desire to take care of Sylvia and makes the actions he takes to nurture his relationship intrinsically valuable and meaningful.

Commitment has one particular quality that makes it an especially adept marker of conviction. Like an elastic band, it is resilient to wear and tear, but it can still be stretched and manipulated. Because commitment is based in the history of the relationship, it affords a reasonably resilient chronic disposition to prioritize the relationship. As a chronic disposition, it functions to keep the relationship on an even keel, much as a rudder steadies a ship (Kelley, 1979; Rusbult et al., 1998; Rusbult & Buunk, 1993; Rusbult & Van Lange, 2003). However, events and situations can still test and stretch commitment. Even people who are highly committed experience doubts and question commitment given the right situations (Arriaga, 2001; Murray, Holmes, Griffin, & Derrick, 2015). Sylvia's caution has become a source of confusion and ambivalence for Brian because he is so invested in his relationship. It has started to trouble him precisely because moving in together made him more dependent. Indeed, in Murray's newlywed sample, people who were most committed at the point of marriage were the most likely to question their commitments over time (Murray et al., 2015).

This resilient elasticity means that commitment can signal the need to make further progress toward value goals in two respects. Through its resilience, commitment can function as a chronic motivational resource that incentivizes the pursuit of value. Much as the endorphins associated with exercise become addictive for the athletically minded, behaving caringly, communally, and responsively may become its own inherent reward for the committed-minded (Linardatos & Lydon, 2011). In Brian's case, his usually strong commitment affords him the optimism needed to believe his actions are inherently meaningful, motivating him to think and behave in ways that sustain conviction. Through its elasticity, commitment *wavering* can signal especially testing "resistance" situations likely to require exerting a greater force of conviction in the future. In such situations, Brian's unexpected and unsettling doubts about his commitment signal insufficient value goal progress and motivate him to reaffirm the importance of acting with Sylvia's best interest in mind (van Harreveld et al., 2014).

Defending Goal Progress

As interdependence increases, people typically encounter more situations that test conviction and thwart value goal progress. These "resistance" situations differ from "risky" situations that test trust and thwart safety goal progress in one principal way. In "risky" situations, the perceiver is more dependent on the partner than the partner is on the perceiver (Chapter 3). In "resistance" situations, the balance of power is shifted and the partner is more dependent on the perceiver than the perceiver is on the partner. In interdependence terms, the perceiver has more "fate" control over the partner's outcomes in "resistance" situations, whereas the partner has more "fate" control over the perceiver's outcomes in "risky" situations. Fate control is the difference between Sylvia deciding whether to make a sacrifice for Brian (a "resistance" situation in which she has high fate control) and Sylvia asking Brian to make a sacrifice for her (a "risky" situation in which she has low fate control). In a "risky" situation, Brian gets to decide Sylvia's fate, which gives him greater power to be selfish or selfless. In a "resistance" situation, Sylvia gets to decide Brian's fate, which gives her greater power.

Typically, "resistance" situations have significant positive and negative features. This ambivalent feature mix tests Sylvia's conviction in the value of caring for Brian and threatens her motivation to act in the relationship's best interest. When Brian seeks Sylvia's sympathetic ear, she knows she'll have less time to spend on her own interests. When Sylvia cleans up after Brian without so much as a word of complaint, she also knows he might take advantage of her tolerance again. Thus, the strong positives and negatives that define "resistance" situations do not afford unequivocal reason for behaving caringly and communally. Instead, these situations cast people into a state of behavioral indecision that could stymie relationship-promotive action.

In the lever model of conviction depicted in Figure 4.1, "resistance" situations elicit dissonance and/or conscious doubts as a means of motivating clear-minded and unconflicted action. For Brian to behave responsively when it might be costly or unwise, he needs to perceive "value" in action. That is, he needs to make prioritizing Sylvia and his relationship the "right" choice. At those times when Brian needs to care for Sylvia when it is costly to him, experiencing dissonance or even doubting his commitment could provide the motivational incentive to make her more valuable and worth the sacrifice.

We now explore how uncertainty and the behavioral ambivalence inherent to resistance situations motivate people to turn conflicted interdependent situations into unconflicted ones. We review the motivated biases in attention, perception, and inference that allow people to perceive their partner as the "right" and "only" person for them. We start with motivated biases that turn the behavioral conflict created by a plethora of possible partners into the clear decision to pursue one "right" partner. We then examine the biases that keep the chosen partner the "right" partner when the going gets tougher.

Fitting Motivation to Context: Decision Deliberation

Uncertainty is inherent to choice. Even a trip to the grocery store presents a dizzying array of options. There's ketchup in its original form, reduced-sugar, low-salt, jalapeño, organic, and ketchup blended with balsamic vinegar. Such a plethora of options invites indecision and behavioral conflict, but most people leave the grocery store believing they chose the right ketchup. In the social world, there are even more potential partners than ketchups to choose from, but most people leave the mating arena reasonably certain they chose the one partner that is "right" for them as well.

Brickman (1987) argued that the impossibility of making a truly unconflicted choice between romantic partners motivates people to believe they have done just that. Indeed, being hopeful, but uncertain, of another's romantic interest motivates people to make the case for pursuing them ironclad. For instance, women inspecting Facebook profiles of potential dating partners value men who "might" like them more than men who "definitely" like them (Whitchurch, Wilson, & Gilbert, 2011). As we see next, making a definite, but uncertain, romantic choice automatically activates the perceptual, cognitive, and behavioral means for people to believe they are making the "right" choice. Uncertainty sensitizes people to cues that diagnose the upsides of an intended commitment and desensitizes people to cues that diagnose its downsides. The automatic detection of such value thus makes it easier to commit to pursue one particular partner over others. In fact, subliminally associating an available partner with desirable traits is sufficient to spur dedicated romantic interest (Koranyi, Gast, & Rothermund, 2012).

Maximizing the Upsides

The prospect of making an uncertain choice among potential partners sensitizes perceivers to partner qualities that make a given choice more valuable and easier to justify. Women primed with thoughts of romance are better able to discriminate heterosexual (a sexually desirable trait) from homosexual men (Rule, Rosen, Slepian, & Ambady, 2011). On speed dates, women are more drawn to men displaying the wide and broad facial signature of dominance (a genetically valuable trait) than men with narrower faces (Valentine, Norman, Penke, & Perrett, 2014). Men and women primed with the desire to seek romantic partners also selectively attend to the most physically attractive of their options (Maner, Gailliot, Rouby, & Miller, 2007). Physiological states that spur romantic choice also increase sensitivity to diagnostic cues to a partner's value. Ovulating women are better able to discern heterosexual from homosexual men than non-ovulating women (Rule et al., 2011). Ovulating women are also more likely to flirt with dominant, "sexy cad" men who show the behavioral markers of genetic fitness than non-ovulating women (Cantu et al., 2014). Men are also more likely to pick up on cues that make women desirable, such as sexual arousal, when women are ovulating than when they are not (Miller & Maner, 2011b).

Minimizing the Negative

The prospect of making an uncertain choice among partners also desensitizes perceivers to qualities that could make a desired choice questionable and hard to justify. In deciding to pursue Sylvia, Brian had to sacrifice some of his personal autonomy to follow his own interests, including pursuing alternate partners. If he were to perseverate on such limitations, he might never commit. However, people contemplating romantic commitments automatically adopt more positive attitudes toward dependence (Koranyi & Meissner, 2015) and direct their attention away from attractive alternatives (Koranyi & Rothermund, 2012b).

Fitting Motivation to Context: Decision Implementation

Objective threats to unconflicted caring and communal action typically increase in frequency and severity as interdependence increases. When Brian first started dating Sylvia, sacrificing his weekends rarely gave him a moment's hesitation because he was so captivated by her. But now that the passion has started to ebb, the costs of sacrificing his weekends are more salient. They have also discovered points of conflict they never entertained before they moved in together. Much to Sylvia's surprise, the appearance of household cleanliness Brian maintained while they were dating was just pure pretense.

The situations partners encounter as they become more interdependent bring reasons *not* to be caring, communal, and responsive into sharper relief. This ambivalent reality makes forceful conviction in the partner's value and meaning even more important for leveraging relationship-promotive behavior (Murray et al., 2015) and satisfying the belongingness imperative (Baumeister & Leary, 1995). It also makes forceful conviction more difficult to sustain because it is more frequently tested (Kelley, 1979). Given such taxing realities, the cognitive burden of value creation needs to be light (Bargh, Schwader, Hailey, Daley, & Boothby, 2012; Bargh & Williams, 2006; Dijksterhuis & Nordgren, 2006). Otherwise Brian wouldn't have much in the way of self-regulatory resources available for anything other than being responsive to Sylvia (Finkel et al., 2006). Fortunately, the "resistance" situations people typically encounter automatically activate biases in attention, perception, and inference that accentuate the positives and minimize the negatives of responsive behavior. In so doing, such biases efficiently and expediently restore the value and purpose of behaving responsively without Brian giving it a second thought.[1] We describe the automatic biases implicit in four commonly encountered "resistance" situations next.

Maximizing the Upsides

The first "resistance" situation involves sacrificing self-interest to meet a partner's needs. Imagine Sylvia made special plans to go on a quiet spa weekend with Brian, but he wants to go mountain biking with his friends. For Brian to sacrifice, the valuing of making Sylvia happy needs to outweigh losing out on adrenaline and time with his friends. If Brian were to perseverate on both the positives and the negatives in this situation, he could get stuck in behavioral conflict. But the "right" course of action would be clear if "sacrifice" situations automatically elicit his tendency to enhance the value of meeting Sylvia's needs. Sacrifice situations have just this effect. People more willingly sacrifice for their partner when they are behaving on automatic pilot because their self-control is taxed (Righetti, Finkenauer, & Finkel, 2013).

The second "resistance" situation arises when one partner inadvertently interferes with the other's goals. Brian's careless disregard for shoes, clothes, and food wrappers strewn about constantly frustrates Sylvia's aspirations of domestic civility. If she perseverated on Brian's apparent disregard for her interests in such "goal interference" situations, she might question prioritizing his needs. However, the "right" course of patience and caring would be immediately clear if goal interference automatically elicits compensatory tendencies to value the partner all the more.

We tested the hypothesis through a combination of experimental and daily diary studies (Murray, Holmes, et al., 2009). In one of the experiments, participants in the "goal-interference" condition completed a biased survey. This survey took participants through a list of exceedingly common ways one partner could interfere with the other partner's personal goals (e.g., "I couldn't watch something I wanted to watch on TV"; "I had my sleep disrupted"; "I had to spend time with friends of my partner I didn't like"). Participants typically indicated that their partner interfered with their goals in many, if not most, of the ways listed. Participants in one of the control conditions completed a survey that simply asked them to indicate whether their goal pursuits had ever been disrupted (e.g., "I couldn't watch something I wanted to watch on TV"; "I had my sleep disrupted"). We then measured automatic compensatory partner valuing by examining how quickly people associated their dating partner with positive traits in a categorization task. People automatically valued their partner *more* when they thought of their partner as the root of their personal frustrations. A partner interfering with one's goals even motivates the victims of such obstruction to perceive greater meaning and value in treating their partner well! In a diary study, newlyweds who valued their partner more when their partner interfered with their goals on Monday actually behaved more responsively toward their partner on Tuesday (Murray, Holmes et al., 2009).

Minimizing the Downsides

The third resistance situation involves being hurt and let down by the other partner's failure to be responsive. Brian encounters such "disappointment" situations whenever he wants Sylvia to do anything adventurous. In such situations, seeing compensatory value in being accommodative, forgiving, and responsive could keep Brian unconflicted and on the "right" behavioral course (Rusbult, Verette, Whitney, Slovik, & Lipkus, 1991). Such resistance situations do indeed elicit automatic inclinations to be accommodating and forgiving. For instance, imagining that a close other forgot to mail one's application for a coveted job opportunity immediately brings thoughts of forgiving the errant partner to mind (Karremans & Aarts, 2007). People also blame themselves when their partner lets them down, concluding that they just did not communicate their needs clearly enough for their partner to understand them (Lemay & Melville, 2014). The impulsive inclination to compensate for a partner's fallibility is so powerful that people even respond with positive facial affect to signs of a significant other's faults in a stranger (Andersen, Reznik, & Manzella, 1996).

The fourth resistance situation takes us outside the relationship to the temptations posed by attractive alternatives. Knowing she has bookish colleagues at work who find her desirable has put Sylvia in something of a quandary. She doesn't want to be attracted to anyone else, but sometimes she wonders if life would be easier if her partner had more similar interests to her own. If she got caught up with such thoughts, she could be locked into behavioral conflict about spending all of her time and energies on Brian. But, rather than being captivated by alternatives, people instead seem to quite automatically minimize what they could gain by pursuing alternate relationships.

The presence of attractive and available alternative partners automatically elicits compensatory tendencies to disregard and disparage (Maner, Gailliot, & Miller, 2009; Maner, Rouby, & Gonzaga, 2008). For instance, people primed with their love for their partner are quicker to deflect their attention away from attractive alternatives than control participants (Maner et al., 2009). People in committed dating and marital relationships also consciously disparage their alternatives, telling themselves they could never find anyone as desirable as the partner they possess (Johnson & Rusbult, 1989; Simpson, Gangestad, & Lerma, 1990). Just being involved in a relationship is enough to keep people from unconsciously mimicking the behaviors of attractive others (Karrenmans & Verwijmeren, 2008) and dull memory for the facial features of attractive others (Karrenmans, Dotsch, & Corneille, 2011). Women primed with commitment even take the unnecessary precaution of physically moving away from a *virtual* alternative partner (Lydon, Menzies-Toman, Burton, & Bell, 2008)! The automatic biases that turn alternative princes (and princesses) into frogs also keep people on an even behavioral keel. When tempting alternatives are salient, people are more likely to report intentions to behave caringly and communally toward their partner (Lydon et al., 2008).

Rebuilding Conviction: Giving Meaning to Action

The evidence that "resistance" situations motivate value creation supports one tenet of the psychological lever metaphor we introduced to explain how conviction motivates responsiveness (Figure 4.1). Threats to conviction, whether they come from the negatives inherent in sacrifice, goal interference, disappointment, or alternatives, automatically motivate people to find greater value in their partner. But the research we highlighted leaves a central question unaddressed: Does the compensatory creation of value actually alleviate threats to conviction and compel unconflicted action? Is it truly functional and adaptive in sustaining consistently responsive relationship interactions? Three lines of research suggest that it might have just this approach-motivating effect.

In the first line of research, Zheng, Fehr, Tai, Narayanan, and Gelfand (2015) hypothesized that the act of forgiveness makes actions feel more physically doable. They manipulated value creation by asking participants to think of a time when they had either forgiven or not forgiven someone who had transgressed against them. Then they surreptitiously measured how forceful people felt in the presence of a physically demanding world. Participants estimated the physical slant of a hill (Experiment 1) and jumped as high as they could (Experiment 2). In the terms of our lever model, the value that forgiveness imbues in the partner should supply greater force to behavior, even overcoming forces of physical resistance. In these studies, forgiveness did exactly that. It effectively unburdened participants, giving greater force to action. Those who recounted a time when they had forgiven a transgressor perceived the hill to be more climbable (i.e., less steep) and they could also jump measurably higher than participants who thought of a time they had not forgiven a transgressor. Consistent with this logic, hills also appear more physically conquerable (i.e., less steep) to people thinking of cherished significant others than the same hills appear to people thinking of less-valued companions (Schnall, Harber, Stefanucci, & Proffitt, 2008).

In the second line of research, Van Tongeren and colleagues (2015) hypothesized that the act of forgiving a romantic partner's most serious transgressions gives greater meaning and purpose to action *in general*. These researchers invited committed couples to participate in a daily diary study. Participants initially completed a "meaning in life scale," which tapped the extent to which they perceived their own life as being meaningful and purposeful. Every two weeks for the next five months participants then completed a standardized inventory, checking off "offenses" their partner had committed over the prior two weeks. They also rated their forgiveness of each offense. At the end of the study, participants then completed the "meaning in life" scale again.

In the terms of our level model, more frequent offenses (i.e., greater exposure to "disappointment" situations) threaten conviction and necessitate the compensatory creation of value in the partner. Forgiving the partner restores value, thereby restoring meaning to action, as captured by the sense that one's life as a whole has purpose. The findings held true to this logic. When people compensated for conviction threats, life became more meaningful. When partners frequently offended, people who were more forgiving of these transgressions later reported a *greater* overall sense of meaning and purpose in their lives than people who were less forgiving. However, when partners rarely offended, forgiveness did not predict changes in the perception of meaning. It was only creating *compensatory* value that worked to restore meaning and purpose (Van Tongeren et al., 2015).

In the third line of research, we hypothesized that questioning commitment automatically motivates people to defend the value of commitment, hardening the resolve to behave caringly and communally over time (Murray et al., 2015). Murray's newlywed study revealed exactly how this commitment-protective equilibrium unfolds (Murray et al., 2015). Both members of the couple reported feelings of commitment just after marriage and each year for the next three years. They also each completed 14 days of daily diaries at each of these time periods. These diaries allowed us to assess automatic intentions to protect commitment through IF-THEN contingencies in each partner's thoughts and behavior. Specifically, these diaries allowed us to index Brian's tendencies to (1) value Sylvia when she proved costly in interference situations; (2) accommodate to Sylvia when she behaved uncaringly in "disappointment" situations; and (3) make Sylvia depend on him when her willingness to sacrifice for him might be in question.

Looking at these marriages from year to year revealed strong evidence for a commitment-protective equilibrium. When people questioned their commitments, they defensively enacted automatic intentions to repair commitment. That is, people responded to years in their marriage when they felt less committed than usual by being more likely to justify costs, accommodate, and promote their partner's dependence in subsequent interactions the next year (Path A in Figure 4.2). Being more likely to act on these automatic commitment intentions in turn hardened subsequent resolve to stay in the relationship. That is, being more likely to justify costs, accommodate, and promote their partner's dependence in daily interactions strengthened feelings of commitment the next year (Path B in Figure 4.2). Thus, the compensatory defense of value fortifies conviction, as our lever model implies. When Brian experiences greater doubt, he thinks and behaves in ways that give greater value to caring and responsive behavior, which in turn, fortify his commitment to treat Sylvia caringly and communally in the face of future doubts.

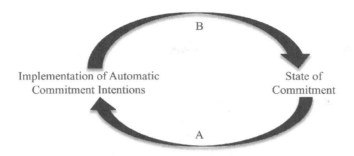

FIGURE 4.2 The Equilibrium Model of Relationship Maintenance. (Adapted from Murray, S. L., Holmes, J. G., Griffin, D. W., & Derrick, J. L. (2015). The equilibrium model of relationship maintenance. *Journal of Personality and Social Psychology, 108*, 93–113. Copyright American Psychological Association; adapted with permission.)

Fitting Motivation to Context: Conviction Calibration

This brings us to our last set of arguments about value goal progress. Conviction is not only elastic and resilient; it is also self-perpetuating. For the most part, people who have made more *overall* progress toward value goals are more likely to think and behave in ways that further future goal progress (Linardatos & Lydon, 2011).

The duality in how commitment marks value goal progress is captured well by a daily diary study reported by Li and Fung (2015). In this study, people who were chronically more committed were more dissatisfied on days when their interactions with their partner were unexpectedly negative. Nonetheless, when daily interactions were unexpectedly negative, people who were more committed initially ended up even *more* satisfied months later. These effects should not be surprising by this point.

More committed people expect interactions with their partner to be caring and responsive (Rusbult & Van Lange, 2003). When negative interactions violate such expectations, more committed people likely experience unsettling feelings of dissonance and doubt. In the equilibrium model, it is experiencing *acute* doubts about commitment that signals the need to protect progress in the pursuit of value goals and motivates people to think and behave in ways that create compensatory value and bolster commitment (Murray et al., 2015). Therefore, being more threatened by daily negative interactions should motivate more committed people to apply still greater force to their convictions. By defensively creating greater value in the partner, more committed people could then restore purpose in caring, communal, and responsive behavior.

Consistent with this logic, chronic commitment helps keep relationships on an even keel. It supplies added incentive to sustain a sense of value and meaning in action by accentuating the positive and minimizing the negative in "resistance" situations. For instance, people who are more committed more readily forgive their partner's betrayals (Finkel, Rusbult, Kamashiro, & Hannon, 2002), sacrifice on their partner's behalf (Van Lange et al., 1997), and discount their partner's imperfections (Arriaga, Slaughterbeck, Capezza, & Hmurovic, 2007). They also better resist the lure of attractive alternatives, derogating and ignoring even the most tempting of these temptations (Linardatos & Lydon, 2011; Lydon, Meana, Sepinwall, Richards, & Mayman, 1999). People who are more committed are also more practiced in suppressing aggressive impulses toward their partner when they are hurt and unjustifiably provoked by partner transgressions (Slotter et al., 2012).

Conviction Is Not Trust

These research examples highlight the last point we need to make about value goal progress. A person's *chronic* level of conviction furthers value goal progress through a different calibration than chronic trust furthers safety goal progress. Possessing *lower* levels of chronic trust signals the need to make greater progress toward safety goals and intensifies this goal pursuit (Chapter 3). However, it is possessing *higher* levels of chronic conviction that signals the need to make greater progress toward value goals and intensifies this goal pursuit. How so?

Trust is largely a prevention-oriented regulatory sentiment; it functions to keep bad things from happening (Murray & Holmes, 2009, 2011). In risky situations, less-trusting people cannot afford for anything bad to happen because they are so readily hurt by rejection (Murray, Griffin, Rose, & Bellavia, 2003). Therefore, being *less* chronically trusting flags insufficient progress toward safety goals to motivate people to take the appropriate defensive action to keep bad things from happening (as we saw with Katy in Chapter 3).

Conviction is largely a promotion-oriented regulatory sentiment; it functions to make good things happen. People with greater chronic conviction thrive on the rewards their relationships offer and they are loath to miss out opportunities for good things to happen (Gable, 2005). Much like a runner addicted to an endorphin high, Brian just thrives on the feeling of contentment he gets when he takes care of Sylvia (Linardatos & Lydon, 2011; Rusbult & Van Lange, 2003). Because people with stronger chronic convictions are more promotion-oriented, they are likely to be more sensitive to the *gains* they might miss (e.g., Brian missing out on Sylvia's happiness) than the losses they might incur (e.g., Brian not be able to go mountain biking) in resistance situations. By sensitizing people to reward, greater chronic conviction signals the likelihood and desirability of making even better things happen. Consequently, people with greater chronic conviction capitalize on available opportunities to revitalize their sense of conviction (Li & Fung, 2015). They are more likely to act on any automatically activated means to maximize the upsides and minimize the downsides of responsive action because they are essentially addicted to the conviction they already possess.

The Measure of Success: Value and Relationship Well-Being

Conviction is such a heady and addictive state because perceiving value in action generates belongingness rewards. Partner interactions are likely to be more caring, communal, and mutually responsive when partners know they are "right" for one another (Rusbult & Van Lange, 2003). Indeed, seeing a partner as intrinsically special and valuable motivates people to behave responsively (Gordon, Impett, Kogan, Oveis, & Keltner, 2012). Even subliminally reminding people of the value to be found in relationships (by priming sex) increases sacrifice and accommodation (Gillath, Mikulincer, Birnbaum, & Shaver, 2008). If the pursuit of value does indeed motivate responsiveness, goal attainment should differentiate well from poorly functioning relationships. Partners who come consistently closer to satisfying the goal to perceive incontrovertible value and meaning in the partner should be involved in more consistently responsive, satisfying, and more *stable* relationships than people who fall short. Is this the case?

This (finally) brings us to the most researched area of motivated cognition in relationships: The benefits of seeing special value in the partner that no one else really sees (de Jong & Reis, 2014; Eastwick & Neff, 2012; Fletcher & Kerr, 2010; Fletcher, Simpson, & Thomas, 2000; Martz et al., 1998; Miller, Niehuis, & Huston, 2006; Murray & Holmes, 1999; Murray, Holmes, Dolderman, & Griffin, 2000; Murray, Holmes, & Griffin,, 1996a, 1996b; Murray et al., 2011; Rusbult, Van Lange, Wilschut, Yovetich, & Verette, 2000). The literature on positive illusions is too extensive to review in entirety here, so we selectively sample highlights instead.

Positive Illusions in Relationships

What makes a partner feel like a "right" and valuable choice? In our research on positive illusions, we maintain that people create lasting value in partners by seeing them as ideal, or very nearly so (Murray et al., 1996a, 1996b). Brian's image of his "ideal" partner epitomizes what he most desires and believes is right for him. Perceiving Sylvia as a close match to his ideals should make Brian happier and more responsive toward Sylvia if idealizing her cements his desired belief that she is exactly right for him.

Findings from Murray's newlywed study illustrate the power that creating such inimitable value has to sustain satisfying relationships (Murray et al., 2011). In this study, we asked each husband and wife to describe himself or herself, his or her partner, and his or her hopes for an ideal partner on a variety of interpersonal qualities (e.g., warm, intelligent, critical and demanding, responsive, lazy). Participants made these ratings at six-month intervals over the first three years of their marriage. They also reported their overall satisfaction in the marriage at each of these seven times.

Constructing a measure of idealization that captured the creation of value in the partner took three steps. First, we correlated Brian's ratings of Sylvia's qualities across the 20 attributes with his ratings of his ideal partner's qualities. This "projection" index captures the degree to which Brian believes that Sylvia has the same profile or relative ordering of qualities he hoped to find in an ideal partner. A strong positive correlation means that Brian ascribes the same profile of qualities to Sylvia and to his ideal partner (e.g., seeing both Sylvia and his ideal as more assertive than warm and more lazy than critical). Second, we correlated Brian's ratings of his ideal partner's qualities with Sylvia's ratings of her own qualities. This "reality" index captures the degree to which Brian actually did find the qualities in Sylvia he had hoped to find (at least, according to Sylvia). Third, we used the "projection" and "reality" indices together to pinpoint whether people who *created* greater value in their partner would be better able to sustain satisfaction over the first three years of marriage. To do this, we predicted the path or trajectory of each person's satisfaction (i.e., declining, stable, increasing) over time from the simultaneous effects of the "projection" and "reality" indices. In this analysis, the association between Brian's ideals and his perception of Sylvia now captures Brian's *motivated creation* of value (because we removed the kernel of truth in his perceptions).

Figure 4.3 presents average declines in satisfaction for people who were more or less likely to idealize their partner at the time they married. Satisfaction declined precipitously for people who idealized their partner the least. However, perceiving greater value in the partner stabilized relationships. People who married optimistically believing that their (less-than-ideal) partner was a veritable mirror of their ideals were just as happy three years into marriage as they were when they married.

These findings provide a great analogue to our lever logic. The more ideal the partner is perceived to be, the more "right" the partner. Idealizing the partner more thus gives greater meaning to caring and communal behavior – tipping the psychological balance in "resistance" situations in its favor more often than not. If Brian's resolve that Sylvia is truly right for him motivates him to be more responsive, it should prove to be contagious. Sylvia should be more satisfied when Brian sees her as a closer match to his ideals because valuing her should make it easier for him to be responsive. She should reap belongingness rewards from his idealization-fueled and clear-minded motivation to treat her well. Consistent with this logic, when people perceived their partner as a near-perfect match to their ideals at marriage, their *partner* also stayed blissfully satisfied. But, when people married without such a sense of resolve, their partner suffered as well.

This newlywed study suggests that creating incontrovertible value and meaning in the partner is crucial for continued satisfaction. Value creation stabilizes relationships in our view because it vanquishes doubt and makes caring for the partner the "right" choice. Further findings buttress this idea. For instance, newlyweds coached to take the perspective of a third party who can see good

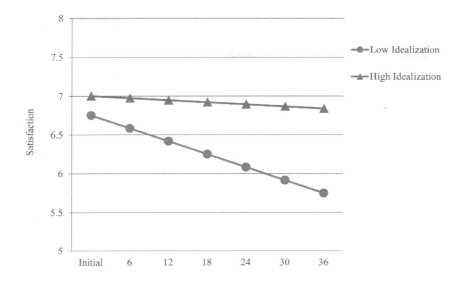

FIGURE 4.3 Declines in Satisfaction as a Function of Initial Idealization. (Reproduced with permission from *Murray*, S. L., Griffin, D. W., Derrick, J., Harris, B., Aloni, M., & Leder, S. (2011). Tempting fate or inviting happiness? Unrealistic idealization prevents the decline of marital satisfaction. *Psychological Science, 22*, 619–626. Copyright Sage Publications.)

intention in a partner's conflict behavior are less distressed by their problems over time. They also report more stable relationship satisfaction over time than newlyweds who are not coached to take such a generous perspective (Finkel, Slotter, Luchies, Walton, & Gross, 2013). Creating greater value in the partner also protects against divorce, which provides perhaps the clearest evidence that value creation sustains purpose and meaning in relationship action. It actually keeps the relationship together. Newlyweds who marry partners they perceive to be spot-on matches to their ideals are less likely to divorce after 3.5 years of marriage than newlyweds who perceive poorer matches (Eastwick & Neff, 2012).

Conclusion

We opened this chapter with the uncertainties that Sylvia and Brian are experiencing now that they have moved in together. We then described how the pursuit of value vanquishes such doubts and restores meaning to action. But we glossed over one obvious fact: Not everyone is equally successful in vanquishing doubts. While some people easily find the conviction they seek, perceiving sufficient value and meaning in the partner proves elusive for others. For the unfortunate, the inability to quash doubts sets relationships on the path to discord. People who consciously feel conflicted – torn between positive and negative feelings about their partner – report greater dissatisfaction (Fincham & Linfield, 1997). Physical health suffers as well; people who report greater ambivalence about their partner's value evidence greater coronary-artery calcification than people who put doubts to rest (Uchino, Smith, & Berg, 2014).

For better or worse, the motivated biases that serve value goals are not immune to the evidence. Some situations and partners are harder to find value in than others, as we will see in Chapter 7 (Murray et al., 1996a). The pursuit of value is not immune to other goal pursuits either. Safety and value are interconnected goal pursuits. People usually need to be *safe* before they let themselves truly believe they found the "right" partner (Murray, Holmes, & Collins, 2006). The imperial priority that safety has over value can make it difficult to sustain *un*conflicted value and meaning in relationship action. Low self-esteem people present a case in point. They evidence the same automatic biases to protect conviction as high self-esteem people. But low self-esteem people experience strong reservations about their partner's value nonetheless, because they too often get entrenched in safety goal pursuits (Murray et al., 1996a, 2000; Murray, Holmes et al., 2009). The possibility of such goal competition brings us to the motivational tension between safety and value – the topic of Chapter 5.

Note

1 Automatic behavioral inclinations are flexible as well as efficient. By flexible, we mean that such behavioral inclinations can be corrected or overturned when people are both motivated and able to do so (Olson & Fazio, 2008). We return to this point in Chapter 5.

5
WHY SAFETY OVERRIDES VALUE

Three years into Skyler and Walt's marriage, they had their first child, a son, Alex. Before Alex was born, Skyler had always had such faith in Walter. She believed that there was nothing he wouldn't do for her. After Alex was born, Skyler realized that there was actually a long list of things that Walt would only do very grudgingly. Diapers, late-night feedings, and early-morning conversation were at the top. Stressed, sleep-deprived, and physically unstable, balancing a baby on her hip, Skyler first started to wonder whether she could really count on Walt. The husbands of her Facebook friends seemed so much more engaged in being fathers and Walt just seemed to be spending more and more time at work. Skyler did not like feeling shaky and uncertain about Walt, but she could not entirely convince herself that she was wrong to feel this way either.

Alex's birth rocked Skyler and Walt's marriage because it changed the structure of dependence. The situational landscape shifted right beneath their feet. Before Alex was born, Walt depended on Skyler to meet his needs just as much as she depended on him. They treated one another as confidants, put tons of time and energy into their careers, enjoyed going out with friends, and happily shared the domestic responsibilities they could not hire someone else to perform. Once Skyler became a stay-at-home mom, this dependence structure shifted. She now had to depend on Walt more than he had to depend on her. Walt was her sole ticket to time for herself and the world of adult conversation, but it seemed so easy for him to beg off, saying he couldn't get up with Alex or spend a few extra minutes chatting in the morning because he had to work.

With her world fundamentally shaken, safety and value became painfully competing goal pursuits for Skyler. Struggling to feel as safe as she used to feel trusting Walt, she was starting to lose sight of what she used to value most about him. Even though Skyler did not like feeling so conflicted, she couldn't help but wonder whether the qualities she most loved in Walt, like his passion for his career, were more vice than virtue. She also couldn't stop herself questioning whether she was ever right in excusing Walt's jealousy as a quirk of his affection rather than a symptom of immaturity. As Alex got older and Walt worked still more, her doubts only compounded.

This chapter explores how changes in the situational landscape can precipitate shifts in the motivational tension between safety and value goal pursuits. In the first part of this chapter, we set the stage for motivational competition by revealing that safety and value are necessarily *interconnected* goal pursuits. Because safety and value function as part of a goal system, they cannot be pursued autonomously. The pursuit of safety informs the pursuit of value and the pursuit of value reciprocally informs the pursuit of safety (Murray, Holmes, & Collins, 2006). We draw on evolutionary and interdependence theories to position safety and value as goals in a natural state of opposition. Much as a balance only sets at rest with equal weight on both sides, safety and value goal pursuits must flexibly shift in relative priority to best satisfy the belongingness imperative.

The pursuit of safety and value so naturally operate in reciprocal tandem that managing a threat to one goal pursuit immediately constrains the opposing goal pursuit. For instance, pursuing the goal to be safe from physical harm can actually push people to sacrifice the goal to see value in nurturing behavior. To pose an embodied threat to safety, Forest and colleagues asked experimental participants to sit at a shaky table, stand on one foot, or sit on an uneven cushion (Forest, Killie, Wood, and Stehouwer, 2015). Control participants sat or stood on even surfaces. Then they measured perceptions of safety (through perceptions of physical instability and predictions for the relationship's longevity) and value in nurturing behavior (through behavioral displays of affection). Participants in unstable bodily positions not only felt physically shaky; they also expected their relationships to *end* sooner than participants in physically stable positions. Feeling psychologically unsafe in the relationship, physically unstable participants then put valuing their partner on the psychological backburner. They withdrew physical affection, preemptively blunting the pain of a potential break-up by acting as though their partner was not worth nurturing.

In the second part of the chapter, we turn to research on the risk regulation model to highlight the motivational sway safety often holds over value. This model asserts that people need to feel safe and invulnerable to hurt before they can truly believe they are in the "right" relationship with the "right" person (Murray et al., 2006). Functionally, this goal constraint means that Skyler needs to be safe before she can bestow kindnesses on Walt with any real degree of conviction in the "rightness" of her actions. Experientially, this goal constraint means that progress in the pursuit of safety limits progress in the pursuit of value. In other words, trust constrains conviction. This chapter will reveal that Skyler is not unique in her existential dilemma. When safety is a struggle, value is often too ambitious a goal to pursue. We draw on literatures examining attachments to God, parents, siblings, friends, and romantic partners to show how markers of trust and safety automatically constrain both the *means* available to pursue value goals and the desired *end*-state of experiencing an unconflicted basis for relationship-promotive action.

In the third section of the chapter, we apply the risk regulation model to explain why relationships so often frustrate the belongingness needs of people most in need of romantic connection. We focus on the role that low self-esteem plays in amplifying risk regulation dynamics because it has been central to our research program (Murray, Holmes, & Griffin, 2000). In Skyler's case, low self-esteem left her relatively ill equipped to bounce back from Walt's disappointing performance as a father because some part of her expected him to disappoint her eventually. We conclude the chapter with a discussion of self-fulfilling prophecies and the effects that one partner's goal pursuits and priorities have on the other partner's goal pursuits. By making our discussion of goal systems more dyadic and interconnected, we set the stage for the next chapter's discussion of how the pursuit of value can sometimes come to take precedence over the pursuit of safety.

The Motivational Tension: Naturally Opposing States

The proverbs "you can't have it both ways" and "you can't have your cake and eat it too" capture a natural challenge to goal pursuit. It is difficult to simultaneously and successfully pursue two opposing goals (Orehek & Vazeou-Nieuwenhuis, 2013). The road not taken is lost, and the cake, once eaten, is gone. Having the cake, while still eating it, requires a delicate balancing act, one where the competing goals to possess and consume the cake (or any other desired end) keep each other in check.

Finding a sense of belonging is tantamount to having one's cake *and* eating it too. From an evolutionary perspective, the goals for safety and value exist in a natural state of opposition across relationship interactions. Nurturing and valuing the peer, familial, romantic, and group relationships we need to survive and reproduce directly increase our exposure to the multiplicity of pathogens and diseases that we must avoid to survive long enough to reproduce (Mortensen, Becker, Ackerman, Neuberg, & Kenrick, 2010; Sacco, Young, & Hugenberg, 2014). Because nurturing and valuing interpersonal connection impede steering clear of germs and disease in social life, simultaneously pursuing both goals would invite behavioral conflict. People would be left stuck in an approach-avoidance conflict, telling others to both "come here" and "go away." For people to have their belongingness cake and eat it too, evolutionary theorists reason that safety and value goals have to be pursued alternately (Mortensen et al., 2010; Sacco et al., 2014). The pursuit of one goal necessarily comes at some cost to the pursuit of the competing goal.

The Belongingness Goal Balance

Mortensen and colleagues (2010) and Sacco and colleagues (2014) shed light on the nature of the goal co-regulation involved in the pursuit of belongingness. The mechanics of a physical balance probably best illustrate our take on the logic of their experimental predictions. Figure 5.1 depicts a balance at rest. The weights on each end of the balance capture the goals to be safe from physical harm (on the left) and perceive value in caring, communal, and responsive interaction (on the right). In social life, safety and value are equally strong, but opposing goal pursuits. The "even" or level balance depicted in Figure 5.1 captures a state of goal conflict. In this standoff, no movement toward either goal is possible until something happens to tip the balance. Imagine safety and value goals as children playing on a seesaw. Seesaws only work if one child descends, allowing the other to ascend; if both children kept their feet firmly planted to the ground, neither would go anywhere. The same is true for progress in safety and value goal pursuits. Actionable goal progress cannot be made until something in the situation tips the balance in favor of pursuing one of these two competing goals.

In the belongingness balance, situations that make disease salient tip the balance in favor of restoring safety, whereas situations that put the value of pursuing interpersonal connection into question tip the balance in favor of restoring value. Tipping the balance in *favor* of one goal is not enough to leverage goal pursuit in its favor though. The balance also needs to be tipped *against* the other goal pursuit. Safety and value goals operate like ends of a seesaw. As one goes "up" in priority, the other must go "down" in priority for measurable progress to be made in the pursuit of the prioritized goal.

Tipping the Balance Toward Safety

In interpersonal life, encountering threats to physical health, such as a coughing, sneezing, and infectious colleague, threaten the potential for physical harm. Thus, threats to physical health tip the belongingness balance in favor of restoring safety over pursuing value. Namely, situations that make contagious disease salient

Equilibrium Point

FIGURE 5.1 The Belongingness Balance

prioritize safety goal pursuits, pushing their activation upward and necessitating a proportionate decrease or offset in the urgency of value goal pursuits.

Making the risk of disease salient motivates people to question the value and meaning of nurturing interpersonal connections. Mortensen and colleagues (2010) and Sacco and colleagues (2014) tipped the balance toward safety goal pursuits by showing experimental participants slideshows highlighting germs and contagious diseases. Control participants either viewed negative or innocuous slides. Then they measured the value people attached to nurturing interpersonal connection through self-reports of extraversion, the need to belong, and automatic approach and avoidance arm motions in response to human faces. Participants threatened with disease sacrificed value for progress in the pursuit of safety. Disease-threatened participants reported weaker needs to belong (Sacco et al., 2014) and less extraverted personalities (Mortensen et al., 2010, Experiment 1) than control participants. The prospect of interpersonal connection even seemed to physically repulse disease-threatened participants. They were quicker to withdraw from pictures of human faces than control participants (Mortensen et al., 2010, Experiment 2). Disease-threatened participants essentially traded value for the physical safety interpersonal distance afforded them. Thus, situations that tip the balance in favor of safety goal pursuits elicit a proportionate offset in the pursuit of value goals.

Tipping the Balance Toward Value

Threats to the value of seeking interpersonal connection should conversely tip the belongingness balance in favor of value over safety goal pursuits. Namely, situations that make enacting caring, communal, and responsive interaction seem questionable thwart value goal pursuits, heightening their activation and necessitating a proportionate offset or decrease in the activation of safety goal pursuits.

Threatening the meaning and integrity of existing social connections does indeed result in people eschewing concerns about physical safety. Sacco and colleagues (2014) tipped the balance toward value goal pursuits by making efforts to nurture interpersonal connections seem questionable. Experimental participants described a time when they had been unjustifiably rejected by others (Experiment 1) or suffered an inexplicable rejection at the hands of virtual Cyberball players (Experiment 2). Control participants experienced relative acceptance. They then measured worries about contracting physical illnesses (Experiment 1) and affinity for "healthy" symmetrical over "unhealthy" asymmetrical faces (Experiment 2) as markers of the priority participants put on preserving physical safety. Experimental participants sacrificed physical safety for the chance to restore value and meaning to nurturing interpersonal connections. They not only reported less concern about catching contagious diseases from others, such as a cold or flu, but they were just as drawn to "unhealthy" asymmetric faces as they were to the "healthy" symmetric ones. Rejected participants automatically traded off the goal to be physically safe from harm for the chance to restore more meaningful connections.

The Risk Regulation Balance

The ideas behind the belongingness balance resonate with the logic of our risk regulation model in many ways (Murray et al., 2006). Just as safety and value goals are in a state of natural opposition across social relationships, we think of safety and value goals being in a state of natural opposition in the context of a *singular* relationship. Skyler is torn about her marriage right now because she hasn't been able to have her cake and eat it too. She wants to feel like she used to feel about Walt, but valuing Walt in the same way she once did only makes it hurt more when he rejects or disappoints her. But, rather than limiting safety to a physical state, the risk regulation model broadens the definition of safety to include a psychological state. The two are naturally bound together in romantic relationships. In fact, people fend off worries about their own mortality (the ultimate physical safety peril) by exaggerating the security of their partner's acceptance and affection (Cox & Arndt, 2012). When it comes to the pursuit of safety in romantic relationships, not being hurt encompasses more than not being infected by disease. The psychological transcends the physical. This broader conceptualization of safety makes all the difference in its co-regulation with value goals.

Imagine Walt has the flu. If Skyler exposes herself to his germs to comfort him when he's sick, trading her *physical* safety for value comes with little future cost to *psychological* safety. Risking the flu does not make Skyler more unilaterally dependent on Walt and more vulnerable to being hurt. However, trading psychological safety for value does make a partner's non-responsiveness more likely and more painful because this goal trade-off increases dependence and vulnerability. If Skyler forgives Walt for missing his son's soccer game, it sets her up for being hurt again (McNulty, 2010a).

The logic of our risk regulation model builds on this distinction. Although value and safety are evenly traded in the belongingness balance, they are not evenly traded in the risk regulation balance. Pursuing value in connection over staying safe from disease cannot make the flu one might contract any more serious and grievous a threat to physical safety. There is actually considerable evidence to suggest the opposite is the case; social bonds increase resilience against infection (Baumeister & Leary, 1995)! However, when Walt disappoints or rejects Skyler, defending her conviction that he is the "right" person can compound threats to her psychological safety by making Skyler more dependent on Walt. When it comes to goal regulation in a specific relationship, prioritizing value over safety is going "all in" in gambling parlance. Valuing Walt above others makes Skyler more vulnerable to him, giving him greater power to hurt her and pose more frequent and grievous threat to her psychological safety. Because prioritizing value over safety "doubles down" on dependence, it sets Skyler further back in her future pursuit of safety.

For this reason, the risk regulation balance depicted in Figure 5.2 diverges from the belongingness balance in two ways. The first divergence is visible:

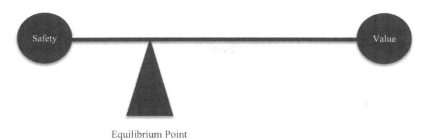

Equilibrium Point

FIGURE 5.2 The Risk Regulation Balance

The equilibrium point of the balance is offset to the left and shifted toward safety. Metaphorically, this means that safety goal pursuits generally have greater leverage or "teetering" power than value goal pursuits. Situations that threaten safety goal pursuits have greater power to deactivate value goal pursuits than situations that threaten value goal pursuits have to deactivate safety goal pursuits. Functionally this means that safety goal pursuits usually come first. In the risk regulation balance, people only let themselves risk valuing and nurturing a specific partner when they *first* feel safe in the knowledge that their partner will also nurture and value them (Murray, Holmes, MacDonald, & Ellsworth, 1998; Murray, Holmes, & Griffin, 2000; Murray, Holmes, Griffin, Bellavia, & Rose, 2001; Murray, Rose, Bellavia, Holmes, & Kusche, 2002; Murray et al., 2006). For instance, people only include their partner in their self-concept when they believe their partner's self-concept already includes them (Tomlinson & Aron, 2013). Safety can even determine whether a relationship comes into existence at all. Even the subtlest cues that a partner might be safe to approach, such as the use of similar pronoun usage in conversation, can move people from acquaintances to relationship partners (Ireland et al., 2011).

Why would psychological safety be such a monopolizing goal? Research into goal systems provides some insights. Individual means of goal fulfillment become more important to a goal (and more behaviorally monopolizing) when there are fewer *other* means available to achieve the same goal (Kruglanski et al., 2002). The goal to feel safe from harm probably has fewer means associated with its fulfillment than the goal to perceive value and meaning in action. Essentially, safety is a less flexibly satisfied goal. For instance, Knowles and colleagues tested whether people could "make up" for the safety threat posed by being hurt by others by affirming their intelligence and efficacy (Knowles, Lucas, Molden, Gardner, & Dean, 2010). Affirming value in personal action was no substitute for safety. The only way people could make themselves feel better in the face of such interpersonal hurts was to directly affirm others would care for them. In relationships, the power of dissonance gives people many means to satisfy value goals. They can ignore a partner's faults, embellish virtues, whitewash the past, change ideals, minimize sacrifices, derogate alternatives, and the list goes on (Brickman, 1987). However, minimizing dependence is the only surefire means to satisfy the goal to be safe from being hurt or let down by a partner, giving this means–goal association greater activation potential and priority.

The second divergence is not visible in Figure 5.2. It has to do with the actual movement of the risk regulation balance. The belongingness balance focuses on how *thwarted* goals tip the balance in favor of their own pursuit. Priming disease prioritizes safety goal pursuits and motivates people to eschew social connection to keep germ-free (Mortensen et al., 2010; Sacco et al., 2014). Conversely, priming fruitless attempts to pursue connection prioritizes value goal pursuits and motivates people to eschew physical safety to keep themselves caringly connected to others (Sacco et al., 2014).

However, satiating a goal can have just as strong an effect on goal regulation as thwarting a goal. In a goal system, satiated goals become deactivated, which can have powerful downstream effects on the pursuit of competing, non-focal goals. Namely, satiating a goal allows competing goals to come online and take motivational center stage (McCulloch, Aarts, Fujita, & Bargh, 2008; Shah, Friedman, & Kruglanski, 2002). In the risk regulation balance, situations can quench as well as thwart safety goals. Once safety is satiated, it can then tip the motivational balance back in favor of pursuing *unquenched* value goal pursuits. Being safe essentially releases people to put value into relationship-promotive action, both literally and figuratively (Murray et al., 2006).

The Imprint of Risk Regulation in Approach and Avoidance

Keeping these two unique features of the risk regulation balance in mind, let's now turn to the literature to see whether such goal co-regulation occurs. We first illustrate the generality of risk regulation by showing its imprint on general behavioral systems for approach and avoidance. Once we demonstrate that safety's imperial control over value has such a large footprint, we then turn to the specifics and examine how safety's regulation of value affects the daily lives of couples like Skyler and Walt.

Tipping the Balance Toward Safety

If safety regulates value through general systems for regulating approach and avoidance behavior, threatening psychological safety should tip the goal balance in favor of avoidance and against approach. Specifically, situations that threaten safety – situations that make dependence, vulnerability, and the potential to be hurt by a partner salient – should increase the activation of avoidance goals and necessitate a proportionate decrease or offset in approach goal strength.

When the possibility of being hurt by a significant other is salient, people prioritize avoidance over approach. Thwarting safety goals activates avoidance and suppresses approach motivations, making the safety-conscious less engaged in vigorously pursuing anything of value at all. In two experiments, Cavallo, Fitzsimons, and Holmes (2010) activated the goal to be safe by leading experimental participants to believe their partner would eventually discover their dark secrets and then become disaffected. Control participants were given no such worry. Then they measured *general* motivations to approach vs. avoid the social world. They assessed reaction times to approach (e.g., "progress," "eager") and avoidance (e.g., "safety," "prevent") words (Experiment 1) and performance on a gain- versus a loss-framed anagram task (Experiment 2). When the possibility of being hurt was made salient, participants were faster to identify avoidance than approach words in a lexical decision task; they also solved more anagrams when they were instructed not to fail than when they were instructed to succeed.

Putting safety at issue also suppresses approach motivations when the threat to safety is largely symbolic. Subliminally priming a picture of maternal rejection changes the content of sexual fantasies. People primed with such reason to feel unsafe and insecure fantasize about having more distant, detached, and less affectionate sex than people primed with pictures of maternal caring (Birnbaum, Simpson, Weisberg, Barnea, & Assulin-Simhon, 2012). Reading biblical passages that highlight the possibility of being rejected and ostracized by God also decreases people's willingness to seek others out to provide care (van Beest & Williams, 2011). People also reactively devalue those who betray them in trust games, seeing less evidence of their own facial features in defectors than cooperators (Farmer, McKay, & Tsakiris, 2014). Women who have been rejected by an attractive potential suitor even derogate the unattractive suitors they have every chance of attracting and catching (MacDonald, Baratta, & Tzalazidis, 2015).

Tipping the Balance Toward Value

If safety regulates value through systems for regulating approach and avoidance behavior, satiating the goal to be psychologically safe should also tip the goal balance in favor of approach over avoidance. Specifically, situations that make the general possibility of being accepted and included by others salient should quench avoidance goal pursuits, deactivating them (at least for the time being), allowing the competing goal to approach to take motivational center stage.

When ongoing situations make interpersonal acceptance certain, people embrace the pursuit of value in behavior. Switching off safety goal pursuits effectively unleashes approach motivations that underlie the capacity to act with force, drive, and conviction. For the religiously inclined, thinking of a loving and accepting God increases (non-moral) risk taking (Chan, Tong, & Tan, 2014; Kupor, Laurin, & Levav, 2015). People primed with God report greater interest in high-adrenaline behaviors like alpine skiing, rock climbing, and skydiving than controls (Kupor et al., 2015). People primed with God are also more likely to keep pumping air into balloons that are about to burst in the hope of gaining financial

94 Why Safety Overrides Value

reward (Chan et al., 2014). God-primed people approach risks that others avoid precisely because thinking of God turns safety into a non-focal goal; they feel safe, so they can act with abandon and decisiveness (Kupor et al., 2015). Being included by *actual* people can also switch off safety goal pursuits and unleash value goal pursuits. For instance, being included by others in a lab setting piques interest in finding attractive people to date and mate (Brown, Young, Sacco, Bernstein, & Claypool, 2009).

Risk Regulation Live! Its Dynamics in Daily Relationship Life

The evidence that safety regulates value through general systems for regulating approach and avoidance behavior gives safety wide powers to regulate value within romantic relationships. In specific situations, progress in the pursuit of safety goals should control willingness to nurture the partner and relationship. Frustrating safety should disable value goal pursuits, making it difficult to be nurturing, whereas quenching safety should enable value goal pursuits, making it easy to be nurturing. We highlighted an embodied version of this dynamic at the beginning of this chapter. People in physically shaky positions withdrew affection from their partners. In so doing, they sacrificed value for safety by reducing dependence on partners and relationships that might rock their worlds even more precipitously (Forest et al., 2015).

In the risk regulation model, the acute experience of trust "tips" the motivational balance between safety and value goal pursuits. Figure 5.3 captures the role such situational trust plays as goal-regulating agent (Murray et al., 2006). Having reason (whether bodily, behaviorally, or introspectively) to question a partner's caring and commitment "tips" the balance toward safety and away from value. Conversely, having reason (whether bodily, introspectively, or behaviorally) to expect a partner's caring and commitment "tips" the balance toward value and away from safety.

When researchers study risk regulation dynamics in context, they often focus on the "risky" situations we examined in Chapter 3 because these situations *strain*

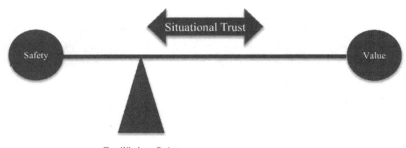

Equilibrium Point

FIGURE 5.3 Trust as a Leveling Agent

or test trust. "Risky" situations are ones where Skyler is more dependent on Walt than he is on her because she needs something, such as attention, support, sacrifice, or forgiveness, that Walt might not be willing to provide. Expecting a partner not to be available or caring in such situations tips the goal balance toward safety and away from value goal pursuits. In such situations, Skyler needs to take some action to reduce her vulnerability to Walt.

Skyler is safest from being hurt by Walt when she needs him no more than he needs her (see Chapter 3). This basic requirement for safety makes *dependence* the currency of goal prioritization in the risk regulation model. Skyler can put safety first by altering the currency of her own dependence. In the risk regulation model, people can directly satisfy safety goals by relying on their partner's care and nurturing less (Murray et al., 2006). Skyler can physically distance herself from Walt by not soliciting his support or sacrifices because he cannot as readily hurt her if she asks little of him. She can also directly push Walt away by withdrawing her affection, criticizing him, or precipitating fights because he cannot as readily disappoint her if he cannot get close to her. But this is not the only means of safety pursuit open to Skyler. In the risk regulation model, people can also satisfy safety goals indirectly by suppressing the pursuit of value. Skyler can reduce her dependence symbolically by psychologically distancing herself from Walt. By giving meaning and purpose to her actions, valuing Walt makes Skyler more invested in her relationship and more dependent on Walt. Questioning Walt's value and the meaning of nurturing and caring for him provides Skyler with a game-stopper route to safety. Walt cannot hurt her nearly as readily if Skyler has already started to question her convictions and entertain the thought that Walt is no longer right for her.

Just as it takes two to tango, it takes satisfying *both* safety and value goals to satisfy belongingness needs in relationships. For interactions to be consistently responsive, Skyler needs to be safe enough to put her outcomes in Walt's hands and value Walt enough to be responsive to him (see Chapters 1 and 2). For the co-regulation of safety and value goals to satisfy the need to belong, moving closer to safety should deactivate its pursuit, allowing the opposing pursuit of value to be situationally activated. Being safe with Walt gives Skyler permission to value him when the unexpected trials and frustrations of relationship life make him costly to her. It in no way guarantees that Skyler will value Walt when unexpectedly costly situations threaten conviction. It simply helps ensure there are no obvious impediments to Skyler finding meaning and value in caring and nurturing Walt when these actions seem questionable to her.

In sum, questioning a partner's availability and commitment tips the goal balance toward the pursuit of safety and against value. When safety is threatened in specific situations, the regulation of dependence should follow suit. Prioritizing safety over value could take the form of support not solicited, affection not provided, value not perceived, or closeness not sought. When safety is threatened across multiple situations in the relationship, its chronic activation should chronically suppress value goals, eroding the relationship's capacity to satisfy belongingness needs. Indeed, when people perceive their partner as less available, caring, and responsive in daily interaction, they report less satisfaction concurrently and over-time (Sadikaj, Moskowitz, & Zuroff, 2015).

A Selective Sampling of Risk Regulation Dynamics

Our first empirical look at risk regulation dynamics was straightforward. We tested the hypothesis that trust in a partner's availability and caring regulates positive illusions in samples of dating and married couples (Murray, Holmes, & Griffin, 2000). We started here because trust marks progress in the pursuit of safety and positive illusions about a partner's "rightness" mark success in the pursuit of value (Chapter 4).

Because feeling valued by one's partner provides an important basis for trusting in their responsiveness (Murray & Holmes, 2009, 2011), we measured trust by asking participants to describe how they believed their partner saw their interpersonal qualities, (e.g., "My partner sees me as . . . 'kind and affectionate'; 'open and disclosing'; 'intelligent'; 'critical and judgmental'; 'lazy'; 'demanding'"). We measured positive illusions by asking participants to describe themselves and their partner on these same qualities. Skipping over the data analytic detail, safety seemed to constrain value. People who felt safer because they believed their partner saw them more positively were more likely to possess positive illusions about their partner. Conversely, people who felt less safe because they believed their partner saw them more negatively hedged their bets; they could not quite let themselves believe that their partner really was quite "right" for them. Since we conducted this initial study, a growing corpus of research has provided much richer demonstrations of safety's priority over value. We highlight some favorites among these studies next.

On the Edge of a Cliff

In the virtual world, partners can be made to be unavailable and rejecting or available and accepting with a few lines of computer code. Kane and colleagues took advantage of virtual-reality technology to create a situation where one partner needed support the other either did or did not provide (Kane, McCall, Collins, & Blascovich, 2012). While immersed in a virtual world, the participant took a walk along a high, high cliff overlooking a canyon. While the participant walked along this visibly perilous path, the participant's partner, represented as an avatar, looked on. The researchers varied the behavior of this virtual partner to manipulate vulnerability and risk. In the "attentive and available" condition, the avatar partner clapped, waved, and oriented its body toward the stressed participant. In the "inattentive and unavailable condition," the avatar ignored the stressed participant and looked off into the distance.

The virtual partner's attentiveness and availability tipped the balance between safety and value goals. Inattentive and unavailable partners frustrated the goal to be safe. Participants experienced the cliff walk as less safe, less secure, and more fraught with risk when their partner ignored than applauded and encouraged them. Struggling to restore safety, participants then vigilantly monitored the behavior of partners who ignored them for further signs of rejection. Participants in the "inattentive and unavailable" partner condition kept looking to see where their partner's gaze was affixed, whereas participants in the "attentive and available" partner condition did not need to look. They simply trusted their partner's gaze was on them. Having had the experience of their partner ignoring them once when they really needed them, participants in the "inattentive and unavailable" partner condition then kept greater physical distance from their partner on a subsequent task. They literally kept themselves out of harm's way, sacrificing their partner's value as a source of support (Kane et al., 2012).

On the Verge of Criticism

In the actual world, there is no end to the situations in which partners can be perceived to be unavailable and unresponsive. Walt's observation that Skyler could stand to be a little less critical (or lose a little weight) can be all it takes to make her worry his support might not always be forthcoming. Perceiving his disapproval or disappointment could then tip Skyler's goal pursuits toward safety and away from value. In fact, when people think their partner is trying to change them, they worry they are falling short of their partner's ideals. This worry then motivates them to psychologically withdraw from their partner and they defensively reduce closeness over time (Overall & Fletcher, 2010; Overall, Fletcher, & Simpson, 2006). Falling short thus motivates people to trade the value they could see in their partner for the safety that comes from needing their partner's approval less (Overall & Fletcher, 2010).

At the Margin of Ingratitude

Partners do not even have to do anything as obviously untoward as being critical or unsupportive to threaten safety. The simple act of doing nothing when they are expected to do something can generate distrust and tip the goal balance. In the initial months after her son was born, Skyler made excuses for Walt's absences. She knew he had to work more given the loss of her salary. But these excuses started to wear thin once Skyler started wondering whether Walt really appreciated everything she did for him. In her case, Walt's seeming ingratitude made him seem unavailable and tipped her goal balance toward safety. Skyler is not alone in this respect. Feeling unappreciated generally results in people distancing themselves from their ungrateful partner. In daily interactions, people who feel less appreciated by their partner reciprocate such ingratitude by finding less to value and appreciate in their partner over time (Gordon, Impett, Kogan, Oveis, & Keltner, 2012). Not feeling as special in a partner's eyes essentially diminishes the partner in one's own eyes. Divesting dependence in this way definitely makes Skyler safer, but it comes with a significant cost to her motivation to take care of Walt. Over time, people who feel less appreciated by their partner become less likely to nurture and care for their partner (Gordon et al., 2012). Feeling unappreciated results in people trading the value they once saw in their partner for the safety to be had in needing their partner's gratitude less.

On the Cusp of Deception

Research on the deleterious effects of concealment further illustrates how a partner's inactions can threaten safety goal pursuits (Finkenauer, Kerkhof, Righetti, & Branje, 2009; Uysal, Lin, & Bush, 2012). In longitudinal studies, people who perceive a partner to be concealing secrets report increased feelings of exclusion (Finkenauer et al., 2009) and diminished feelings of trust over time (Finkenauer et al., 2009; Uysal et al., 2012). By undercutting trust, the perception that a romantic partner is hiding something then tips the goal balance toward safety and away from value. Consequently, people who fear they are not privy to their partner's secrets divest themselves of the partner and relationship over time. They start to keep more secrets themselves (Uysal et al., 2012), engage in more conflict (Finkenauer et al., 2009), and see less reason to be happy in the relationship (Finkenauer et al., 2009).

In the Fear of Stigma

Even if Walt had been a more involved father, Skyler's shift in identity from professional career woman to stay-at-home mom might still have made it difficult for her to trust in Walt's availability and care. People with stigmatized social identities experience a less safe, less equitable world (Crocker & Major, 1988). For people who already question their relationship's safety and stability, like Skyler, social identity threats may turn into relationship threats. Doyle and Molix (2014) made this point by priming the social stigma attached to being female (Experiment 1) or African-American (Experiment 2). When people already had reason to question their partner's availability (because they were in shorter-term relationships), making a stigmatized social identity salient tipped the goal balance toward safety and away from value. Stigmatized people in shorter-term relationships divested dependence when their worlds were made to feel more unsettled. They reported being involved in less intimate and satisfying relationships when their stigmatized social identity was primed than when it was not primed. Sadly, people kept themselves safe from partners who had done nothing at all wrong when the world was made to seem all the more unsafe and hostile toward them.

An Accumulation of Insecurities

These various findings suggest that "risky" situations tip the goal balance toward safety and away from value. Whether the threat to safety comes from a failed support attempt, a critical word, an unspoken secret, a forgotten thank you, or a stigmatized social identity, activating safety goal pursuits deactivates value goal pursuits. The sheer diversity of these effects suggest that the safety over value trade-off likely insinuates itself into relationship life more broadly. Indeed, when concerns about a partner's availability and caring transcend any one specific context or situation, the consequences for dependence should be particularly cataclysmic. The fates of less trusting newlyweds are emblematic of the eventual costs of persistently prioritizing safety over value.

When newlyweds have trouble trusting their partner, it sets them up for a lifetime of protecting against hurts. Derrick and colleagues examined how trust regulates the state of dependence across nine years of marriage (Derrick, Leonard, & Homish, 2012). Being generally uncertain of a partner's availability and caring predicted subsequent declines in dependence – as captured by reduced intimacy, diminished self-disclosure, and decreased satisfaction. In fact, less trusting newlyweds were eventually more likely to divorce because they had so consistently divested dependence.

The imperial power safety holds over value is not unique to romantic relationships or Western cultures either. It is evident in relationships that blood ties presumably secure. People actually distance themselves from family members, like parents and siblings, on days when they are less certain of their acceptance (Overall & Sibley, 2009b). It is also evident across cultures. In Eastern cultures, people not only need to trust in their partner's availability to risk dependence. They also have to trust that their family members will be there to support the relationship (MacDonald & Jessica, 2006).

One caveat before we proceed. The "resistance" situations we discussed in detail in Chapter 4 do not get a free pass from safety's influence. "Resistance" situations are ones where Skyler is *less* dependent on Walt than he is on her because he needs something from her. For instance, Skyler encounters "resistance" situations in her marriage when Walt needs her to give him a reprieve from childcare duties so he can spend an evening with friends. Such sacrifice situations test or strain Skyler's conviction in Walt and automatically tip the goal balance in favor of value to ensure that Skyler will be responsive to Walt. Although valuing Walt moves Skyler closer to its desired end of unconflicted action, it also moves her further away from safety. With every unexpected cost of interdependence that increases Walt's value to her (through the basic processes of dissonance reduction we saw in Chapter 4), Skyler becomes all the more invested and dependent on Walt. For this reason, the pursuit of safety can sometimes subvert the pursuit of value in "resistance" situations as well (Murray, Derrick, Leder, & Holmes, 2008; Murray, Holmes et al., 2009). We will see reversals in goal priorities play out next as we turn to the role that self-esteem plays in regulating the tension between safety and value goal pursuits.

Tipping the Balance: Self-Esteem and Safety

We have been acting as though situations are the only force that tips the goal balance to build the empirical case that risk regulation is a general or normative principle of relationship life. But anyone who has ever spent time on a seesaw knows that the partners on the seesaw control its potential for precipitous swings. In the risk regulation balance, each partner's *chronic* goal priorities can similarly "weigh in" and tip the goal balance in the direction opposite to the situationally prioritized goal.

Let's go back to the belongingness balance taking the perspective of someone who never fears getting sick. The threat of catching a cold or flu poses a less serious threat to physical safety for people who feel invulnerable to illness than it does for the hypochondriacs among us. For the fearless, activating the situational goal to be safe offers less opposition to value because safety is a less personally "weighty" goal. It's akin to the physics of a lighter child trying to hold a heavier child up on a seesaw. The weightier goal will tip the balance back just like the heavier child. Chronic goal priorities similarly "weigh in" on safety's regulation of value goal pursuits. For instance, people who feel invulnerable to disease put less weight on safety; they value others just as much when the threat of disease is salient as they do when it is absent (Mortensen et al., 2010).

In relationships, less trusting people who *chronically* question their partner's availability and commitment are the relationship equivalents of hypochondriacs. Just as hypochondriacs feel especially vulnerable to illness, the less trusting feel especially vulnerable to being hurt by their partner. People who chronically trust in their partner's availability and caring are akin to those intrepid, resilient souls who never worry about being sick. The more trusting rarely seriously question their partner's availability and responsiveness. In any ongoing situation, such divergent expectations of partner availability make safety a "weightier" goal pursuit for less trusting people (Murray et al., 2006). The risk of being hurt pushes less trusting people much further away from the goal to be safe because they are already handicapped in its pursuit (Murray, Griffin, Rose, & Bellavia, 2003). By contrast, highly trusting people can afford to pursue safety less vigilantly because resilient expectations of acceptance better allow them to roll with the proverbial punches. If safety is a more pressing goal for the especially safety-conscious, less trusting people should put the restoration of safety at a greater premium than highly trusting people. They do. In the aftermath of being hurt, people who chronically feel less valued by their partner treat their partner with hostility, effectively pushing him or her away. However, people who chronically feel more valued by their partner better resist this inclination (Murray, Bellavia, Rose, & Griffin, 2003, see Chapter 3).

The power *not* being safety-consciousness has to reverse goal priorities can be understood by taking our goal systems logic one step further. Safety and value goals are interconnected goals in memory (Murray et al., 2008). However, the strength of opposition between safety and value goals likely differs as a function of each person's overall progress toward safety. The further Skyler is from the goal to be safe *overall*, the weightier her situational goal to be safe, and the greater power it has to inhibit value goal pursuits. Conversely, the closer Walter is to the goal to be safe *overall*, the less weighty his situational goal to be safe, and the less power it has to inhibit value goal pursuits.

Self-Esteem and Safety

This brings us finally to why low self-esteem people have particular trouble in relationships. Low self-esteem people are not only less likely to idealize their partner than high self-esteem people (Murray, Holmes, & Griffin, 1996a, 1996b), but they are also less likely to nurture and care for their partner with conviction (Murray et al., 2006). Preoccupied by safety goal pursuits, low self-esteem people seem to act as though they are waiting for the evidence that finally proves their partner really was not the "right" person after all. Why does this happen?

In the sociometer model, self-esteem functions to forecast one's esteem in the eyes of others (Leary & Baumeister, 2000; Leary, Tambor, Terdal, & Downs, 1995). Because high self-esteem people can easily point to qualities they value in themselves, they expect others to be accepting and valuing of them. However, low self-esteem people assume that others will see them in the same relatively negative light as they see themselves (Swann, Hixon, & De La Ronde, 1992). Consequently, low self-esteem people underestimate how positively their partner regards them (Murray et al., 2001) and how much their partner loves them (Murray et al., 2001) even after their marriages have already lasted a decade.[1]

Struggling to explain their partner's commitment to them, low self-esteem people are more likely than high self-esteem people to slip into the role of the relationship hypochondriac. For instance, trying to take another's perspective and see things through their eyes is usually a relationship good. But it backfires for low self-esteem people. Taking their partner's perspective on a day's events preoccupies low self-esteem people with negative thoughts about what their partner sees in them (Vorauer & Quesnel, 2013). Similarly, when low self-esteem people overestimate how clearly they communicated their support needs, they misinterpret their partner's perfectly understandable lack of support provision as rejection (Cameron & Robinson, 2010). However, high self-esteem people can more readily afford to be a bit slipshod in their pursuit of safety because they are so much further along in its pursuit (Cameron, Stinson, Gaetz, & Balchen, 2010). In our thinking, different rates of safety goal progress impose different constraints on the activation and inhibition of safety and value goals. It is these goal system constraints that make it so much more difficult for low than high self-esteem people to sustain the connection needed to secure their relationship's future. In the next few pages, we first sketch out the hypothesized nature of these goal constraints for low and high self-esteem people. We then describe the empirical research that has provided some promising initial support for these hypothesized goal constraints.

Safety reigns supreme in the goal system of a low self-esteem person like Skyler. In such a safety-conscious goal system, safety occupies the position of a superordinate goal that limits pursuit of the subordinate goal for value. Situations that activate safety goals strongly *inhibit* value goals (to remove any impediment to safety's unconflicted and unabashed pursuit). In turn, situations that activate value goals can often also *activate* safety goals, creating acute motivational tension or conflict (Murray et al., 2008). Such tension serves to remind a less trusting, low self-esteem Skyler to guard against being overly dependent on Walt. Safety does *not* reign supreme in the goal system of a high self-esteem person like Walt. In such a value-conscious goal system, value instead competes for priority as the superordinate goal. Situations that activate value goals strongly deactivate safety goals (to remove any impediment to value's unconflicted pursuit). In turn, situations that activate safety goals can also *activate* value goals, creating acute motivational tension or conflict. Such tension serves to remind a more trusting, value-conscious Walt to guard against cutting his losses too soon.

Because the source of acute motivational tension differs for low and high self-esteem people, the situations that motivate *reversing* goal priorities also differ. For low self-esteem people, it is the threat of valuing their partner too much in a "resistance" situation that supplies the reverse motivation to be safe and distanced. But, for high self-esteem people, it is the threat of trusting their partner too little in a "risky" situation that supplies the reverse motivation to nurture and care. In either case, goal reversal is not likely to happen without an available opportunity and executive resources for self-regulation (Olson & Fazio, 2008). So how does all this speculation about goal constraints stand up against the literature?

Reversing Goals in "Risky" Situations

"Risky" situations are ones where Skyler is more dependent on Walt than he is on her (see Chapter 3). Skyler often finds herself in such "risky" situations in her marriage when she wants Walt's undivided attention after he has had a tiring day at work. "Risky" situations test or threaten trust because they heighten the potential to be hurt and disappointed. Thus, such situations automatically activate the goal to impose a safer distance (see Chapter 3). In risky situations, reducing dependence and moving away from the partner should be an *unconflicted* automatic intention for low self-esteem people because safety is a personally weightier goal than value. However, for high self-esteem people, value is a personally weightier goal than safety. Therefore, reducing dependence and moving away from the partner should be a more *conflicted* automatic intention for high self-esteem people. Consequently, in risky situations, high self-esteem people should reverse goal priorities and pursue value when they have an opportunity available to do so (Cavallo, Holmes, Fitzsimons, Murray, & Wood, 2012).

In a series of three experiments, we first threatened safety goals by leading experimental participants to believe their partner was upset with them. Control participants had no such apprehension. We then measured the inhibition (vs. activation) of value goal pursuits through self-reports of partner idealization and closeness (which, given their explicit nature, afford the opportunity to self-regulate goal pursuits). Low self-esteem people pursued the safety goal the situation automatically prioritized. Low self-esteem people idealized their partner less and reported feeling less close to their partner in the safety threat than control conditions. However, threatening safety actually furthered value goal pursuits for high self-esteem participants. They drew closer to their partner in the safety threat than control conditions (Murray, Rose, Bellavia, Holmes, & Kusche, 2002).

Subsequent research made this point even more persuasively. High self-esteem people actually approach and embrace risky bets when they think their partner might be upset with them, whereas low self-esteem people make safe bets (Cavallo, Fitzsimons, & Holmes, 2009). Similarly, high self-esteem people approach and draw closer to God when the threat of partner rejection is salient, whereas low self-esteem people avoid this source of connection (Laurin, Schumann, & Holmes, 2014). High self-esteem people so efficiently reverse safety goals pursuits that they automatically turn attention away from their partner's negative qualities when safety is threatened (Lamarche & Murray, 2014).

Reversing Goals in "Resistance" Situations

"Resistance" situations, such as ones where Skyler needs to sacrifice for Walt, test her conviction in Walt's "rightness" for her. Thus, such situations automatically activate the goal to construct compensatory value in relationship-promotive action (see Chapter 4). Pursuing value in resistance situations should be an *unconflicted* automatic inclination for high self-esteem people because value is a personally weightier goal pursuit than safety for high self-esteem people. However, valuing the partner should be a *conflicted* automatic inclination for low self-esteem people because being more attached and dependent moves low self-esteem people further away from their personally weightier goal to be safe. Consequently, low self-esteem people should reverse goal priorities and pursue safety over value when they have the opportunity available to correct.

In one of our favorite experiments, we threatened value goal pursuits by leading experimental participants to focus on all the ways in which their partner interfered with their personal goals. Control participants simply focused on ways in which their goals had been thwarted (through no fault of their partner). We then administered both implicit and explicit measures of partner valuing, with the assumption that the explicit measures could give low self-esteem people the opportunity to reverse goal priorities (Murray, Holmes, et al., 2009). High and even low self-esteem participants primed with the ways in which their partner interfered with their goals automatically compensated. Cost-primed participants were quicker to identify positive qualities in their partner than controls regardless of self-esteem (as we saw in Chapter 4). But, on the explicit measure of positive illusions, low self-esteem people reversed goal priorities. Low self-esteem people consciously reported valuing their partner less when primed with the ways in which their partner thwarted their goals (as compared to control participants). Even in the harried day-to-day course of married life, high self-esteem people still manage to compensate. In our daily diary study of newlyweds, high self-esteem people valued their partner more on days after their partner thwarted more of their goals. However, low self-esteem people failed to compensate for such infringement, which then made it harder for them to nurture and care for their partner (Murray, Holmes, et al., 2009). Sadly, low self-esteem people are so practiced in reversing value in favor of safety that they consciously report feeling less close to their partner when the goal to approach is subliminally primed (Murray et al., 2008).

Transactive Goal Pursuits: Safety and Self-Fulfilling Prophecies

With Skyler on the brink in her marriage, it is time to consider Walt's role in the current dilemma. Though it is easy to cast him as the villain (heartlessly leaving Skyler at home while he goes off to live life like he did before they had children), it would not be fair. While not blameless, Walt is not entirely at fault either. He was deliriously happy when Alex was born and hated that he had to miss out on time with him to work. He only put in extra hours on weekdays to avoid getting called into work on the weekend. He made special efforts to be attentive and generous to Skyler, getting her new books, music, and movies, because he knew that being home alone with a baby was hard on her. He wanted to do more with their son, but Skyler seemed to get so irritated with him when he didn't do things the "right" way. He thought he was listening and being supportive; he kept gently reminding Skyler to focus on all the great things they had going for them, but it seemed like so much of what he said and did went unnoticed. For a long while, he stayed focused on everything he loved about Skyler. But lately it has gotten harder. He really wants to be there for her still, but he needs her to be there for him too. For the first time ever he's started to question what he wants out of his marriage.

Walt's side to this story reveals that the co-regulation between safety and value involves more than one partner's goal pursuits. In relationships, goal pursuit is transactive (Fitzsimons, Finkel, & van Dellen, 2015). Partners facilitate, impede, and catch one another's goals interacting as two parts of an interdependent whole. This transactive reality makes the pursuit of safety a dyadic rather than solitary enterprise. Skyler's pursuit of safety limits the progress Walt can make in his pursuit of value just as his pursuit of value limits the progress Skyler can make in her pursuit of safety.

It is probably easiest to illustrate how partners can facilitate, impede, and catch one another's safety and value goals by reviewing how Skyler and Walt got to where they are now. Low in self-esteem, Skyler always had inklings of doubt, wondering if she could really trust Walt, and her son's birth finally gave voice and validity to her concerns. When Walt started working so much more, she could not help but wonder whether he was trying to avoid her. She just assumed he was feeling guilty when he brought her home books and movies and she did not understand why he kept trying to brush off her concerns with his optimistic words that all would be well once Alex got a little older. She gets impatient and irritated with him more readily now and usually forgets to check whether he needs comfort or support. High in self-esteem, Walt has really tried to be reassuring when she got upset, but what he said or did seemed to not make any difference. After months of trying, he is starting to feel defeated. Skyler just never seems happy when he tries to give her support and he cannot help but keep much of what he is thinking to himself for fear he might inadvertently say or do something that would upset Skyler.

In pursuing safety, Skyler secured the very outcome she wanted to avoid. Walt is now less invested in taking care of her needs than he was before. Skyler's safety goal pursuits deactivated Walt's value goal pursuits just as they deactivated her own value goal pursuits. Partners can catch one another's goal priorities because one partner's actions (and reactions) limit the degrees of freedom the other partner has to pursue and satisfy goals for both safety and value. Motivated cognition is situated after all.

The first constraint on goal pursuit comes from the pragmatics of self-perception. It is hard to see behavior as efficacious and meaningful when it seems to have no discernable effect. Similarly, for someone stuck with the Sisyphusian task of trying to make a less trusting partner feel safe, it is difficult *not* to question the value of nurturing and caring behavior. For instance, the partners of low self-esteem people face constant frustrations providing support. They try to prop low self-esteem people up and get them to see the half-full glass, but low self-esteem people insist on seeing it as half-empty (Marigold, Cavallo, Holmes, & Wood, 2014). The partners of low self-esteem people also have to constantly censor themselves, being careful to avoid saying anything that could be construed as negative or hurtful (Lemay & Dudley, 2011). The partners of low self-esteem people cannot even share the joys and accomplishments that make their life meaningful without fear of low self-esteem people raining on their parade (MacGregor & Holmes, 2011). Given Walt's many fruitless attempts to comfort and nurture Skyler, it is no wonder that he has started to question whether caring for her really does make sense.

The second, likely more powerful, constraint comes in how self-fulfilling prophecies foreclose one's behavioral options. In a self-fulfilling prophecy, the perceiver's expectations for an interaction shape his or her behavior, which in turn pushes the partner to behave in a way that confirms the perceiver's expectations (Murray et al., 2003; Snyder & Stukas, 1999). For instance, rejection-sensitive women expect their partner to reject them so they treat their partner hostilely, which limits their partner's capacity to do anything other than reject them in return (Downey, Freitas, Michaelis, & Khouri, 1998).

Relationships may be especially vulnerable to safety goal contagion because of the power insecurity has to perpetuate itself. As we introduced in Chapter 3, feeling safe is not the same as *being* safe. However, it is *feeling* safe (i.e., trust) that tips the balance toward the pursuit of value. Skyler's post-baby cynicism made her objectively safer because she asks very little of Walt now that she expects the worst from him. However, being objectively safer and less dependent did not make her *feel* any safer. Instead, it left her feeling more uncertain of his caring because she gave Walt so few opportunities to show his caring (Holmes & Rempel, 1989). In this way, the steps vulnerable people take to progress toward safety may backfire and chronically activate safety goal pursuits. Because safety and value exist in a natural state of opposition, being preoccupied with safety too often puts defending the value of caring and nurturing behavior on the psychological backburner. Unfortunately, the kind and nurturing behaviors feeling unsafe motivates Skyler to withhold are the very behaviors needed to help Walt feel safe and satisfy his safety goal pursuits in the face of their current stressors (Wieselquist et al., 1999). Seeing so little evidence of Skyler's acceptance essentially pushed Walt into safety concerns of his own; this then motivated him to start questioning the kindnesses he had bestowed without thinking. In this way, vulnerable people's preoccupation with safety can confirm their fears (Stinson, Cameron, Wood, Gaucher, & Holmes, 2009).

Conclusion

We opened this chapter with the idea that situations can rock relationships, potentiating the natural opposition between safety and value goals. We then explored goal system dynamics that tip the motivational balance back and forth between the pursuit of safety and value. In so doing, we highlighted the tyranny safety generally holds over value and the trouble prioritizing safety can cause in relationships. But we neglected one important consideration. Value can sometimes take precedence over safety too. In the next chapter, we see exactly when, why, and for whom this goal reversal happens.

Note

1 Low self-esteem people are especially trust-disadvantaged when their conscious beliefs about their partner's availability, caring, and responsiveness are assessed. However, as we will see in Chapter 6, low self-esteem people may be uniquely trust-advantaged when their automatic attitudes toward their partner are assessed.

6
WHEN VALUE OVERRIDES SAFETY

Arya never expected it to last when she started dating Aaron. Before she met him, she endured one short-lived relationship after the other. She could never completely convince herself that her past partners cared for her and keeping her distance always seemed like the best way to avoid being hurt. Aaron was somehow different. Even though Arya cannot exactly explain why Aaron wants to be with her, her doubts no longer dissuade her from wanting to be with him. The value she sees in caring for him has come to mean more to her than the safety to be had in keeping some distance.

Low in self-esteem like Skyler, Arya has no trouble seeing the potential to be hurt in the situations populating her married life. Unlike Skyler, the pursuit of safety usually does not hold her hostage. While Skyler withdraws in situations that threaten hurt, Arya typically draws even closer to Aaron. Safety has lost its imperial sway over value because valuing Aaron has come to give so much meaning and purpose to her actions in and outside her relationship. Aaron is such a central part of Arya's life that she no longer wants to take her doubts about his feelings for her too seriously. The thought of losing the meaning he gives to her life pains her more than the thought of being let down by him. For Arya, the balance of power between safety and value gradually shifted in ways that gave sustaining her sense of conviction greater power to monopolize goal pursuit.

Arya's experience is not unique. In every relationship, there are times when value has to take precedence over safety for the relationship to thrive. This chapter explores the special circumstances that result in value becoming a monopolizing goal. In so doing, it gives new dynamism to the risk regulation balance. Figure 6.1 captures this potential for dynamism by giving the equilibrium point "wheels" and momentum. In this balance, safety is not fixed as the goal with greater

108   When Value Overrides Safety

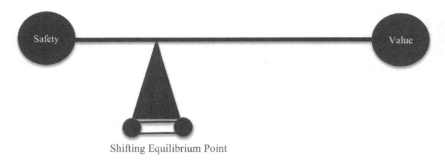

Shifting Equilibrium Point

FIGURE 6.1   Dynamism in the Risk Regulation Balance

leveraging power to tip attention, inference, and behavior in its favor. Instead, the equilibrium point can shift in value's decided favor when personal or relationship contexts *consistently* make sustaining a sense of conviction in the value of caring and nurturing behavior more important than not being hurt.

The easiest place to see the monopolizing power of value is in the earliest stage of relationships. People who are newly romantically involved defy every known principle of risk regulation. They are both wildly anxious and uncertain about their partner's caring *and* obsessively convinced that their partner is perfect for them (Brickman, 1987: Eastwick & Finkel, 2008). This is no random coincidence. For a relationship to form, people need to leap before they look. They need to risk seeking connection, with smiles, touches, self-disclosure, and overt expressions of interest, while knowing a potential partner might not reciprocate. For bonds to form in the face of such a clear safety threat, an especially weighty and dramatic force is needed to shift the balance of power in the competition between safety and value goals consistently and decidedly in value's favor.

The physiological and psychological experience of romantic infatuation does just that. Neuroimaging (i.e., fMRI) studies suggest that passionate love activates subcortical areas of the brain that control reward sensitivity and goal-directed behavior (Aron et al., 2005; Bartels & Zeki, 2000; Fisher, Aron, & Brown, 2005). On a dopamine-induced high, someone passionately in love can only think about reasons to connect, obsessively focusing on all that is wonderful about the partner, an intoxicating preoccupation that leaves no psychological oxygen left for entertaining concerns about safety (Fisher, 1998; Fisher, Aron, Mashek, Haifang, & Brown, 2002). In fact, thwarting safety goal pursuits actually intensifies (rather than deactivates) value goal pursuits in fledgling relationships. People report being more passionately in love with new potential partners when they are *more* uncertain their affections are reciprocated (Eastwood & Finkel, 2008). Romantic infatuation imbues partners with such incontrovertible reasons to connect that the safety concerns that spurred the obsession with the partner's perfection are masked (Brickman, 1987).

In this chapter, we expand this theme by exploring the contexts that shift the equilibrium point of the risk regulation balance decidedly in value's favor. We start with life contexts outside the relationship that intensify the goal to possess an unequivocal sense of conviction within the relationship. We explore how self-relevant goal pursuits, such as the quest for self-integrity and the desire to perceive an orderly world, turn the pursuit of conviction and value in the relationship into a monopolizing concern. Next, we delve into the relationship itself to explore ongoing situations, such as the intensification of hopes and the accumulation of personal investments, that motivate people to put solidifying their convictions ahead of safety. This allows us to explore how sustaining conviction can motivate people to confabulate evidence of safety, putting themselves at greater objective risk of being hurt (Lemay & Clark, 2015).

We conclude the chapter by exploring how transactive goal regulation can also turn value into a monopolizing goal pursuit. Because partners in interdependent relationships can catch, satiate, and switch one another's goals (Fitzsimons, Finkel, & van Dellen, 2015), Aaron's pursuit of value can also motivate Arya to set aside her pursuit of safety. Explaining exactly how such goal transmission could occur brings us back to the automatic partner attitudes that underlie trust (see Chapter 3). Arya's positive automatic attitude toward Aaron captures his long history of responsive behavior. Such an attitude signals that Aaron is not only safe to approach but *worth* keeping (Murray, Holmes, & Pinkus, 2010). By giving partners implicit value, more positive automatic attitudes motivate vulnerable people to discount the possibility of rejection in the very situations that pose the greatest threat to the pursuit of safety (Murray, Gomillimon, Holmes, & Harris, 2015; Murray, Gomillion, Holmes, Harris, & Lamarche, 2013).

Putting Life Meaning Ahead of Safety

Relationship-specific goals for safety and value are pursued as part of a broader goal system (Fitzsimons et al., 2015). They occur alongside goal pursuits that transcend the relationship, such as being a person of worth (Steele, 1988), feeling competent and autonomous (Ryan & Deci, 2000), and seeing purpose and meaning in life (Heine, Proulx, & Vohs, 2006). Within this goal system, relationship-transcendent goals can commandeer safety and value goal pursuits as a means to meet more general motivational ends (Leary & Baumeister, 2000). As we see next, pursuing the goal to be a person of worth, doing sensible things, and living in a meaningful world can shift the equilibrium point of the risk regulation balance in favor of value. It certainly did for Arya. Her father fell unexpectedly ill just when she was contemplating asking Aaron to move in. With her expectations about her family shaken, Arya needed something else in her life to make sense. Committing to Aaron allowed her to see herself as part of a benevolent, orderly, and meaningful world, an end important enough to override her concerns about being hurt.

The Power of Self-Affirmation

The power that relationship-transcendent goal pursuits have to suppress safety and intensify value goal pursuits first surfaced in research on self-affirmation. Steele (1988) offered self-affirmation theory to explain why people justify their actions in dissonance paradigms (e.g., deciding a lie was not a lie or a chosen option is infinitely preferable to a forgone one). Steele reasoned that people do *not* justify their actions to make behavior consistent with their thoughts and feelings as dissonance theorists assumed. Instead, he reasoned that people justify their actions to restore self-integrity – to reaffirm the belief that they are good people living sensible, value-driven lives. Steele's insight led to decades of research exploring how simple acts of self-affirmation, such as reflecting on the values that serves as one's most important guiding life principles, can alleviate all manners of self-protective defenses (see Sherman & Cohen, 2006, for a review).

Self-affirmation has similar power to suppress self-protection. The simple act of self-affirming inoculates people against concerns about physical and psychological safety, motivating them to approach social connection. For instance, when people reflect on the value that serves as the most important guiding principle in their lives, they step outside themselves; they report greater feelings of love and connection to others (Crocker, Niiya, & Mischkowski, 2008). The guarantee of social connection afforded by self-affirmation is such an effective prophylactic that it can even make the mortality risks posed by unhealthy behaviors seem like a more remote threat (Crocker et al., 2008).

Contemplating guiding life values can also push vulnerable people like Arya and Skyler to forgo safety for value goal pursuits in relationships. Jaremka and colleagues activated safety goal pursuits by leading participants in the threat condition to believe their partner would discover their dark secrets and become disaffected (Jaremka, Bunyan, Collins, & Sherman, 2011). Control participants had no such apprehension. Next, they introduced a competing, relationship-transcendent goal pursuit. Participants in the self-affirmation condition described how their most important personal value gave their life meaning. Participants in the neutral goal condition described why their own least important value would be important to others. Low self-esteem people who did *not* reflect on their most important life value sought safety over value, like Skyler. When faced with rejection, they derogated their partner and distanced themselves from the possibility of being hurt. However, low self-esteem people who reflected on their important life value behaved more like Arya. They evaluated their partner just as positively when they expected to be rejected as they did when they had no such safety concerns. Being immersed in a self-affirmation goal pursuit effectively motivated low self-esteem people to forgo safety for meaning and value within the relationship.

Encouraging vulnerable people to engage in self-affirmation goal pursuits even frees them from the socially crippling effects of mistrust. Stinson and colleagues instructed experimental participants to reflect on the life value that was most important to them (Stinson, Logel, Shepherd, & Zanna, 2011). Control participants reflected on a life value that was important to someone else. They then tracked people's trust in the caring of those closest to them (e.g., friends, romantic partners) and comfort interacting with a new acquaintance. Self-affirming motivated less trusting people to forgo safety for value in relationships. Less trusting people who reflected on the personal value they held most dear came to believe in the integrity of their social connections *more* over time and they evidenced greater physical comfort engaging the social world (Stinson et al., 2011).

The Power of Violated Expectancies

Although the dynamics underlying the power of self-affirmation are still a bit of a mystery, one possibility seems clear (Crocker et al., 2008). Self-affirmation's symbolic guarantee of social connection could function as a prophylactic. Safety might be a moot goal for the self-affirmed because reflecting on personal values actively connects people to an orderly and meaningful world. Being actively engaged in this broader world can then testify that nothing bad will happen and little can be lost in forging ahead (Critcher & Dunning, 2015). In this way, the act of self-affirming allows people to put the cart (value goals) ahead of the horse (safety goals) because engaging in the pursuit of shared life goals makes safety seem beside the point, suspending this goal pursuit.

If active engagement in the social world functions as such a relationship prophylactic, what happens to the relative priority people put on pursuing safety versus value in the relationship when the stability of the social world is threatened? Does being trapped in a less orderly and predictable world shift the equilibrium point of the risk regulation balance even closer to safety? Or might such a disquieting world motivate people to pursue a compensatory sense of relationship conviction with greater force, shifting the equilibrium point of the risk regulation balance in value's decided favor?

The research evidence points to the latter possibility. When ongoing events thwart the relationship-transcendent goal to perceive an orderly and meaningful world, vulnerable people appear to eschew safety for the hope of restoring value and meaning through the relationship (Murray, Lamarche, Gomillion, Seery, & Kondrak, 2016). The meaning maintenance model assumes that people need the world to make sense to act purposefully and efficaciously within it (Heine et al., 2006). The world makes sense when events unfold much as people expect, as happens when it rains on a cloudy day, syrup tops pancakes, and nasty people receive their just desserts. When events do not unfold as people expect, the world stops making sense and people are thrown into an aversive state of behavioral indecision. Consequently, violations of expectancy motivate people to restore meaning and order to their worlds so they might act with purpose within it once again. In fact, expectancy violations as benign as pairing words that do not naturally belong together (e.g., quickly blueberry, juicy running) motivate people to impose associations they expect to see on the world. For instance, people primed with incongruent word pairings punish prostitutes more severely for violating social convention, restoring order and stability to shaken perceptions (Randles, Proulx, & Heine, 2011).

Because relationship-specific and -transcendent goals are interconnected (Cavallo, Fitzsimons, & Holmes, 2009; Fitzsimons et al., 2015), the general desire to restore meaning and order to the world should commandeer safety and value goals for its own ends. People threatened by a disorderly and unpredictable world might compensate for disorder in the world by imposing greater order on their relationships. However, when expectancy violations impose disorder on the world, threatened perceivers impose meaning and order on only those situations that need reordering (Heine et al., 2006). For instance, people exposed to meaning threats punish social deviants, but not those who adhere to social convention.

Thus, when expectancy violations impose disorder on the world, some relationships may be in greater need of reordering than others. People who are blissfully satisfied in their relationships live in a consonant or ordered state. They go about life maintaining relationships that meet their expectations in most respects. However, people who are less satisfied live in a comparative state of disorder. They go about life maintaining a relationship that is not necessarily the one they wanted or expected to inhabit. The amount of dissonance experienced as a result of living with such a violation should be directly in proportion to the state of dissatisfaction in the relationship. Thus, the ongoing motivational push to reduce dissonance by crystallizing conviction in the relationship should intensify as satisfaction with the relationship *decreases*.

Consequently, when expectancy violations impose disorder on the world, people in less satisfying relationships likely need to make sense of their ongoing involvement in the relationship. They can do this by clarifying and exaggerating just how much their partner really does mean to them. The pressure they face to compensate and clarify conviction should also increase in proportion to their state of dissatisfaction. However, people who are highly satisfied in their relationship have relatively little to set right in their relationships when expectancy violations impose disorder on the world. Affirming already unequivocal relationship convictions should be all it takes to remind satisfied perceivers that life really is orderly and full of meaning and purpose.

To test these hypotheses, we created situations where the world did not turn out as expected (Murray et al., 2016). In two experiments, we violated the conventional moral that hard work pays off. Experimental participants read an abridged version of Kafka's *An Imperial Message*, a story about a messenger who overcomes a series of herculean obstacles only to ultimately fail in his mission to deliver a message to the king. Control participants read a conventional narrative about a persevering tortoise triumphing over a ne'erdowell hare. In a third experiment, expectancy violation participants viewed surrealist art that presented a familiar image in an unexpected configuration (i.e., an apple floating in front of a face). Control participants viewed realist art (i.e., a landscape with a double rainbow). Participants in a fourth experiment had their expectations confounded while they watched a bizarre clip from the David Lynch movie *Rabbits*, while controls viewed a clip from the tried and true *Wizard of Oz*. In the fifth experiment, participants violated bodily expectations by physically approaching negative and avoiding positive stimuli (rather than vice versa). Participants in the expectancy violation condition pulled a joystick toward them (simulating approach) whenever a negative word appeared on a computer screen and pushed the same joystick away from them (simulating avoidance) whenever a positive word appeared, a behavioral violation. Conversely, participants in the control condition pulled a joystick toward them (simulating approach) whenever a positive word appeared and pushed the same joystick away from them (simulating avoidance) whenever a negative word appeared, the behavioral convention.

Next, we measured the priority participants put on the pursuit of safety versus value within the relationship. Participants rated their own feelings of closeness and commitment and their perceptions of their partner's feelings of closeness and commitment. Because being more committed than one's partner poses an objective threat to safety (see Chapter 3), Arya's willingness to risk such vulnerability captures the heightened priority she puts on the pursuit of value goals. Therefore, we used the difference between Arya's feelings of closeness and commitment and her perceptions of Aaron's feelings of closeness and commitment to index goal prioritization. More positive difference scores captured compensatory conviction – feeling closer and more committed despite being relatively less certain of the partner's closeness and commitment.

Figure 6.2 illustrates the nature of the effects we found across experiments. It depicts the association between pre-test relationship satisfaction and compensatory conviction for participants in the expectancy violation and control conditions in the first surreal stories experiment. For less satisfied perceivers, violating expectancies triggered the prioritization of value over safety. Less satisfied perceivers made stronger compensatory expressions of conviction in the expectancy violation than control condition. This meaning-restorative response also intensified in magnitude as initial satisfaction decreased (and dissonance likely increased). However, such a compensatory reaction was not at all in evidence for more satisfied perceivers. More satisfied perceivers did not report greater conviction in the expectancy violation condition, presumably because they had found enough solace in their unadulterated convictions.

The components of the compensatory conviction difference score present a still clearer picture of the psychological dynamics at play. For less satisfied perceivers, violating expectancies made the partner seem less safe and predictable. Even though the expectancies we violated had nothing at all to do with the partner, less satisfied perceivers believed their partner felt less close and less committed to them in the expectancy violation than control condition. These doubts also magnified as initial satisfaction decreased. Despite having greater reason to

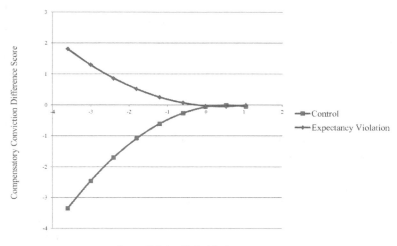

FIGURE 6.2 Meaning Threats Motivate Less Satisfied People to Express Compensatory Conviction

prioritize the pursuit of safety within their relationship, less satisfied perceivers in the expectancy violation conditions nonetheless pursued value. Less satisfied perceivers reported feeling even closer and more committed to their partner in the expectancy violation than control condition. This doubt-defying, meaning-restorative response also increased in intensity as initial satisfaction decreased. The conviction expressed in the expectancy violation conditions truly was compensatory. When the world seemed uncertain, people in less satisfied relationships compensated for their relationship's greater seeming fragility with strengthened commitment. They doubled down on dependence to make sense of life.

So let's recap. In the self-affirmation experiments, engaging the symbolic pursuit of a superordinate important life value motivated people low in self-esteem to eschew safety for the pursuit of value. In the expectancy violation experiments, thwarting the desire to perceive a meaningful and orderly world similarly motivated people low in relationship satisfaction to prioritize value. These research programs make it clear that goal pursuits outside the relationship can reverse the usual lock safety has over the pursuit of value. We now turn to relationship circumstances that have comparable power to shift the equilibrium point of the risk regulation balance decidedly in value's favor.

Putting Justifying Caring Ahead of Safety

The self-affirmation and expectancy violation experiments reveal conditions outside the relationship that motivate vulnerable people to prioritize value over safety. In these experiments, transcendent goals inject themselves into the relationship, infusing value goal pursuits with added momentum to drive behavior. In daily relationship life, well-meaning experimenters are not always around to prompt vulnerable people (or anyone else) to eschew safety for the pursuit of value. Fortunately, increasing interdependence often gains the natural potential to decouple value from safety goal pursuits when it is left to its own devices. As we will see, justifying individual acts of caring and commitment can create a self-perpetuating momentum that gradually shifts the equilibrium point of the risk regulation balance in value's decided favor.

Behavior creates the psychological impetus to construct its justification (Brickman, 1987; Harmon-Jones, Harmon-Jones, & Levy, 2015). Arya's prior acts of caring laid the foundation for future responsiveness by motivating her to believe that Aaron was worth it. Through this self-perpetuating cycle, investments of caring and conviction in the partner's value become progressively intertwined over time (Rusbult & Van Lange, 2003; Wieselquist, Rusbult, Foster, & Agnew, 1999). As we will see, this cycle reaches a motivational tipping point once people have invested so much of themselves in caring that they cannot afford to question their conviction in their partner's value. For the highly invested, conviction is no longer not just an end in itself. It also affords a central means for satisfying the relationship-transcendent goal to be a valuable person leading a sensible and meaningful life (Brickman, 1987). Arya's investment in her marriage, including her hopes for its future, her willingness to put her career aside for Aaron, and her immersion in Aaron's family, represent everything personally that could be lost if she let herself question her convictions. It is this personal investment in conviction that allows value to take safety's place as a monopolizing goal pursuit. Indeed, Arya's marriage has now become so important to her that she is motivated to emphasize how much she can trust Aaron.

Such a qualitative shift in conviction happens as partners become increasingly emotionally intimate and progressively less able to separate themselves from their relationship (Lydon & Linardatos, 2012). Scholars use the term "relationship-specific identification" to capture commitment's transformation from a simple evaluation of the relationship to an evaluation of the self within the relationship (Linardatos & Lydon, 2011). Arya is now "identified" with her relationship; her marriage is now part of who she is and she could not change her mind about Aaron without fundamentally shaking her sense of herself and her life. Once commitment to the partner becomes self-defining, protecting the self requires protecting the *relationship*. In fact, the relationship-identified do not find personal comfort in distancing themselves from their partner in risky situations. Questioning the partner's value actually threatens self-esteem and hurts more than the transgression that provoked it (Lydon & Linardatos, 2012).

With such a transformation in what it means to be hurt, safety can takes a back seat to value because the pursuit of value goals is *both* self- and relationship-protective for the relationship-identified. This allows relationship maintenance in threatening situations to become automatic and functionally independent from trust. For instance, people who are highly identified with their relationship automatically turn their attention away from attractive and available alternative partners (Linardatos & Lydon, 2011). Simply priming *generic* thoughts about the partner also motivates the relationship-identified to respond more constructively to their partner's transgressions (Linardatos & Lydon, 2011). People who are more identified with their relationship even compensate and evaluate their partner more positively when told that their partner's values about having a baby with Down's syndrome differ from their own (Auger, Hurley, & Lydon, 2016). People who have already invested a lot in caring for their partner also misperceive their partner's behavior as being more supportive than it was (Lemay & Neal, 2013, 2014). They blame themselves when their partner disappoints them, deciding they simply did not communicate their needs clearly enough (Lemay & Melville, 2014). Furthermore, even low self-esteem people who include their partner as part of their identity resist devaluing their partner when faced by the possibility of being hurt by their partner's transgressions or negative behavior (Baker & McNulty, 2013).

I am Committed, So I Must Be Safe and It Must Be Right

The investments of caring that build relationship-specific identification usually occur gradually as relationships develop over time. However, it is also possible to rapidly accelerate interdependence in the lab and invest people in caring for a new partner. In such formative relationships, being personally invested motivates people to defend investment by exaggerating evidence of safety (Lemay & Clark, 2015). People who have already taken the risk of caring for a new partner convince themselves that partner is safe to approach *after the fact* of their responsiveness. Rather than being a motivational priority in its own right, safety becomes a temporary means to value's end.

Lemay and Clark (2008) made this point through their research on the projection of communal responsiveness. These authors reason that people justify their own investment in caring behaviors by projecting similarly caring motivations on to the recipient of their responsiveness. In one experiment, unacquainted participants reported in pairs to the laboratory for a study of social interaction (Lemay & Clark, 2008). In the "personal investment" condition, the researchers quickly escalated investment in this new relationship by instructing participants to behave in a positive and responsive way to the other participant. In the control condition, the target participant was instructed to behave neutrally. Then the pairs interacted. Participants instructed to be responsive reported greater attraction to their partner than controls, suggesting greater personal investment in this new relationship. Participants instructed to be responsive also justified this greater investment by projecting their own responsiveness on to their partner. They perceived their partner as behaving more responsively toward them (as compared to controls).

Significant transition points in the relationship, such as moving in together, marrying, or parenting a child, also quickly escalate personal investment in the relationship, intensifying the necessity to put value pursuits ahead of safety. Gagne and Lydon (2001) mimicked such a goal-transforming transition in the lab. They asked dating participants about to graduate from college to contemplate the future of their relationship. Participants in the "investment" condition devised a plan of action for maintaining their relationship in the future, adopting an implemental mindset that treated commitment as a foregone conclusion. Participants then rated their partner's status relative to the typical partner on physical attractiveness, intelligence, warmth, and sense of humor. Invested participants justified the decision they had just imagined implementing in their life. They exaggerated their partner's value relative to controls who had not had a mindset invoked, seeing their partner as even more superior to the typical partner than they had thought.

When commitment escalates markedly in real life, personally treating it as a foregone and unassailably sound decision also forecasts the relationship's fate. For instance, people cement the "rightness" of impending commitments by projecting their own responsiveness on to their partner. In a longitudinal study reported by Lemay and Clark (2008), people who were about to be married reported on their own motivation to be responsive to their partner (e.g., "How far would you be willing to go to help your spouse?") and their partner's motivation to be responsive to them (e.g., "How far would your spouse be willing to go to help you?"). Two years after marriage, they completed the same measures again. This allowed the researchers to identify who cemented their investment in caring for their partner by exaggerating their partner's reciprocal motivation to care for them. People who initially reported stronger motivations to care for their partner justified and protected this investment by exaggerating their partner's later caring and responsiveness to them. These invested participants decided they *had* to be safe in their partner's hands because they were already committed to caring for their partner. They compromised safety and increased actual vulnerability by assuming rather than ensuring safety. However, doing so helped guarantee they would not have any reason to question the meaning and value inherent in treating their partner responsively in the future. Those invested participants who projected their caring on to their partner behaved more responsively through the tribulations of their marriage's initial years.

The priority newlyweds put on personally investing in commitment even when it makes them less safe also forecasts marital fate. Schoebi, Karney, and Bradbury (2012) measured personal intentions to maintain commitment in a sample of newlyweds (e.g., "It makes me feel good to sacrifice for my partner"; "My marriage must often take a back seat to other interests of mine"). Then they observed how constructively couples behaved during the discussion of a marital problem and they tracked marital satisfaction and relationship stability. Newlyweds who were personally invested in doing whatever it took to protect their commitments did just that. Women with stronger intentions to maintain their commitment risked being hurt in conflict situations. They behaved visibly more constructively while discussing a serious marital problem, seeking greater closeness to their partner despite the risks. Newlyweds with stronger intentions to maintain their commitments also reported greater satisfaction later after four years and they were also less likely to divorce after 11 years (Schoebi et al., 2012).

Automatic Attitudes and Partner Goal Contagion

The research we just reviewed reveals how being invested in caring for the partner can tip the equilibrium point of the risk regulation balance in value's decided favor. However, we still need to resolve the puzzle that introduced this chapter. How did a low self-esteem Arya come to invest enough in caring for Aaron to set aside her temptation to keep safe and maintain a self-protective distance? Answering this question takes us back to transactive goal pursuits and the role Aaron's responsive behavior ultimately played in nurturing Arya's investment in caring for him.

Partners in interdependent relationships can catch, satiate, and switch goal pursuits (Fitzsimons et al., 2015). Because Arya's goal pursuits occur alongside Aaron's goal pursuits, his pursuit of value could suppress her conflicting pursuit of safety. Such partner goal transmission could conceivably happen through multiple mechanisms. Being motivated to protect his investment in caring for Arya might motivate Aaron to forgive her transgressions, benevolence that she might feel obliged to reciprocate. Aaron might also make big and small sacrifices for her, practicing a communal relationship norm that limits conflicts and occasions where Arya feels vulnerable enough to distance. However, Aaron's greatest power to shift his partner's goal pursuits may reside in the power his own responsive behavior has to change his value to Arya without her necessarily even realizing her investment has increased.

The possibility for such implicit influence and goal contagion brings us back to the automatic partner attitudes that underlie trust (see Chapter 3). People develop more or less positive automatic attitudes through experience interacting and living with their partner. Being treated with greater care and responsiveness conditions more positive automatic attitudes toward the partner, whereas being treated with less care and responsiveness conditions more negative automatic attitudes (Murray et al., 2010; Murray, Gomillion, et al., 2013). Because automatic partner attitudes summarize the history of the partner's behavior, they probably also encapsulate the partner's predominant goal pursuits. Arya's highly positive automatic attitude toward Aaron captures his long history of responsive behavior and the strong behavioral priority he put on the pursuit of value. Such a positive automatic attitude not only signals that Aaron is safe to approach (Chapter 3), but it also suggests that he is *worth* keeping (Murray et al., 2010). Such an implicit investment in Aaron's value might just be enough to motivate Arya's caring and nurturing behavior in situations that tempt her to self-protect.

To explore this possibility in our research program on automatic partner attitudes, we targeted people who normally prioritize safety goal pursuits in risky situations – those who are low in self-esteem (Murray et al., 2015) or self-regulatory capacity (Finkel & Campbell, 2001; Murray, Gomillion, et al., 2013). In one of these studies, we had married couples complete an Implicit Association Test (IAT) to measure automatic partner attitudes and a 14-day diary study to measure safety and value goal pursuits in everyday interaction (see Chapter 3 for a detailed description of the IAT). Each day participants reported on their trust in their partner's caring, their partner's supportive and communal and rejecting and selfish behavior toward them, and their supportive and communal and rejecting and selfish behavior toward their partner.

We originally reasoned that highly positive automatic partner attitudes allow vulnerable people to feel safer in risky situations. Rewriting these hypotheses in terms of partner goal transmission suggests a further possibility. Because automatic attitudes are grounded in the partner's prior goal pursuits (Murray et al., 2010), they should have the power to transmit the goals the partner prioritizes to the perceiver. This grounding in experience should give highly positive automatic partner attitudes the power to transmit a resilient and committed partner's personal investment in caring to a vulnerable perceiver in need of a motivational "assist" to set safety goals aside. In other words, a low self-esteem Arya could catch Aaron's value goal pursuits because his past acts of caring conditioned her highly positive automatic attitude toward him, implicitly increasing her personal investment in him and hardening her resolve to care for him.

Regardless of the mechanism, the findings are clear. When vulnerable people possess more positive automatic partner attitudes, safety goal pursuits no longer monopolize perception and behavior in risky situations. This is just as true for people who are low in self-esteem as it is for people who are low in self-regulatory capacity.

Consider a classic means of restoring safety – being vigilant and quick to perceive rejection in risky situations. Vulnerable people who possess more positive automatic attitudes are actually *insensitive* to rejection when they have just been hurt and have every reason to prioritize safety. Figure 6.3 presents the rejection-sensitivity findings for low and high self-esteem people in *high-risk* situations in our diary study (i.e., days after participants reported personally and unusually high levels of uncertainty about their partner's caring). Low self-esteem people with more positive automatic attitudes perceived their partner as less rejecting and selfish on days after they had been personally hurt by their partner (relative to low self-esteem people with more negative automatic attitudes).

We found a conceptually parallel effect on rejection sensitivity for people low in working memory, which imposes a cognitive constraint on self-regulatory strength (Murray, Lupien, & Seery, 2012). We manipulated the risk of partner rejection by leading experimental participants to believe their partner had compiled a lengthy list of their faults. Control participants had no such apprehension

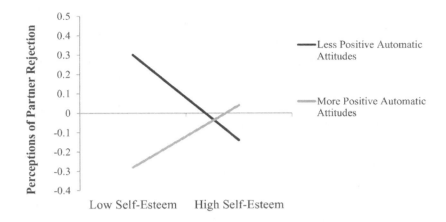

After High Risk Days

FIGURE 6.3 Low Self-Esteem People with More Positive Automatic Partner Attitudes Evidence Less Rejection Sensitivity. (Adapted from Murray, S. L., Gomillion, S., Holmes, J. G., & Harris, B. L. (2015). Inhibiting self-protection in romantic relationships: Automatic partner attitudes as a resource for low self-esteem people. *Social Psychology and Personality Science, 6,* 173–182. Copyright Sage Publications; adapted with permission.)

(see Chapter 3 for details on this manipulation). While this was happening, we measured psychophysiological threat reactions (as indexed through the heart working less efficiently). Next, we asked participants to give a speech about their career plans while their partner watched and report how they expected their partner to react to their speech (while we continued to measure psychophysiological threat reactions). For the self-regulation-impaired, more positive automatic attitudes fostered *insensitivity* to perceiving rejection in the face of their partner's overtly rejecting behavior. When people low in working-memory capacity had more positive automatic partner attitudes, their hearts worked more efficiently, pumping more blood with less arterial resistance, indicating greater bodily resilience (relative to people low in working-memory capacity with more negative automatic attitudes). People low in working-memory capacity with more positive automatic attitudes also expected their partner to be more approving of their speech even though their partner had just rejected them (Murray et al., 2012).

Across these studies, vulnerable people with more positive automatic attitudes eschewed safety pursuits. By minimizing the possibility of rejection, they behaved as though restoring trust in their partner was more important than keeping safe

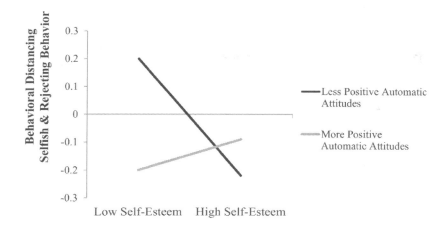

After High Risk Days

FIGURE 6.4 Low Self-Esteem People with More Positive Automatic Partner Attitudes Evidence Less Defensive Distancing. (Adapted from Murray, S. L., Gomillion, S., Holmes, J. G., & Harris, B. L. (2015). Inhibiting self-protection in romantic relationships: Automatic partner attitudes as a resource for low self-esteem people. *Social Psychology and Personality Science, 6*, 173–182. Copyright Sage Publications; adapted with permission.)

from being hurt. Further findings from the diary study suggest that more positive automatic partner attitudes allow vulnerable people to do more than simply eschew safety in high-risk situations. By suppressing safety goals, highly positive automatic attitudes also release and facilitate value goal pursuits. Figure 6.4 presents prototypic findings for such value preservation. It captures the results for behavioral distancing in *high-risk* situations for people low versus high in self-esteem in the diary study. Low self-esteem people with more positive automatic attitudes sustained connection in risky situations. They engaged in less rejecting and selfish behavior on days after they had been personally hurt (relative to people low in self-esteem with more negative automatic attitudes). In fact, people low in self-esteem with more positive automatic attitudes responded just as constructively to being hurt as high self-esteem people did! A parallel effect emerged for people low in self-regulatory capacity. When the self-regulation-impaired possessed more positive automatic attitudes, they suppressed the temptation to distance. They drew closer to partners who had just rejected them, prioritizing value over safety goal pursuits (Murray, Gomillion, et al., 2013).

So, let's recap. In high-risk situations, vulnerable people who are normally preoccupied with safety instead prioritize value – when, and only when, they

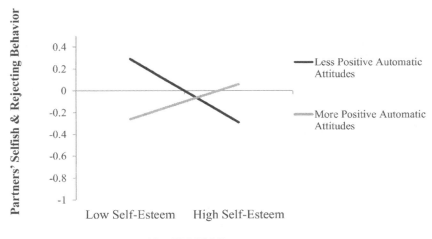

FIGURE 6.5 The Partners of Low Self-Esteem People with More Positive Automatic Partner Attitudes Also Evidence Less Defensive Distancing. (Adapted from Murray, S. L., Gomillion, S., Holmes, J. G., & Harris, B. L. (2015). Inhibiting self-protection in romantic relationships: Automatic partner attitudes as a resource for low self-esteem people. *Social Psychology and Personality Science, 6*, 173–182. Copyright Sage Publications; adapted with permission.)

possess more positive automatic attitudes toward their partner. But does this mean they are actually catching their partner's goal pursuits? The diary data suggest that this might just be the case. Figure 6.5 presents the rejecting and selfish behavior of the *partners* of low and high self-esteem people on high-risk days. The *partners* of low self-esteem people with more positive automatic attitudes engaged in less rejecting and selfish behavior on days after people with low self-esteem had felt more hurt. A quick comparison between Figures 6.4 and 6.5 reveals that low self-esteem people with more positive automatic attitudes practically mirror their *partner's* behavior, suggesting they might have caught their partner's goals.

Conclusion

In this chapter, we explored personal and relationship contexts that can tip the equilibrium point of the risk regulation balance in value's decided favor. We described how safety and value goals operate as part of an interconnected goal system. Within this goal system, relationship-transcendent pursuits for self-integrity and a purposeful and meaningful life can infuse and transform relationship-specific goal pursuits.

When ongoing situations make the relationship a central *means* for satisfying transcendent goals, value gains monopolizing power over safety in goal pursuit. Simple acts of self-affirmation immerse low self-esteem people in the pursuit of a value-driven life, allowing them to forgo safety in risky situations and connect. Conversely, thwarting the goal for a sensible and meaningful world by violating expectancies motivates vulnerable people to prioritize value. When the world does not turn out as expected, people who are uncertain of their relationship's meaning clarify and solidify conviction, drawing closer in the face of doubt. For the relationship-identified, interdependence reaches a tipping point where the relationship becomes a central source of personal meaning and value in life as a whole. At this tipping point, protecting conviction becomes monopolizing and the relationship-identified even distort evidence of safety and embellish their value to their partner to avoid questioning their partner's value to them.

Not everyone reaches such a tipping point. For the most fortunate of the safety-conscious, highly positive automatic partner attitudes transmit one partner's greater personal investment in caring to the more vulnerable partner. However, in some relationships, safety retains its monopoly over value even when circumstances dictate it could and should lose such a stranglehold. Skyler is a case in point. Alex's birth should have motivated her to clarify her convictions and increase her personal investment in Walt. His birth instead threatened her investment because she could not let safety concerns go long enough to see the value Walt brought to her life. In Chapter 7, we turn to the reality constraints the person, partner, and relationship impose on goal pursuit. As we will see, safety and value goal pursuits can lose their natural compensatory balance or even completely backfire when their pursuit is not sensitive to reality's affordances.

7
REALITY CONSTRAINTS

When Skyler and Walt first started dating, their friends and family thought they were perfect for one another. They both loved sports and happily supported one another's careers. They shared such similar preferences, values, and personalities that they could quite literally finish one another's sentences. Nobody ever would have expected them to struggle, least of all them. The same could not be said for Arya and Aaron. They seemed to disagree about everything and had such different personalities that everyone expected their relationship to fizzle out before they ever married.

How could Skyler and Walt, two veritable peas in a pod, end up with the unhappy relationship fate portended for Arya and Aaron, two seeming misfits? This chapter answers this question. It explores the constraints reality imposes on safety and value goal pursuits. For people to believe what they want, reality needs to be amenable to wish fulfillment (Kunda, 1990). For Skyler to see herself as meeting her weight loss goals, the readings on her bathroom scale need to be trending down, not up. An amenable bathroom scale gives her license to exaggerate her success, misremembering herself as being heavier than she was post Alex's birth. But an uncooperative bathroom scale makes it much harder for her to convince herself (or anyone else) that she is svelte.

Just as the reality imposed by bathroom scales constrains desired beliefs about weight, the reality imposed by partners and relationships constrains progress in safety and value goal pursuits. Reality limits goal progress by dictating which particular goals can be most readily and successfully pursued in a given situation and relationship (Murray, Gomillion, Holmes, & Harris, 2015; Murray & Holmes, 2011). As we will see, despite a rockier start, Arya ultimately experienced a happier fate than Skyler because the goals Arya prioritized proved to be a much better fit to the reality of her partner and relationship.

McNulty (2010b) first popularized the idea that context (or reality) matters in relationships. His research suggests that there is no magic bullet that guarantees marital happiness for everyone. Ongoing realities in the relationship instead control whether specific ways of thinking or behaving ultimately prove to be therapeutic or toxic (McNulty, 2011; McNulty & Fincham, 2012; McNulty & Karney, 2004; McNulty, O'Mara, & Karney, 2008). For instance, optimistically expecting the best from a partner forecasts increased satisfaction for couples with strong problem-solving skills, but sets couples with weak problem-solving skills up for distress (McNulty & Karney, 2004; McNulty et al., 2008). Similarly, being kind, and constructive in conflict discussions forecasts increased satisfaction for couples with minor problems, but such solicitude puts those with more serious problems at risk (McNulty & Russell, 2010).

This chapter articulates a situated, functionalist perspective on motivated cognition in relationships. It explores how the reality constraints imposed by the situation, partner, and relationship control whether the perceiver's active goal pursuits satisfy or frustrate basic goals for safety and value and ultimately satiate or frustrate belongingness goals. We argue that relationship life is more likely to satisfy these three interconnected goals when perceivers match current goal pursuits to the goal affordances created by the partner they chose and the relationship they inhabit. In making this argument, we put a new, interdependence-based, twist on the meaning of context. We define context in terms of the unique situational challenges created when partners with unique preferences and personalities form one interacting unit.

In the first part of the chapter, we reiterate how the reality of specific situations affords particular goal pursuits over others (see Chapters 3 and 4). We then describe how relationship realities differ because partner preferences, interests, and personalities combine to create each relationship's unique situational terrain. Because Skyler chose an easier, more compatible partner than Arya, the situations each encountered routinely afforded systematically different opportunities to pursue safety and value goals. In the second part, we explore how mismatches develop between the goals perceivers pursue and the goals their partner and relationship afford. We bring these dynamics to life by using the relationships of Arya and Aaron and Skyler and Walt as examples of goal–reality fit and misfit, respectively. We conclude with empirical examples of how the match between perceiver goal pursuits and partner realities controls a marriage's eventual capacity to satisfy the need to belong (Murray et al., 2015; Murray, Gomillion, Holmes, Harris, & Lamarche, 2013).

The Objective Reality: Actual Goal Affordances

Situations afford different interpersonal goals because the situations that arise in any relationship differ in objective structure. Situation structure varies along three primary dimensions: Content, influence, and compatibility (Kelley, 1979).

Situations vary in *content* because partners are interdependent in life tasks, personality, and relationship aspirations. Partners must coordinate responsibility for inglorious life activities, like cooking and cleaning. They must also negotiate activity preferences, like coordinating Arya's love for hiking with Aaron's preference for more cerebral afternoons with a book, and values, like matching her socialist leanings to his more strident conservative philosophy. Partners also need to find ways to mesh the expression of their individual personalities. Something of a provocateur, Aaron likes to needle Arya about politics and religion and Arya's more reserved manner means that she rarely gets the last word when they disagree. Finally, partners need to negotiate shared visions for themselves as a unit, as happened as Aaron proved that Arya could count on him to provide support. Situations vary in degree of *influence* because partners have more or less unilateral control over one another's outcomes. Once Arya and Aaron started spending more recreational time together, she had to depend on his willingness to participate in her favored outdoor pursuits to feel like herself. Situations vary in *compatibility* because partner preferences can be more or less aligned. For instance, Arya and Aaron have compatible kitchen preferences because Arya loves to cook and Aaron enjoys cleaning up and returning the kitchen to sparkling condition. So, they readily reached a happy assignment of dinner duties. However, they have incompatible yard maintenance preferences since neither one of them likes to garden or cut the grass. So they routinely argue over the allocation of those responsibilities.

These three structural properties combine to determine the objective magnitude of risk and force of resistance present in any given situation.[1] From Arya's perspective, the prototypic risk situation is one where she needs Aaron to sacrifice his self-interest. The magnitude of situational *risk* present in such a situation increases proportionate to the importance of the *domain*, Aaron's relative *influence* over Arya, and the *compatibility* of their interests. Asking Aaron to keep his opinions to himself around her parents poses greater situational risk than asking him to cut the grass for two reasons. First, her parents are more important to her than the lawn (so Aaron has greater influence over her welfare in the "keeping his mouth shut" than "cut the grass" case). Second, Aaron is more strongly wedded to brash self-expression than he is averse to grass cutting (so Aaron's interests are less compatible with her interests in the "keeping his mouth shut" case).

The prototypic resistance situation for Arya is one where Aaron needs her to somehow sacrifice her self-interest. The force of situational *resistance* present for Arya in such a situation increases proportionate to the importance of the *domain*, her relative *influence* over Aaron, and the *compatibility* of their interests. Appreciating Aaron's conservative political views creates greater situational resistance for Arya than skipping a weekend hike to go to a museum with him for two reasons. First, Aaron hardly ever wants her to go with him to a museum, but he always needs her validation of his political way of thinking (so Arya has greater influence over Aaron's political than museum welfare). Second, Arya is more strongly wedded to her own socialist philosophy than she is attached to hiking (so Arya's interests are less compatible with Aaron's interests when it comes to validating his conservatism than his museum preferences).

The objective magnitude of risk and force of resistance present in any given situation determines the goals it affords.[2] Situations that are high in objective risk and low in resistance better afford the pursuit of safety than value. Consequently, her parents' upcoming visit automatically motivates Arya to make Aaron need her, taking over his grass cutting for the week, so he might feel indebted enough to her to express his opinions out of earshot of her parents (see Chapter 3; Murray, Aloni et al., 2009). However, situations that are low in objective risk and high in resistance better afford the pursuit of value than safety. Consequently, anticipating Aaron's latest soliloquy on his political views automatically motivates Arya to see Aaron's brashness as refreshing rather than aggravating (see Chapter 4; Murray, Holmes, et al., 2009). Because situations are implicitly linked to goal affordances, the specific goal that monopolizes attention should shift as situations shift, adaptively promoting goal progress.

The Situational Terrain of the Relationship

Just as situations vary within relationships, they also vary between relationships (Murray & Holmes, 2009, 2011). When Arya and Aaron first met, friends and family could not understand why they had been so immediately drawn to one another. They seemed like the oddest possible match. But when Skyler and Walt first met, everyone who knew them thought they were perfect for each other. They were so similar, except for the fact that Skyler had a less robust sense of self-worth. They both loved sports and music and shared similar political philosophies, circles of friends, and career passions. They never argued (until after Alex was born) because they agreed on most everything. Walt was also such an easygoing and optimistic person that lending his sympathetic ear and emotional support to Skyler came naturally.

Partner compatibility differs across relationships for two main reasons. First, partner *interests* can be more or less divergent and more or less readily accommodated. When they first got married, Arya and Skyler both preferred to spend their leisure time with their spouse. However, agreeing on leisure activities was easier for Skyler than Arya because Skyler and Walt had highly overlapping activity preferences. Sharing her opinions with Walt also came more naturally to Skyler because she never expected him to disagree with her at every turn as Arya expected with Aaron. Second, partners can also be more or less difficult and more or less readily accommodated. Some partners are harder to interact with than others because they bring more difficult emotional repertoires and dispositions to the relationship (Murray & Holmes, 2011). For instance, partners who are more neurotic are quicker to cast blame for mistakes (Karney & Bradbury, 1997). Low self-esteem or anxiously attached partners resist self-disclosure

(Forest & Wood, 2011) and push partners away when they feel hurt (Ford & Collins, 2010). They also provide inconsistent support (Collins & Feeney, 2004), but demand unrelenting support (Lemay & Dudley, 2011; Marigold et al., 2014) and use guilt punitively to manipulate their partner into doing what they want (Overall, Lemay, Girme, & Hammond, 2014).

Unfortunately, people caught up in the rush of infatuation do not usually possess the foresight needed to pick a partner who would provide the most compatible fit to them (Brehm, 1988). Even though people usually pick partners who are similar to them in some obvious ways (such as age and religion), people do not usually pick partners who are good fits to them in ways that might really matter. Indeed, partners in real marriages are no more similar in personality than partners in pseudo-marriages Lykken and Tellegen (1993) created through the luck of a draw. The happenstance nature of partner selection thus guarantees variability in personality compatibility across relationships.

Because some partners are more compatible than others, the situations couples encounter also vary systematically in the safety and value goal pursuits they afford (Murray & Holmes, 2011). In relationships with a relatively rocky situational terrain, partners have largely incompatible preferences or possess more difficult dispositions (e.g., low self-esteem, high neuroticism, low agreeableness) or both. People with an *incompatible* partner encounter more situations that afford objective opportunities to pursue both safety and value goals. Indeed, Arya has occasion to defend Aaron's value to her every time he starts pontificating his conservative philosophy and she has occasion to keep herself safe every time she contemplates relying on Aaron to keep his opinions to himself around her parents. However, in relationships with a relatively smooth situational terrain, partners have largely compatible preferences or possess easier dispositions (e.g., high self-esteem, low neuroticism, high agreeableness) or both. People with a *compatible* partner encounter fewer situations that afford strong conflicts between safety and value goals. Indeed, Skyler rarely even had the occasion to defend Walt's value when they first married because he so seldom infringed on her goals.

Fitting Active Goal Pursuits to Relationship Realities

Even though situations objectively afford specific goal pursuits, perceivers may not always detect and enact such goal affordances. Competing relationship-specific and relationship-transcendent goal pursuits can instead bias the perception of such situational affordances (Balcetis & Dunning, 2013; Balcetis & Lassiter, 2010; Kunda, 1990).

Such a mismatch between actual and perceived goal affordances exists for Skyler. Low in self-esteem and uncomfortably dependent on Walt after Alex's birth, she perceived his offers to help with Alex as slights against her parenting acumen. Through such a transformation, Skyler turned situations that could have made her feel safer into situations that instead thwarted safety goal pursuits.

People can transform situational goal affordances because goal pursuit is a property of the *person* as well as the objective situation. Less trusting people like Skyler feel more vulnerable to being hurt in most situations. The chronic activation of safety goal pursuits acts as a motivational vacuum, appropriating situations that better afford value goal pursuits into new opportunities to satisfy the motivational imperative for safety (see Chapter 5 for an extended discussion).

The MODE (Motivation and Opportunity as DEterminants) model of the attitude–behavior relationship sheds light on exactly how such goal substitution can occur. This model posits that people can override situationally activated attitudes and goals when they have both the motivation and opportunity available to do so (Olson & Fazio, 2008). According to this model, someone with a strongly positive automatic attitude toward eating M&Ms could nonetheless resist gobbling up this confection provided she had the motivation to diet and the self-regulatory capacity available to enact this conscious dieting intention. The right combination of motivation and opportunity can similarly allow people to override situationally activated goals in relationships. Indeed, as we saw in Chapter 5, low self-esteem people override the situationally activated goal to value their partner when they have the self-regulatory resources available to prioritize more pressing safety goal pursuits (Murray, Derrick, Leder, & Holmes, 2008; Murray, Holmes, et al., 2009).

Matching Safety Pursuits to Reality

Skyler's preoccupation with safety put her relationship at risk because it was not appropriate to her relationship's objectively easy situational terrain. In relationships with an easy terrain, compatible partner interests make it natural for partners to be responsive. Consequently, needlessly prioritizing safety in such a relationship limits opportunities to pursue the value goal pursuits such relationships better afford. Imagine that Walt is more than willing to help with Alex, but Skyler assumes that he will refuse. Keeping safe, and making him owe her before she asks for his help, would leave her uncertain whether indebtedness rather than caring motivated his responsiveness. By prioritizing safety in situations that better afforded the pursuit of alternate goals, Skyler thus turned safe and value-affording situations into ones that foreclosed opportunities for closeness.

Nevertheless, a chronic preoccupation with safety could be quite advantageous in a different relationship context. Low in self-esteem, Arya also prioritized safety in her early interactions with Aaron. However, her relationship thrived rather than faltered because the difficult situations she and Aaron faced better afforded the pursuit of safety goals. In relationships with a rockier situational terrain, incompatible partner interests make it more difficult for partners to be responsive. In such a relationship, taking steps to ward off non-responsive behavior is appropriate. Imagine that Aaron is likely to ignore Arya's wishes to keep his opinions to himself when her parents next visit. Staying safe, and hedging her

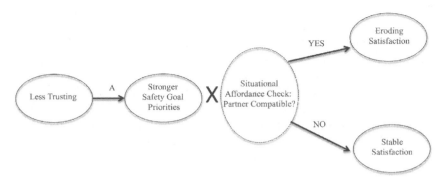

FIGURE 7.1 The Contextual Model of Safety Goal Pursuit

bets by cutting the grass for him the week before her parents arrived, could help to guarantee his commitment and buy his silence (Murray, Aloni, et al., 2009). By prioritizing safety in situations that actually afforded the pursuit of this goal, Arya thus turned high-risk situations into opportunities for greater closeness.

Figure 7.1 captures the contextual model of safety goal pursuit that formalizes these contrasting stories (Murray, Holmes, et al., 2013). It has two primary predictions. The first prediction has to do with the ease of activating safety goal pursuits. As we introduced earlier, safety goal pursuits are not just a function of a situation's objective affordances. They are also a function of the goal affordances perceivers expect to see in a situation. Because less trusting people like Skyler are the equivalent of relationship hypochondriacs (see Chapter 5), they are likely to see the necessity to keep safe in many of the situations they face in their relationships. Consequently, Path A in Figure 7.1 assumes that less trusting people are more likely to prioritize safety goal pursuits across situations in their relationships than more trusting people.

The second prediction has to do with the appropriateness of pursuing safety goal pursuits in specific situations in the relationship. People are justified in prioritizing safety in situations that put incompatible partner interests in opposition. However, people can also perceive opportunities to further safety pursuits in situations that do *not* actually afford the pursuit of this goal because partner interests are compatible. Depending on the situations people face in their relationship, pursuing safety can be either appropriately prudent and judicious or inappropriately and inordinately cautious. Figure 7.1 captures this contextual idea through a situational affordances "reality check." In this reality check, possessing a more or less compatible partner creates situational affordances that control the effects that prioritizing safety goal pursuits has on relationship well-being. Specifically, for compatible partners, prioritizing safety should erode satisfaction because the situations compatible partners encounter rarely necessitate its pursuit. However, for incompatible partners, prioritizing safety should preserve satisfaction because the situations incompatible partners encounter so often necessitate its pursuit.

So how did we test this contextual model of safety goal pursuit? We invited just-married couples into the Murray lab and contacted them again every six months for three years. At the point of marriage, we measured partner compatibility through (1) conflict frequency and (2) the *partner's* self-reported attachment anxiety, behavioral inhibition sensitivity, self-esteem, and neuroticism. We classified people as possessing a relatively *incompatible* partner when they reported greater conflict in their relationship and their *partner* reported lower levels of self-esteem and higher levels of rejection sensitivity, anxiety, and neuroticism. Conversely, we classified people as possessing a more *compatible* partner when they reported less conflict in their relationship and their *partner* reported higher levels of self-esteem and lower levels of rejection sensitivity, anxiety, and neuroticism. At the initial and each subsequent time point, we also measured explicit trust in the partner's commitment (e.g., "Though times may change and the future is uncertain, I know my partner will always be ready and willing to offer me strength and support") and satisfaction (e.g., "I am extremely satisfied with my relationship").

The newlyweds also completed interaction diaries just after they married that allowed us to index safety goal priorities through three IF-THEN contingencies in their daily thoughts and behavior. First, Arya puts greater priority on safety the more she responds to feeling inferior to Aaron by doing something to put him in her debt and make him depend on her (see Chapter 3). Using the diary reports, we indexed each person's IF-THEN tendency to prioritize safety in this specific way with a statistical coefficient associating one day's feelings of inferiority (e.g., "I'm not good enough for my partner") to the next day's communal behavior (e.g., "I searched for something my partner had lost"). Second, Arya also puts greater priority on safety the more she responds to feeling hurt by pushing Aaron away (see Chapter 3). Again, using the diary reports, we indexed each person's IF-THEN tendency to prioritize safety in this specific way through a statistical coefficient associating one day's feelings of rejection (e.g., "I feel rejected or hurt by my partner") to the next day's cold and distant behavior (e.g., "I snapped or yelled at my partner"; "I ignored or didn't pay attention to my partner"). Third, Arya puts greater priority on safety the *less* she values Aaron when he infringes on her personal goal pursuits (see Chapter 4). Again, using the diary reports, we indexed each person's IF-THEN tendency to prioritize safety in this specific way with a statistical coefficient associating goal infringement (e.g., "My partner used the last of something I needed and did not replace it") and partner devaluing (e.g., "My partner is a (not) great person"). Finally, we created an overall index of safety goal pursuit for each person by summing these three indices such that higher scores reflected stronger tendencies to prioritize safety goal pursuits across situations in the relationship.

The findings supported both primary predictions of the model. First, people who were less trusting were more likely to prioritize safety goals in daily interaction in the initial weeks after they married. Being less trusting, Skyler and Arya were both more likely to indebt their partner to them, keep at a safe distance, and value their partner less when he interfered with their goals in daily interactions. Second, partner compatibility functioned as a reality check, controlling whether prioritizing safety in daily interaction early in marriage ultimately stabilized or eroded later marital satisfaction.

Figure 7.2 presents changes in satisfaction as a function of partner compatibility and safety goal pursuit. The findings for incompatible partners are on the left. Prioritizing safety in such a rocky relationship terrain helped preserve satisfaction. When people had an *incompatible* partner, those who wisely put greater priority on safety goal pursuits reported less of a decline in satisfaction than people who put less priority on safety. The findings for *compatible* partners are on the right. Prioritizing safety in such a smooth relationship terrain proved toxic. When people had a *compatible* partner, those who put undue and needless priority on safety goal pursuits reported much steeper declines in satisfaction than people who appropriately put less priority on pursuing safety.

The final hypothesis we tested sought to illustrate exactly why Skyler ended up less satisfied than Arya even though they were both less trusting at the beginning of their marriages. We reasoned that being less trusting should only get people into trouble in their relationships when it inspires them to pursue safety goals with a *compatible* partner. That is, being less trusting should only forecast declines in satisfaction when people prioritize safety goal pursuits despite relationship realities that better afford value goal pursuits. The results supported this logic. When people had a compatible partner, those who were initially less

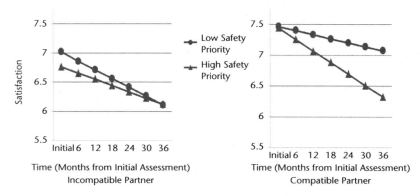

FIGURE 7.2 Prioritizing Safety Accelerates Satisfaction's Decline in More Compatible Relationships and Slows Satisfaction's Decline in Less Compatible Relationships. (Adapted with permission from Murray, S. L., Holmes, J. G., Derrick, J. L., Harris, B., Griffin, D. W., & Pinkus, R. T. (2013). Cautious to a fault: Self-protection and the trajectory of marital satisfaction. *Journal of Experimental Social Psychology, 49,* 522–533.)

trusting reported steeper declines in satisfaction over time precisely because they prioritized safety in situations that did not afford this goal pursuit.

Motivating Value Pursuits

Although taking a contextual perspective on safety goal pursuit does a good job of explaining why Skyler ended up distressed, it does not fully explain how Arya ended up happier than she started. She began her relationship with Aaron disposed to question his responsiveness and the situations she encountered only reinforced such hesitations. Nonetheless, Arya evidenced a complete reversal in her goal priorities over time.

How could this happen? Life with an incompatible partner presents multiple opportunities to detect objective threats (Murray & Holmes, 2011). Less trusting people also keep a careful watch out for such threats in the interest of keeping safe. This means that being hesitant to trust an incompatible partner should ensure a higher hit rate in detecting realistic threats to commitment. A less trusting Arya should be more likely to notice every time Aaron interferes with her plans or makes her want to retaliate against his unthinking slight against her intelligence. Perceiving such threats to commitment (IF) automatically activates the associated reparative response in memory (THEN) for mitigating such threats and protecting commitment (see Chapter 4). Through basic principles of habit formation (Wood & Neal, 2007), repeatedly encountering situations that prime value rules and reinforce their implementation should make for well-practiced automatic intentions to protect commitment. Less trusting people with compatible partners are not so situationally advantaged. Though compatible partners still behave badly on occasion, such behavior should be the exception, not the rule. Because objective threats help inspire the perception of threats to commitment (Murray & Holmes, 2011), less trusting people paired with compatible partners (like Skyler) are handicapped. The limited objective difficulties they encounter afford the realistic perception of threats too infrequently to condition strong automatic intentions to protect commitment when it counts.

And therein lies the likely explanation for why our hypothetical Arya ended up happier than our hypothetical Skyler. The situations Arya encountered were probably more likely to motivate a transformation in her goal pursuits than the situations Skyler encountered. Delving further into the newlywed data bore this out (Murray et al., 2015). Because the newlyweds completed the interaction diaries every year for three years, we could identify people who reversed goal priorities from safety to value over time – people who became more likely to *inhibit* impulses to retaliate against their partner's transgression (IF rejected, THEN accommodate) and more likely to reactively value their partner when he/she infringed on their personal goals (IF costs, then value partner). When people had an incompatible partner, less trusting people like Arya evidenced gradual transformation in goal priorities over the initial years of marriage, shifting from safety to value. They became more likely to justify costs and accommodate to their partner's transgressions. However, when people had a compatible partner, less trusting people like Skyler became even more preoccupied with the pursuit of safety over value. They became less likely to justify costs and accommodate to their partner's transgressions from one year to the next. In sum, being mindful, watchful, and quick to perceive threats serves less trusting perceivers with incompatible partners well because it provides the situational impetus to later defend their deepening commitments (Murray et al., 2015).

Conclusion

The goals that infuse attention, inference, and behavior need to be attuned to reality's affordances for safety and value goal pursuits to satiate the need to belong. When less trusting people paired with incompatible partners judiciously prioritize the pursuit of safety, they report more stable satisfaction over time. They also gradually reverse their goal priorities, putting preserving the value of hard-won commitments ahead of the pursuit of safety. Life does not turn out nearly as well for less trusting perceivers who prioritize safety in relationships that better afford value goal pursuits. Less trusting, safety-preoccupied people paired with compatible partners grow less satisfied over time and become ever the more likely to prioritize the pursuit of safety, making conviction at best a faint hope. In the last chapter, we continue on these contextual themes as we step back and sketch a new model of motivated cognition in relationships.

Notes

1 As we introduced in Chapters 3 and 4, high-"risk" situations are ones where Skyler is *more* dependent on Walt than he is on her because she needs something from him that he is not necessarily inclined to provide. High-"resistance" situations are ones where Skyler is *less* dependent on Walt than he is on her because he needs something from her that she is not necessarily inclined to provide.
2 Risk and resistance situations can also be viewed from the perspective of the dyad. Situations that are high in risk for Arya are high in resistance for Aaron and vice versa. We discussed these situations in greater detail in Chapters 3 and 4, respectively.

8
LOOKING FORWARD

It is now five years after Katy and Todd first had coffee sitting at that wobbly table. They just got married, but their path to the altar was anything but straightforward. They broke up shortly after Katy hesitated to ask Todd to meet her parents. At the time of that fateful weekend, Todd was so preoccupied by his bar exams that he did not pick up on Katy's hopes or why she was so hurt and disappointed in him. He just thought she was too needy. A year later they ran into each other at the grocery store and fell to chatting. Katy had just finished her graduate degree and she spoke so passionately about her new job that Todd could not help but be captivated by her. She was just as physically alluring as she had ever been, but now she seemed so much more self-confident. He could not figure out why he had ever let her go. Katy too was pleasantly surprised, finding Todd much more attentive and thoughtful than she remembered. Ten months after they reunited in the produce section, they moved in together, and nine months after that, they married. What might their future hold? Will the trepidations they had about one another in the first failed incarnation of their relationship come back to bite them? Or will the newfound happiness they found together prove lasting?

Relationships rarely provide cause to make a definitive prediction one way or another. To our knowledge, there is no singular behavior, trait, or circumstance that guarantees a relationship's success or ensures its failure. As we saw in Chapter 7, even the most difficult of partners and challenging of circumstances can inspire thoughts and behavior that build and strengthen relationships (McNulty, 2010b; Murray, Gomillion, Holmes, & Harris, 2015). In this final chapter, we use the knowledge gained writing this book to explain why we will now be looking for *synergistic* markers of relationship success.

This chapter integrates central arguments from each of the preceding chapters into an "interactionist goal system" model of motivated cognition in relationships. We chose the term "interactionist" given its historical meaning in philosophy, sociology, and social psychology. Philosophically, "interactionist" means that the mind influences the body and the body influences the mind. Sociologically, "interactionist" means that every day social interaction provides the substrate for group life. Social psychologically, "interactionist" means that people may respond to the same situation differently because they see the situation through their own idiosyncratic lens, one shaped by their personal attitudes, dispositions, and goals (Ross & Nisbett, 1991). The model we propose unites these three themes. It assumes that safety and value goal pursuits are *embodied* (in affect, psychophysiology, and cognition) and *embedded* (in the context of a person's current attitudes, disposition, and goal pursuits, the partner's current attitude, disposition, and goal pursuits, and the relationship's history). The model we sketch is not intended as a final statement on how the pursuit of safety and value goals infuses attention, inference, and behavior in romantic life. Instead, we offer it as a working template for structuring research questions that might one day soothsay the fates of couples like Katy and Todd.

In the pages that remain, we outline the basic structure of the goal system that regulates the pursuit of safety and value within relationships. We then consider how this system can leverage either responsive or unresponsive behavior depending on the specific situation at hand, relationship-transcendent goal pursuits, and broader relationship interaction patterns. As we will see, studying the pursuit of safety and value goals in synergistic *interaction* might offer the best hope for predicting whether Katy and Todd's relationship will ultimately prove to satisfy or frustrate the need to belong.

The Basic Elements of an Interactionist Goal System

Before we delve into the model itself, we define our terms, starting with a working definition of a goal system. Goal theorists characterize people as goal strivers (Kruglanski et al., 2002). Although some behavior can be aimless to be sure, most behavior has a point, whether that point is conscious (e.g., comfort a friend), unconscious (e.g., taunt an enemy), lofty (e.g., get promoted at work), indulgent (e.g., spend more time just having fun), or prohibitive (e.g., avoid irritating a spouse). Because people are limited in the simultaneous activities they can pursue at any given time, goal striving requires an agenda of a sort. Goal systems provide this agenda.

Consider the goal system surrounding Katy's personal desire to be independent and self-possessed, illustrated in Figure 8.1. This higher-order goal is connected to three lower-level goals – to exercise, to succeed at work and school, and to control her diet – that function as separate means to meeting her higher-order goal. These lower-level goals are each in turn associated with specific means to

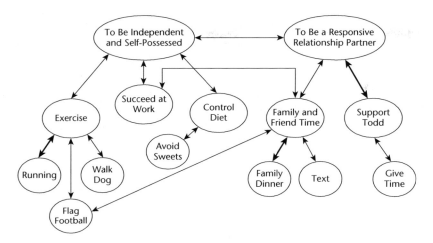

FIGURE 8.1 An Example Goal System

their pursuit. For Katy, running in the morning, walking her dog at night, and playing flag football on the weekend all serve as means to meeting her goal to exercise. However, Katy's personal goal to be independent and self-possessed also connects to her similarly high-level goal to be a good, caring and nurturing daughter, friend, and wife. This higher-order goal is connected to two lower-level goals – to spend quality time with family, and support Todd's autonomy – which serve as means to her higher-order goal. These lower-level goals are each in turn associated with specific means to their pursuit. For Katy, committing to a family dinner twice a week, texting her best friend daily, and giving Todd time to pursue his career and be on his own with his friends all serve as means to meeting her goal to be a good, caring, and nurturing relationship partner.

Goal systems have three structural properties applicable to our interactionist model. The first is *interconnection*. Goals and their associated means interact through a network of cognitive associations (Shah, Kruglanski, & Friedman, 2003). Multiple means may serve a given goal in a goal system. Katy has three viable means to pursue her goal to exercise, but only one viable means for controlling her diet, making it easier for her to progress in the former than latter goal. A given means may also serve multiple goals in a goal system. Katy's flag football games serve her goals to exercise and spend quality time with friends, making this activity especially important to her. The interconnections among goals and means can be strong or weak and excitatory or inhibitory and the nature of these associations can change over time (Shah et al., 2003). Activating Katy's goal to exercise activates her intention to run, an excitatory connection, strengthened by achieving her personal best in her most recent race. However, activating her goal to succeed at work suppresses her goal to be a more present relationship partner, an inhibitory connection that weakened once she realized Todd supported her ambitions.

The second is *dynamism*. Goals (i.e., desired end states) shift in momentary or state accessibility as making progress in the pursuit of a current goal allows an alternate goal to take behavioral priority (Fishbach, Eyal, & Finkelstein, 2010). Goals also shift in momentary or state accessibility as situations make one goal pursuit more pressing than others (Fishbach et al., 2010; Shah et al., 2003). Being in the company of her high school friends activates Katy's goal to be a good and caring relationship partner, while being in the company of her work colleagues activates her goal to be independent and self-possessed. Similarly, the accessibility of means (i.e., paths to the goal) shift as situations better afford one means of pursuing one particular goal over others.

The third is *prioritization*. Goals vary in overall weight or importance because people can be more committed to one (or more) goal pursuits over others regardless of the situation at hand (Shah et al., 2003). Because Katy is more committed to her goal to be successful at work than her goal to control her diet, she readily partakes in the office birthday cakes she would otherwise avoid. Means also vary in weight or importance because some means are more strongly and facilitatively tied to a particular goal pursuit than others. Katy is more committed to running than cycling as a means of exercise because she associates the former activity with greater fitness gains than the latter.

Embodying and Embedding Motivated Cognition in Relationships

Figure 8.2 sketches the interactionist goal system model of motivated cognition in relationships. Its operation follows the principles of interconnection, dynamism, and prioritization common to goal systems (Shah et al., 2003). However, explaining the fate of a romantic dyad necessitated adding a fourth principle – embeddedness.

Interconnection

Because belongingness is the central adaptive problem to be solved in relationships (Baumeister & Leary, 1995), it occupies the center of the goal system, functioning as its operational hub. Belongingness is a dyadic goal in this system. For partner interactions to afford belonging Katy needs to feel safe depending on Todd and Todd needs to value Katy enough to prioritize her needs. Similarly, Todd needs to feel safe depending on Katy and Katy needs to value Todd enough to prioritize his needs. Thus, it is not enough for Katy to be happy interacting with Todd or Todd to be happy interacting with Katy. They both need to experience their interactions as rewarding and mutually responsive to feel secure in their bond together. Consequently, it takes *both* Katy and Todd – two interacting partners and two interconnected goal systems – to fully satiate or frustrate the need to belong in adult romantic relationships.

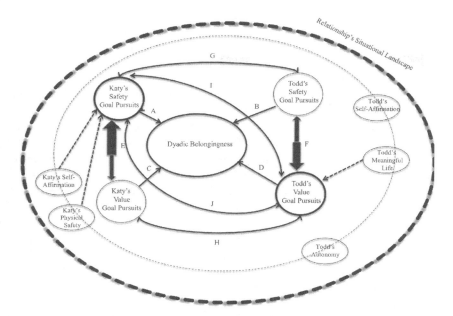

FIGURE 8.2 An Interactionist Goal System for Relationships

The pursuit of safety and value represents adaptive solutions to the problem of belongingness. The pursuit of safety ensures that Todd is just as dependent on Katy as she is on him, giving Katy reason to feel safe putting her outcomes in Todd's hands in risky situations. The pursuit of value leverages Todd's responsive behavior by ensuring that he sees enough value in Katy to make caring for her worth the cost to him. Because making joint progress in the pursuit of safety and value affords greater opportunities for responsiveness (Murray & Holmes, 2009), these goals occupy the immediate orbit of the goal system, applying its centripetal force. Safety and value are individually pursued goals or end-states in this interactionist system. For Katy to connect to Todd, she needs to feel sufficiently safe from harm; Todd's sense of safety might supplement her sense of safety, but it cannot substitute for it. Similarly, for Todd to take care of Katy's needs when it costs him, he needs to value her; the value she sees in him might supplement his sense of conviction, but it cannot substitute for it.

In the center of this goal system, Katy and Todd's individual pursuits of safety and value serve as means to their dyadic pursuit of belongingness. The unidirectional connections from safety goals to belongingness (Paths A and B) and value goals to belongingness (Paths C and D) capture these vertical constraints. In the immediate outer orbit of the goal system, individual pursuits of safety and value compete for self-regulatory resources. Consequently, these goals dynamically shift back and forth in accessibility as a function of progress in the competing goal.

140 Looking Forward

The bidirectional connections between safety and value goal pursuits *within* an individual capture these potential inhibitory or excitatory lateral associations (Paths E and F). Frustrating safety increases the accessibility of this goal, while suppressing value. Conversely, frustrating value increases the accessibility of this goal, while suppressing safety. In this way, Katy's pursuit of safety constrains her pursuit of value (and vice versa) and Todd's pursuit of safety constrains his pursuit of value (and vice versa).

The bidirectional connections between safety and value goals within an individual share a distinguishing feature. The thickness of the arrow varies from root to tip. This variability captures the equilibrium point of the risk regulation balance. In Todd's case, the arrow's greater thickness as it approaches value captures value's greater sway over safety than vice versa. Consequently, Todd's goal to preserve the value and meaning he sees in Katy has greater capacity to inhibit his goal to stay safe than his goal to stay safe from hurt has to inhibit his goal to preserve the meaning and value he sees in Katy. Rather than being fixed within the goal system, this equilibrium point can change as major relationship transitions, such as parenthood, alter the situational landscape.

In this immediate outer orbit, one partner's individual goal pursuits collude and collide with the other partner's individual goal pursuits. For instance, Katy's pursuit of value might motivate her to make a sacrifice for Todd, furthering his pursuit of safety. Conversely, Katy's pursuit of safety could frustrate Todd's pursuit of value if she asks so little of him that he seldom has to justify his caring. The bidirectional connections between safety and value goal pursuits *across* partners capture these potential inhibitory or excitatory lateral associations (Paths G through J).

Dynamism

Now let's delve into the specifics of goal pursuit in a given situation. In a goal system, the accessibility of means for pursuing a given goal depends on the current state of goal progress in that situation (Shah et al., 2003). Figures 8.3 and 8.4 (see below) use this situation-specific lens to zoom into safety and value goal pursuits, respectively.

In Figure 8.3, the acute experience of trust in a specific situation marks safety goal progress and controls the accessibility of the means for its pursuit. Trust dynamically marks safety goal progress by mirroring the perceived risks of depending on the partner in a specific situation. The perception of risk can shift as a function of automatic associations to the situation (Path K), automatic associations to the partner (Path L), and conscious beliefs about the partner's likely responsiveness in that situation (Path M). The power each marker has to define the experience of trust changes dynamically from one situation and perceiver to the next (captured by the varying widths of the progress paths). Katy and Todd have contentious conflicts over finances because she is a spender

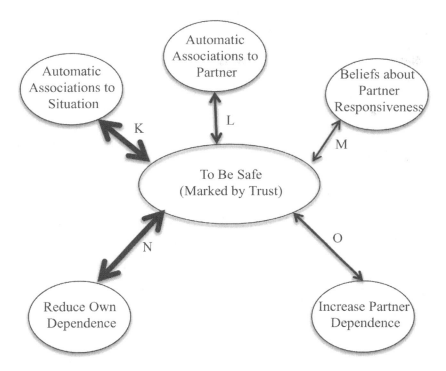

FIGURE 8.3 The Pursuit of Safety Goals

and he is a saver. Her highly accessible negative automatic attitude toward this situation leaves her acutely apprehensive and distrusting any time it comes up. However, in support situations, her strongly positive automatic evaluative association to Todd readily overrides any conscious reservations, leaving her feeling more trusting. In contrast, Todd's trust in Katy is more immune to automatic evaluations provoked by the situation because his greater self-control allows him to discount such impulses.

The acute experience of trust peaks when accessible associations and/or beliefs are more positive, rendering the means for securing safety less accessible. However, the acute experience of trust flags when accessible associations are more negative, rendering the means for securing safety more accessible. In such situations, feeling less trusting activates perceptual and behavioral means for Katy to increase Todd's dependence on her (Path O) and reduce her dependence on Todd (Path N). The specific means for restoring safety that become accessible can change dynamically from one situation and one perceiver to the next (captured by the varying widths of the means paths). When the topic of finances comes up, Katy castigates Todd for not living in the moment, a behavioral means of reducing her dependence on him. For less contentious issues, she is more likely

142 Looking Forward

to simply forgive and excuse any perceived transgression on Todd's part, a perceptual means for convincing herself that Todd really does depend on her.

In Figure 8.4, the acute experience of conviction in a specific situation marks value goal progress and controls the accessibility of means for its pursuit. Conviction dynamically marks value goal progress by mirroring the purpose and meaning Katy sees in treating Todd with care in specific situations. The experience of conviction can shift as a function of the affective state of dissonance or uncertainty (Path P) and the cognitive state of commitment (Path Q). The power each marker has to activate the means for value goal pursuits also varies from one situation and perceiver to the next (captured by the varying width of the progress paths). For instance, Todd never expected Katy to co-opt his desire to be a couch potato and he now gets an unsettled feeling in the pit of his stomach at the sight of his running shoes. However, this vague glimmering of uncertainty about her enforcing her athleticism on him is starting to pale in comparison to the increasingly preoccupying doubts he has about Katy's spendthrift ways.

Conviction peaks when accessible associations and/or beliefs are more positive, rendering the means for securing conviction less accessible. However, conviction flags when accessible associations are more negative, rendering the means for securing value more accessible. The acute experience of Todd questioning

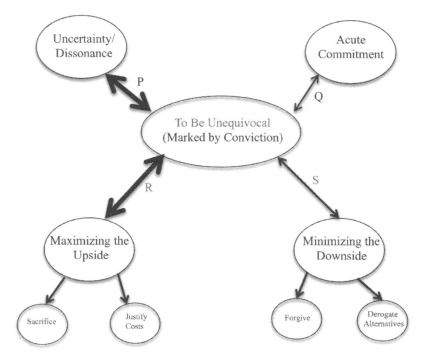

FIGURE 8.4 The Pursuit of Value Goals

the meaning and value he sees in caring for Katy activates associated means for maximizing the positive (Path R) and minimizing the negative in the partner and relationship (Path S). The specific means for restoring value that become accessible can change dynamically from one situation and perceiver to the next. Now that he has endured a few weekend runs with Katy (without dying), the sight of Katy's running shoes has come to remind Todd how much he appreciates Katy's drive, an automatic justification of her infringement on his couch potato goals. He has not yet found a way to convince himself that her online shopping has redeeming value, but he can at least try to see the care she puts into choosing gifts for him. While Todd relies on perceptual transformations to bolster Katy's value to him, Katy more often protects her sense of Todd's value by suppressing her urge to criticize him when his lackadaisical attitude toward household chores violates her expectations.

Prioritization

In a goal system, the accessibility of means depends on more than just proximity to the goal in the current situation (Shah et al., 2003). The accessibility of means also depends on the general priority goal strivers attach to particular goals independent of the specific situation at hand. The varying widths of the circles surrounding safety and value goal pursuits in Figure 8.2 capture such individual differences in goal prioritization. Wider circles capture higher-priority goals with more chronically accessible means, whereas narrower circles capture lower-priority goals with less chronically accessible means. What makes safety or value a more or less generally pressing goal priority?

Pursuing safety functions to minimize non-responsive partner behavior in risky situations (see Chapter 3). For instance, if Katy plays it safe and keeps her need for Todd's support to herself, he has less power to hurt her when she is feeling down. This prevention-oriented pursuit is typically a higher-priority goal for less trusting people because they are more motivated to avoid being hurt by non-responsive partner behavior (Murray & Holmes, 2009, 2011). In contrast, pursuing value functions to maximize responsive partner behavior in resistance situations (see Chapter 4). For instance, Todd is more likely to accede to Katy's entreaty to go running if he values her early-morning athleticism more than he values his sleep. This promotion-oriented pursuit is typically a higher-priority goal for more committed people because they are more motivated to ensure that they are treating their partner responsively (Rusbult & Van Lange, 2003).

Goal weights can also vary across partners and across times in the relationship. In the first incarnation of her relationship, a more distrusting Katy placed much greater weight on her own pursuit of safety than value. This rendered the means for safety more chronically accessible than the means for value. Prioritizing safety thus made it inordinately difficult for the insecure Katy to keep what Todd meant to her central to her mind. Now Katy is much more trusting and she is just as committed to the pursuit of value as she is to the pursuit of safety. Consequently, she can keep what Todd means to her foremost in situations that once tempted her to self-protect.

Embeddedness

This finally brings us to the outermost orbits of the goal system. These outer orbits capture the embedding of safety and value goal pursuits in a broader context. The first of these outermost "context" orbits captures the embedding of these goals in relationship-transcendent goal pursuits, such as desires to be safe and healthy (Sacco et al., 2014), feel autonomous and competent (Ryan & Deci, 2000), perceive the world as sensible and meaningful (Heine, Proulx, & Vohs, 2006), and affirm self-integrity (Steele, 1988).

Ongoing goal pursuits compete for limited self-regulatory resources (Orehek & Vazeou-Nieuwenhuis, 2013). When Katy is immersed in the goal to stay healthy, sanitizing every surface in the house, she has fewer resources available to keep safe from being rejected by Todd. For people to make sufficient progress toward multiple goals given such limits, goal pursuits that can be either satisfied or obviated through *other* connected goal pursuits should be suppressed within the goal system. The dotted arrows connecting relationship-specific and transcendent goal pursuits capture such suppression potential (Shah et al., 2003). In Katy's case, ridding her house of germs can afford a sense of physical safety that obviates her need to do anything else to distance herself from Todd when they discuss the household finances (Gomillion & Murray, 2016). Similarly, her daily career activities so fully engaged her self-affirmation goals that she no longer needs to put as much of a premium on staying safe (Jaremka, Bunyan, Collins, & Sherman, 2011).

The second of these outermost "context" orbits captures the embedding of safety and value goal pursuits in the broader relationship context – its situational landscape of "risk" and "resistance" situations. Partners differ in compatibility (Kelley, 1979) and the stressfulness of the circumstances they face (Karney & Bradbury, 1995). This makes satisfying the dyadic goal of belongingness a more herculean task for some partners because the transitions and contexts they face make it objectively more difficult for them to be responsive (Murray & Holmes, 2009, 2011). The relationship context thus envelops the entire goal system serving belongingness because the situations partners encounter most often control the *viability* of means for satiating this dyadic goal.

To optimize any goal pursuit, people should employ the means that reliably afford the goal over the means that unreliably afford it (Shah et al., 2003). That is why Katy prefers running to cycling; running makes her feel fitter faster. To optimize the dyadic pursuit of belongingness, partners should also favor the goals and employ the means that reliably afford belongingness over the goals and means that unreliably afford it. However, the goals and means that reliably afford belongingness depend on the broader relationship context. The relationship partners inhabit – whether populated by a trusting and a mistrusting partner, an extravert and an introvert, a spendthrift and a tightwad, two free spirits, or two neurotic parents of newborn twins – dictates the goal priorities, goal interconnections, and available means that best afford the dyadic goal of belongingness.

Unfortunately, people do not always pursue the goals that best serve their ultimate aims. Katy can succumb to the temptation to cycle even though she knows she burns more calories running. Similarly, she can still succumb to the temptation to keep her distance from Todd even though she knows better, and even though so little in his behavior warrants it. Because safety and value are end-states unto themselves, they can be pursued indiscriminately. When this happens, safety (or value) becomes the end in itself rather than the means to belongingness. This happened to Katy in the first incarnation of her relationship. The unfortunate coupling of her low self-esteem and Todd's preoccupation with his exams resulted in her becoming so preoccupied by safety that she literally could not see concrete evidence of Todd's caring. In the end, her pursuit of safety consequently frustrated rather than satiated belongingness goals.

The relationship context orbit envelops the goal system because the situational landscape imposes "satisfaction constraints" on the goal pursuits (and associated means) that will best serve belongingness. For instance, the uneasy coupling of an anxious and an avoidant partner is likely to afford more high-risk situation exposure than the tactically easier couplings of two secure partners. For both sets of partners to feel as though they belong together nonetheless, the goals (and associated means) prioritized within the goal systems regulating each partner's attention, inferences, and behavior should fit or match the specific circumstances they face (Murray, Holmes, et al., 2013; Murray et al., 2015). This outermost orbit is drawn with a dotted line to reflect the fluid nature of these contextual constraints. Circumstances change across relationships as partners within the relationship change (becoming more or less similar or more or less entrenched in a difficult personality trait), face new transitions or stressors (like the birth of a first child, a career change, an illness, or a retirement), and become more or less trusting or more or less committed. Progress in the dyadic pursuit of belongingness thus depends on the match between the goal pursuits each partner prioritizes and the relationship circumstances they currently inhabit. Namely, prioritizing safety over value affords a more efficient first path to belongingness in a relationship fraught with incompatibilities and risk than a relationship rich with easy and ready opportunities for reward.

Soothsaying Katy and Todd's Future Relationship

So if we were to catch a glimpse of Katy and Todd's future through the lens afforded by the interactionist goal system depicted in Figure 8.2, what would we see? It depends on a synergy of forces that control how fortuitously each partner's safety and value goal pursuits interact with the other partner's safety and value goal pursuits, relationship-transcendent goal pursuits, and the general relationship landscape of risk and resistance situations. Let's imagine a worst- and a best-case scenario for the fulfillment of dyadic belongingness goals to see what this might mean.

Project ahead from Katy and Todd's current state of newlywed bliss to the birth of their first child, Emma, three years hence. Katy decided, with some trepidation, to start working from home shortly after Emma was born. She had loved the feeling of independence working outside her home gave her, but she could not bring herself to leave Emma so soon. Todd had been struggling to adapt to being a father and Katy being a mother. She seemed so much more demanding now, just like she had been when they first dated. Now that Katy wanted him to do half of the household chores, he bristled at her overly exacting standards for household cleanliness. With this unexpected infringement on his time, Todd sometimes found himself tempted not to give Katy as much emotional support as she wanted navigating her new role as a working mom. As things stand now, they are both madly in love with Emma, but frustrated with one another. Todd is starting to feel unappreciated and overly put upon when it comes to household chores. Katy is feeling personally adrift, missing the professional identity that provided much of her sense of self-esteem and meaning in her life. With so many reasons to feel unsure of herself and Todd, the danger is that Katy could once again become preoccupied with safety goal pursuits, thwarting belongingness for both.

A Worst Case: Mutually Nonresponsive Interactions

For this transition to move Katy and Todd further from the dyadic goal of belongingness, Katy need only fall back into her old habit of indiscriminately prioritizing safety goal pursuits. If she does, she is likely to subvert Todd's goal priorities as well. Such negative eventualities are likely to unfold in relationships when forces within the goal system come together in a destructive synergy that is a *mismatch* to the risks and opportunities afforded by the relationship's evolving situational landscape. We outline one of many possible scenarios that might allow this to happen next.

After Emma was born, Katy cut back her work hours. Without this financial cushion, the manageable conflicts they once had about money became unmanageable. Now that Todd fully understood how much damage Katy's spendthrift ways did to their savings account, he was starting to question why he ever valued Katy's judgment in the first place. Seeing his frustration, Katy was growing increasingly insecure. She was not only struggling to adjust to her role as a new mother, but she felt like she could not count on Todd the way she used to count on him for emotional support. Todd seemed so resistant to her slightest request for help around the house that she hesitated to tell or ask him anything at all. She tried to keep her distance from Todd most of the time now, which was easy to do given how much Emma needed her. Todd knew that he had not been behaving reasonably lately, but he had gotten so tired of feeling like nothing he did could make Katy happy. He had expected having Emma to draw them closer together, but it really only seemed like Katy was a lot more interested in spending time alone with Emma than she was in sharing this experience with him.

The first feature of the goal system that set Katy and Todd on this path involves the landscape of situations that populate their relationship. This landscape constrains the goals (and associated means) that afford the most efficient path to belongingness. In this worst-case future, the differences between Katy and Todd turned out to be more deeply rooted than Katy being more spendthrift. They have fundamentally opposite personality dispositions. Katy is a rollercoaster of emotion and activity; she is expressive, passionate, impulsive, and quick to draw conclusions. This disposes her to be readily hurt and quickly angered in her relationships. She has always relied on her relationship partners to help level out her emotions. Todd is the opposite; he is methodological, some might say plodding, and keeps his emotions to himself. Given these basic differences in personality, the goal system needs to mitigate threats to safety without imperiling the strong sense of conviction each needs to make the many sacrifices required to mesh their incompatible personalities. Thus, Katy needs to find ways to keep herself safe from being hurt without questioning Todd's value to her or causing Todd to question her value to him. Furthering belongingness thus requires the means for safety restoration to be available, but less chronically accessible than the means for value preservation. Such challenging circumstances are bested by a goal system where people define themselves in terms of their commitment to their partner because self-defining commitments tip the equilibrium point of the risk regulation balance in value's favor (see Chapter 6).

Unfortunately, the forces working within the goal system are not so fortuitously configured for Katy and Todd in this future scenario. Instead, three forces within the goal system are working synergistically to thwart belongingness goals. The first involves the interconnection between safety and value goal pursuits in Katy's mental representation of her relationship. It is strongly asymmetrical: Safety has much greater power to inhibit value than value has to inhibit safety goal pursuits. Before Emma, pursuing her identity as a business professional and a dedicated runner provided self-affirmation and infused her goal to perceive meaning and value in Todd with greater impetus and weight. Overwhelmed by her new responsibilities as a working mom, she felt stymied in all of her professional and exercise goals. Without this source of self-affirmation to infuse her value goal pursuits, she started to question the value of caring for Todd (when he seemed to be so unfeeling). This deprived Todd of her support on those occasions when he sought her out for solace about his work-related problems.

The second compromising feature of the goal system is the controlling and corrosive influence Katy's monopolizing pursuit of safety had on Todd's competing and compensatory pursuit of value. Out of fear of being rebuffed, Katy withdrew her support from Todd, which eventually resulted in him questioning his trust in her. Now more vulnerable to being hurt, Todd shifted his goal priorities, putting a greater weight on safety than he had since they first dated. With his goal priorities shifted, Todd started inhibiting his inclination to forgive Katy's faults and protect his sense of conviction. It became harder for him to remember why he had ever thought that Katy had gotten over her old needy and selfish ways. With Katy's value to him in question, it's no wonder he resisted doing the household chores that she seemed to value so much.

The third feature of the goal system involves the number of situations now implicated in the conflict over spending. With no financial cushion left since Katy returned to work part-time, even the most innocuous household discussion now escalates as Todd accuses Katy of needing more self-control and Katy accuses Todd of being too obsessive and controlling. Just the thought of allocating the responsibilities to be shared activates negative associations now because they both expect to be personally attacked on an almost daily basis. With them both feeling so vulnerable, the means for safety goal pursuit are now highly accessible for each, suppressing the competing means for value goal pursuit. Whenever something needs to be done or decided, whether bills to be paid, a house to clean, or friends to entertain, their first inclination is to avoid one another. Neither is inclined to sacrifice. Consequently, Katy's frustration about her disproportionate responsibility for household chores has only worsened. It is getting more difficult for Katy to remember whether she had ever thought she could trust Todd and Todd has similarly given up trying to convince himself that Katy is worth trusting. Consequently, their interactions have become progressively less responsive and more ridden with conflict, frustrating the dyadic pursuit of belongingness.

A Best Case: Mutually Responsive Interactions

For parenthood to move Katy and Todd measurably closer to the dyadic goal of belongingness, Katy must sustain her trust in Todd and resist her temptation to fall back into her old habits, indiscriminately prioritizing safety. Todd must sustain his motivation to prioritize his value goal pursuits. Such positive eventualities are likely to unfold in relationships when forces within the goal system come together in constructive synergy that is a *match* to the risks and opportunities afforded by the relationship's evolving situational landscape. Imagine one possible scenario for how this might happen.

Katy and Todd are no strangers to conflict. They have had their fair share of disagreements about finances. Once Emma was born, neither expected household chores to be such an additional point of contention though. Katy is feeling powerless because she can no longer keep the house as neat and well organized as she likes without Todd's help. For Katy, allocating such responsibilities to

Todd automatically heightens the accessibility of safety (and its associated means). When she entreats Todd to do the laundry in addition to the dishes, she hedges her bets beforehand by cooking his favorite meal, indebting him to her before she even solicits any such domestic sacrifice. She also sensibly refrains from asking Todd to take on any cooking responsibilities given his much greater aversion to cooking than cleaning up after meals. These safety-restoring tactics on Katy's part have helped to avert more than one conflict. Ironically, Todd's feeling aggravated and put upon by the new infringements on his time have also helped localize conflicts to the household domain. Having to sacrifice some of his own free time to take up some of Katy's former household responsibilities automatically heightens the accessibility of his goal to value Katy and make caring for her just as meaningful as ever.

As we saw in the worst-case future, Katy prioritizing of safety outside the one risky domain of household chores is *not* in the best interests of belongingness. Keeping a safe distance across situations from Todd would only deprive Katy of the support he so generously provided before Emma was born. In this best-case version of events, three features of the goal system are now working synergistically to limit Katy's safety goal pursuits to only those specific domains where she most needs to protect against non-responsive behavior.

The first is the priority a high self-esteem Todd usually puts on the pursuit of value. High in self-esteem (and trust and commitment as a result), Todd is likely to act on his automatic inclinations to justify the costs in caring for Katy. In recent times, seeing Emma's toys on the floor and bottles among the dishes reminds him of everything Katy brought to his life, increasing his willingness to take the dish soap and the laundry basket in hand the next time. The priority Todd puts on the pursuit of value also conditioned Katy's highly positive automatic attitude toward him. In risky situations, the activation of this attitude makes Katy feel closer to safety, rendering her means for the safety goal pursuit less accessible and less likely to influence her behavior (Murray et al., 2011). Within the goal system, Todd's pursuit of value thus inhibits Katy's pursuit of safety by inhibiting its means.

The second involves the opportunities Katy is now creating to begin to reaffirm her sense of herself. Getting back into her routine of taking an early-morning run has moved her closer to her goal to feel independent and self-possessed. Affirming the value and meaning in her life in these ways has infused her value goal pursuits within her relationship with extra force, further inhibiting competing safety goal pursuits. The third is the landscape of the situations that generally populate their relationship. Even though Katy and Todd may never agree on finances, they are compatible in many other respects. This means that the greater weight that Todd puts on value than safety goal pursuits is unlikely to come back to bite him, so to speak (Murray et al., 2015). His disposition to see the best is suited well to a relationship where there are few problems to detect. Consequently, Katy and Todd continue to treat one another well, even in the domains that used to give them trouble, satisfying the dyadic pursuit of belongingness. As the complexities involved in soothsaying Katy and Todd's relationship illustrate, the power relationship science has to prognosticate a relationship's future is both limited and limitless. It is limited because the field has only just begun to explore how features of the situation, person, partner, and context might synergistically interact to control a relationship's fate. It is also limitless because relationship scientists now have the conceptual and methodological tools at our disposal to develop and test more synergistic models. We can draw on the wealth of knowledge about dissonance, motivated attention, embodiment, goal systems, and meaning maintenance (among other theories) to push out of the safety of our theoretical comfort zones. Writing this chapter was just this kind of exercise for us and we are excited to see where it takes us.

Conclusion

Although we are concluding this book with a new interactionist goal system model of motivated cognition in relationships, it is not intended to be the end. We instead hope it affords new research beginnings. Relationships are challenging to inhabit (as partners) and challenging to study (as scientists) because they are dyadic enterprises. This more than doubles the ways that safety and value goal pursuits infuse romantic life for both the good and ill of the relationship. This book will fulfill its purpose if it sheds at least a little light on new paths to be explored in uncovering the dynamics of how romantic relationships can both satisfy and thwart people's fundamental need to belong.

REFERENCES

Alexopoulos, T., & Ric, F. (2007). The evaluation–behavior link: Direct and beyond valence. *Journal of Experimental Social Psychology, 43*, 1010–1016.

Andersen, S. M., Reznik, I., & Manzella, L. M. (1996). Eliciting facial affect, motivation, and expectancies in transference: Significant-other representations in social relations. *Journal of Personality and Social Psychology, 71*, 1108–1129.

Aron, A., Fisher, H., Mashek, D. J., Strong, G., Li, H., & Brown, L. L. (2005). Reward, motivation, and emotion systems associated with early-stage intense romantic love. *Journal of Neurophysiology, 94*, 327–337.

Arriaga, X. B. (2001). The ups and downs of dating: Fluctuations in satisfaction in newly formed romantic relationships. *Journal of Personality and Social Psychology, 80*, 754–765.

Arriaga, X. B. (2013). An interdependence theory analysis of close relationships. In J. A. Simpson & L. Campbell (Eds.), *The Oxford Handbook of Close Relationships* (pp. 39–65). Oxford: Oxford University Press.

Arriaga, X. B., Slaughterbeck, E. S., Capezza, N. M., & Hmurovic, J. L. (2007). From bad to worse: Relationship commitment and vulnerability to partner imperfections. *Personal Relationships, 14*, 389–409.

Auger, E., Hurley, S., & Lydon, J. E. (2016). Compensatory relationship-enhancement: An identity-motivated response to relationship threat. *Social Psychological and Personality Science, 7*, 223–231.

Baker, L. R., & McNulty, J. K. (2013). When low self-esteem encourages behaviors that risk rejection to increase interdependence: The role of relational self-construal. *Journal of Personality and Social Psychology, 104*, 995–1018.

Balcetis, E., & Dunning, D. (2006). Seeing what you want to see: Motivational influences on visual perception. *Journal of Personality and Social Psychology, 91*, 612–625.

Balcetis, E., & Dunning, D. (2007). Cognitive dissonance and the perception of natural environments. *Psychological Science, 18*, 917–921.

Balcetis, E., & Dunning, D. (2010). Wishful seeing: Desired objects are seen as closer. *Psychological Science, 21*, 147–152.

Balcetis, E., & Dunning, D. (2013). Wishful seeing: How preferences shape visual perception. *Current Directions in Psychological Science, 22*, 33–37.

Balcetis, E., & Ferguson, M. J. (2009). Seeing what you want and what you are: Motivated perception as guided by current states and active desires. Unpublished manuscript.

Balcetis, E., & Lassiter, G. D. (2010). *Social psychology of visual perception*. New York, NY: Psychology Press.

Banaji, M. R., & Heiphetz, L. (2010). Attitudes. In S. T. Fiske, D. T. Gilbert, & G. Lindzey (Eds.), *Handbook of social psychology* (5th ed., Volume One, pp. 353–393). Hoboken, NJ: John Wiley.

Bargh, J. A., Gollwitzer, P. M., & Oettingen, G. (2010). Motivation. In S. Fiske, D. T. Gilbert, & G. Lindzey (Eds.), *Handbook of social psychology* (5th ed., Volume One, pp. 268–316). New York, NY: Wiley.

Bargh, J. A., Schwader, K. L., Hailey, S. E., Dyer, R. L., & Boothby, E. J. (2012). Automaticity in social-cognitive processes. *Trends in Cognitive Science, 16*, 593–605.

Bargh, J. A., & Williams, E. L. (2006). The automaticity of social life. *Current Directions in Psychological Science, 15*, 1–4.

Barsalou, L. W. (2008). Grounded cognition. *Annual Review of Psychology, 59*, 617–645.

Bartels, A., & Zeki, S. (2000). The neural basis of romantic love. *Neuro Report, 11*, 3829–3834.

Baumeister, R. F. (1993). *Self-esteem: The puzzle of low self-regard*. New York, NY: Plenum Press.

Baumeister, R. F., & Bargh, J. A. (2014). Conscious and unconscious: Toward an integrative understanding of human life and action. In J. Sherman (Ed.), *Dual process theories of the social mind* (pp. 35–49). New York, NY: Guilford.

Baumeister, R. F., & Leary, M. R. (1995). The need to belong: Desire for interpersonal attachments as a fundamental human motivation. *Psychological Bulletin, 117*, 497–529.

Baumeister, R. F., & Masicampo, E. J. (2010). Conscious thought is for facilitating social and cultural interactions: How mental simulations serve the animal–culture interface. *Psychological Review, 117*, 945–971.

Beck, L. A., & Clark, M. S. (2009). Choosing to enter or avoid diagnostic situations. *Psychological Science, 20*, 1175–1181.

Becker, D. V., Anderson, U. S., Neuberg, S. L., Maner, J. K., Shapiro, J. R., Ackerman, J. M., Schaller, M., & Kenrick, D. T. (2010). More memory bang for the attentional buck: Self-protection goals enhance encoding efficiency for potentially threatening males. *Social Psychological and Personality Science, 1*, 182–189.

Beckes, L., & Coan, J. A. (2011). Social baseline theory: The role of social proximity in emotion and economy of action. *Social and Personality Psychology Compass, 5*, 976–988.

Bellavia, G., & Murray, S. L. (2003). Did I do that? Self-esteem related differences in reactions to romantic partners' moods. *Personal Relationships, 10*, 77–96.

Berscheid, E., & Walster, E. H. (1969). *Interpersonal attraction*. Reading, MA: Addison-Wesley.

Birnbaum, G. E., Simpson, J. A., Weisberg, Y. J., Barnea, E., & Assulin-Simhon, Z. (2012). Is it my overactive imagination? The effects of contextually activated attachment insecurity on sexual fantasies. *Journal of Social and Personal Relationships, 29*, 1131–1152.

Bowlby, J. (1969). *Attachment and loss* (Vol. 1: Attachment). London: Hogarth Press.

Brehm, S. S. (1988). Passionate love. In R. J. Steraberg & M. L. Barnes (Eds.), *The psychology of love* (pp. 232–263). New Haven, CT: Yale University Press.

Brickman, P. (1987). *Commitment, conflict, and caring*. Englewood Cliffs, NJ: Prentice-Hall.

Brinke, L. T., Stimson, D., & Carney, D. R. (2014). Some evidence for unconscious lie detection. *Psychological Science, 25*, 1098–1105.

Brown, C. M., Young, S. G., Sacco, D. F., Bernstein, M. J., & Claypool, H. M. (2009). Social inclusion facilitates interest in mating. *Evolutionary Psychology, 7*, 11–27.

Bruner, J. S., & Goodman, C. C. (1947). Value and need as organizing factors in perception. *Journal of Abnormal and Social Psychology, 42*, 33–44.

Bruner, J. S., & Postman, L. (1947). Tension and tension-release as organizing factors in perception. *Journal of Personality, 15*, 300–308.

Bullens, L., van Harreveld, F., & Forster, J. (2011). Keeping one's options open: The detrimental consequences of decision reversibility. *Journal of Experimental Social Psychology, 47*, 800–805.

Bullens, L., van Harreveld, F., Forster, J., & van der Pligt, J. (2013). Reversible decisions: The grass isn't merely greener on the other side: It's also very brown over here. *Journal of Experimental Social Psychology, 49*, 1093–1099.

Bullens, L., van Harreveld, F., Higgins, T. E., & Forster, J. (2014). How decision reversibility affects motivation. *Journal of Experimental Psychology: General, 143*, 835–849.

Cacioppo, J. T., Priester, J. R., & Berntson, G. (1993). Rudimentary determinants of attitudes II: Arm flexion and extension have differential effects on attitudes. *Journal of Personality and Social Psychology, 65*, 5–17.

Cameron, J. J., & Robinson, K. J. (2010). Don't you know how much I need you? Consequences of miscommunication vary by self-esteem. *Social Psychological and Personality Science, 1*, 136–142.

Cameron, J. J., Stinson, D. A., Gaetz, R., & Balchen, S. (2010). Acceptance is in the eye of the beholder: Self-esteem and motivated perceptions of acceptance from the opposite sex. *Journal of Personality and Social Psychology, 99*, 513–529.

Campbell, L., Simpson, J. A., Kashy, D. A., & Fletcher, G. J. O. (2001). Ideal standards, the self, and flexibility of ideals in close relationships. *Personality and Social Psychology Bulletin, 27*, 447–462.

Cantu, S. M., Simpson, J. A., Griskevicius, V., Weisberg, Y. J., Durante, K. M., & Beal, D. J. (2014). Fertile and selectively flirty: Women's behavior toward men changes across the ovulatory cycle. *Psychological Science, 25*, 431–438.

Cavallo, J., Fitzsimons, G. M., & Holmes, J. G. (2009). Taking chances in the face of threat: Romantic risk regulation and approach motivation. *Personality and Social Psychology Bulletin, 35*, 737–751.

Cavallo, J. V., Fitzsimons, G. M., & Holmes, J. G. (2010). When self-protection overreaches: Relationship-specific threat activates domain-general avoidance motivation. *Journal of Experimental Social Psychology, 46*, 1–8.

Cavallo, J., Holmes, J. G., Fitzsimons, G., Murray, S. L., & Wood, J. (2012). Managing motivational conflict: How self-esteem and executive resources influence self-regulatory responses to risk. *Journal of Personality and Social Psychology, 103*, 430–451.

Cesario, J., Plaks, J. E., Hagiwara, N., Navarrete, C. D., & Higgins, E. T. (2010). The ecology of automaticity: How situational contingencies shape action semantics and social behavior. *Psychological Science, 21*, 1311–1317.

Cesario, J., Plaks, J. E., & Higgins, E. T. (2006). Automatic social behavior as motivated preparation to interact. *Journal of Personality and Social Psychology, 90*, 893–910.

Chan, K. Q., Tong, E. M. W., & Tan, Y. L. (2014). Taking a leap of faith: Reminders of God lead to greater risk taking. *Social Psychological and Personality Science, 5*, 901–909.

Chen, M., & Bargh, J. A. (1999). Consequences of automatic evaluation: Immediate behavioral predispositions to approach or avoid the stimulus. *Personality and Social Psychology Bulletin, 25*, 215–224.

Chen, Z., Poon, K. T., & DeWall, C. N. (2015). Cold thermal temperature threatens belonging: The moderating role of perceived social support. *Social Psychological and Personality Science, 6*, 439–446.

Collins, N. L., & Feeney, B. C. (2004). Working models of attachment shape perceptions of social support: Evidence from experimental and observational studies. *Journal of Personality and Social Psychology, 87*, 363–383.

Cox, C. R., & Arndt, J. (2012). How sweet it is to be loved by you: The role of perceived regard in terror management in relationships. *Journal of Personality and Social Psychology, 102*, 616–632.

Crawford, M. T., McCarthy, R. J., Kjaerstad, H. L., & Skowronski, J. J. (2013). Inferences are for doing: The impact of approach and avoidance states on the generation of spontaneous trait inferences. *Personality and Social Psychology Bulletin, 39*, 267–278.

Critcher, C. R., & Dunning, D. (2015). Self-affirmations provide a broader perspective on self-threat. *Personality and Social Psychology Bulletin, 41*, 3–18.

Crocker, J., & Major, B. (1988). Social stigma and self-esteem: The self-protective properties of stigma. *Psychological Review, 96*, 608–630.

Crocker, J., Niiya, Y., & Mischkowski, D. (2008). Why does writing about important values reduce defensiveness? Self-affirmation and the role of positive other-directed feelings. *Psychological Science, 19*, 740–747.

de Jong, D. C., & Reis, H. T. (2014). Sexual kindred spirits: Actual and over-perceived similarity, complementarity, and partner accuracy in heterosexual couples. *Personality and Social Psychology Bulletin, 40*, 1316–1329.

Derrick, J. L., Leonard, K. E., & Homish, G. G. (2012). Dependence regulation in newlywed couples: A prospective examination. *Personal Relationships, 19*, 644–662.

Derrick, J. L., & Murray, S. L. (2007). Enhancing relationship perceptions by reducing felt inferiority: The role of attachment style. *Personal Relationships, 14*, 531–549.

Deutsch, M. (1973). *The resolution of conflict*. New Haven, CT: Yale University Press.

DeWall, C. N., MacDonald, G., Webster, G. D., Masten, C. L., Baumeister, R. F., Powell, C., . . . & Eisenberger, N. I. (2010). Tylenol reduces social pain: Behavioral and neural evidence. *Psychological Science, 21*, 931–937.

DeWall, C. N., Maner, J. K., & Rouby, D. A. (2009). Social exclusion and early-stage interpersonal perception: Selective attention to signs of acceptance. *Journal of Personality and Social Psychology, 96*, 729–741.

Dijksterhuis, A., & Nordgren, L. F. (2006). A theory of unconscious thought. *Perspectives on Psychological Science, 1*, 95–109.

Ditto, P. H., & Lopez, D. F. (1992). Motivated skepticism: Use of differential decision criteria for preferred and non-preferred conclusions. *Journal of Personality and Social Psychology, 63*, 568–584.

Doss, B. D., Rhoades, G. K., Stanley, S. M., & Markman, H. J. (2009). The effect of the transition to parenthood on relationship quality: An 8-year prospective study. *Journal of Personality and Social Psychology, 96*, 601–619.

Downey, G., Freitas, A. L., Michaelis, B., & Khouri, H. (1998). The self-fulfilling prophecy in close relationships: Rejection sensitivity and rejection by romantic partners. *Journal of Personality and Social Psychology, 75*, 545–560.

Doyle, D. M., & Molix, L. (2014). Love on the margins: The effects of social stigma and relationship length on romantic relationship quality. *Social Psychological and Personality Science, 5*, 102–110.

Drigotas, S. M., & Rusbult, C. E. (1992). Should I stay or should I go? A dependence model of break-ups. *Journal of Personality and Social Psychology, 62*, 62–87.

Drigotas, S. M., Rusbult, C. E., & Verette, J. (1999). Level of commitment, mutuality of commitment, and couple well-being. *Personal Relationships, 6*, 389–409.

Dunning, D., & Balcetis, E. (2013). Wishful seeing: How preferences shape visual perception. *Current Directions in Psychological Science, 22*, 133–137.

Dunning, D., Meyerowitz, J. A., & Holzberg, A. D. (1989). Ambiguity and self-evaluation: The role of idiosyncratic trait definitions in self-serving assessments of ability. *Journal of Personality and Social Psychology, 57*, 1082–1090.

Eastwick, P. W., Eagly, A. H., Finkel, E. J., & Johnson, S. E. (2011). Implicit and explicit preferences for physical attractiveness in a romantic partner: A double dissociation in predictive validity. *Journal of Personality and Social Psychology, 101*, 993–1011.

Eastwick, P. W., & Finkel, E. J. (2008). The attachment system in fledgling relationships: An activating role for attachment anxiety. *Journal of Personality and Social Psychology, 95*, 628–647.

Eastwick, P. W., & Hunt, L. L. (2014). Relational mate value: Consensus and uniqueness in romantic evaluations. *Journal of Personality and Social Psychology, 106*, 728–751.

Eastwick, P. W., & Neff, L. A. (2012). Do ideal partner preferences predict divorce? A tale of two metrics. *Social Psychological and Personality Science, 3*, 667–674.

Egan, L. C., Santos, L. R., & Bloom, P. (2007). The origins of cognitive dissonance: Evidence from children and monkeys. *Psychological Science, 18*, 978–983.

Eibach, R. P., & Mock, S. E. (2011). Idealizing parenthood to rationalize parental investments. *Psychological Science, 22*, 203–208.

Eisenberger, N. I. (2012). Broken hearts and broken bones: A neural perspective on the similarities between social and physical pain. *Current Directions in Psychological Science, 21*, 42–47.

Elliot, A. J., & Devine, P. G. (1994). On the motivational nature of cognitive dissonance: Dissonance as psychological discomfort. *Journal of Personality and Social Psychology, 67*, 382–394.

Elliot, A. J., & Niesta, D. (2008). Romantic red: Red enhances men's attraction to women. *Journal of Personality and Social Psychology, 95*, 1150–1164.

Elliot, A. J., Tracy, J. L., Pazda, A. D., & Beall, A. T. (2013). Red enhances women's attractiveness to men: First evidence suggesting universality. *Journal of Experimental Social Psychology, 49*, 165–168.

Farmer, H., McKay, R., & Tsakiris, M. (2014). Trust in me: Trustworthy others are seen as more physically similar to the self. *Psychological Science, 25*, 290–292.

Fay, A. J., & Maner, J. K. (2012). Warmth, spatial proximity, and social attachment: The embodied perception of a social metaphor. *Journal of Experimental Social Psychology, 48*, 1369–1372.

Fazio, R. H. (1986). How do attitudes guide behavior? In R. M. Sorrentino & E. T. Higgins (Eds.), *The handbook of motivation and cognition: Foundations of social behavior* (pp. 204–243). New York, NY: Guilford Press.

Fazio, R. H. (2007). Attitudes as object-evaluation associations of varying strength. *Social Cognition, 25*, 603–637.

Fazio, R. H., Ledbetter, J. E., & Towles-Schwen, T. (2000). On the costs of accessible attitudes: Detecting that the attitude object has changed. *Journal of Personality and Social Psychology, 78*, 197–210.

Fazio, R. H., Sanbonmatsu, D. M., Powell, F. C., & Kardes, M. R. (1986). On the automatic activation of attitudes. *Journal of Personality and Social Psychology, 50*, 229–238.

Fessler, D. M. T., & Holbrook, C. (2013). Friends shrink foes: The presence of comrades decreases the envisioned physical formidability of an opponent. *Psychological Science, 24*, 797–802.

References

Festinger, L. (1957). *A theory of cognitive dissonance*. Evanston, IL: Row Peterson.

Fincham, F. D., & Linfield, K. J. (1997). A new look at marital quality: Can spouses feel positive and negative about their marriage? *Journal of Family Psychology, 11*, 489–502.

Finkel, E. J., & Campbell, W. K. (2001). Self-control and accommodation in close relationships: An interdependence analysis. *Journal of Personality and Social Psychology, 81*, 263–277.

Finkel, E. J., Campbell, W. K., Brunell, A. B., Dalton, A. N., Scarbeck, S. J., & Chartrand, T. L. (2006). High maintenance interaction: Inefficient social coordination impairs self-regulation. *Journal of Personality and Social Psychology, 91*, 456–475.

Finkel, E. J., Cheong, E. O., Emery, L. F., Carswell, K. L., & Larson, G. M. (2015). The suffocation model: Why marriage in America is becoming an all-or-none institution. *Current Directions in Psychological Science, 24*, 238–244.

Finkel, E. J., & Eastwick, P. W. (2008). Speed-dating. *Current Directions in Psychological Science, 17*, 193–197.

Finkel, E. J., Rusbult, C. E., Kamashiro, M., & Hannon, P. A. (2002). Dealing with betrayal in close relationships: Does commitment promote forgiveness? *Journal of Personality and Social Psychology, 82*, 956–974.

Finkel, E. J., Slotter, E. B., Luchies, L. B., Walton, G. M., & Gross, J. L. (2013). A brief intervention to promote conflict reappraisal preserves marital quality over time. *Psychological Science, 24*, 1595–1601.

Finkenauer, C., Kerkhof, P., Righetti, F., & Branje, S. (2009). Living together apart: Perceived concealment as a signal of exclusion in marital relationships. *Personality and Social Psychology Bulletin, 35*, 1410–1422.

Fishbach, A., Eyal, T., & Finkelstein, S. R. (2010). How positive and negative feedback motivate goal pursuit. *Social and Personality Psychology Compass, 4*, 517–530.

Fishbach, A., & Ferguson, M. G. (2007). The goal construct in social psychology. In A. W. Kruglanski & E. T. Higgins (Eds.), *Social psychology: Handbook of basic principles* (pp. 490–515). New York, NY: Guilford.

Fishbach, A., Friedman, R. S., & Kruglanski, A. W. (2003). Leading us not into temptation: Momentary allurements elicit overriding goal activation. *Journal of Personality and Social Psychology, 84*, 296–309.

Fisher, H. E. (1998). Lust, attraction, and attachment in mammalian reproduction. *Human Nature, 9*, 23–52.

Fisher, H., Aron, A., & Brown, L. L. (2005). Romantic love: An fMRI study of a neural mechanism for mate choice. *Journal of Comparative Neurology, 493*, 58–62.

Fisher, H. E., Aron, A., Mashek, D., Haifang, L., & Brown, L. L. (2002). Defining the brain systems of lust, romantic attraction, and attachment. *Archives of Sexual Behavior, 31*, 413–419.

Fiske, S. T., Cuddy, A. J. C., & Glick, P. (2006). Universal dimensions of social cognition: Warmth and competence. *Trends in Cognitive Science, 11*, 77–83.

Fitzsimons, G. M., Finkel, E. J., & van Dellen, M. R. (2015). Transactive goal dynamics. *Psychological Review, 122*, 648–673.

Fitzsimons, G. M., & Shah, J. Y. (2008). How goal instrumentality shapes relationship evaluations. *Journal of Personality and Social Psychology, 95*, 319–337.

Fletcher, G. J. O., & Kerr, P. S. G. (2010). Through the eyes of love: Reality and illusion in intimate relationships. *Psychological Bulletin, 136*, 627–658.

Fletcher, G. J. O., Simpson, J. A., & Thomas, G. (2000). Ideals, perceptions, and evaluations in early relationship development. *Journal of Personality and Social Psychology, 79*, 933–940.

Ford, M. B., & Collins, N. L. (2010). Self-esteem moderates neuroendocrine and psychological responses to interpersonal rejection. *Journal of Personality and Social Psychology, 98*, 405–419.

Forest, A. L., Kille, D. R., Wood, J. V., & Stehouwer, L. R. (2015). Turbulent times, rocky relationships: Relational consequences of experiencing physical instability, *Psychological Science, 26*, 1261–1271.

Forest, A. L., & Wood, J. V. (2011). When partner caring leads to sharing: Partner responsiveness increases expressivity, but only for individuals with low self-esteem. *Journal of Experimental Social Psychology, 47*, 843–848.

Gable, S. L. (2005). Approach and avoidance social motives and goals. *Journal of Personality, 74*, 175–222.

Gagne, F. M., & Lydon, J. E. (2001). Mind-set and close relationships: When bias leads to (in)accurate predictions. *Journal of Personality and Social Psychology, 81*, 85–96.

Gawronski, B., & Bodenhausen, G. V. (2006). Associative and propositional processes in evaluation: An integrative review of implicit and explicit attitude change. *Psychological Bulletin, 132*, 692–731.

Gilbert, D. T., & Ebert, J. E. J. (2002). Decisions and revisions: The affective forecasting of changeable outcomes. *Journal of Personality and Social Psychology, 82*, 503–514.

Gillath, O., Mikulincer, M., Birnbaum, G. E., & Shaver, P. R. (2008). When sex primes love: Subliminal sexual priming motivates relationship goal pursuit. *Personality and Social Psychology Bulletin, 34*, 1057–1069.

Gillath, O., Mikulincer, M., Fitzsimons, G. M., Shaver, P. R., Schachner, D. A., & Bargh, J. A. (2006). Automatic activation of attachment-related goals. *Personality and Social Psychology Bulletin, 32*, 1375–1388.

Gollwitzer, P. M. (1990). Action phases and mindsets: In E. T. Higgins & R. M. Sorrentino (Eds.), *Handbook of motivation and cognition* (Vol. 2, pp. 53–92). New York, NY: Guilford.

Gomillion, S., & Murray, S. L. (2016). *Exercising caution: A dynamic model of self-protection goal pursuit in romantic relationships*. Unpublished manuscript, University at Buffalo, SUNY.

Gordon, A. M., Impett, E. A., Kogan, A., Oveis, C., & Keltner, D. (2012). To have and to hold: Gratitude promotes relationship maintenance in intimate bonds. *Journal of Personality and Social Psychology, 103*, 257–274.

Gregg, A. P., Seibt, B., & Banaji, M. R. (2006). Easier done than undone: Asymmetry in the malleability of implicit preferences. *Journal of Personality and Social Psychology, 90*, 1–20.

Griffin, D. W., & Ross, L. (1991). Subjective construal, social inference and human misunderstanding. In M. P. Zanna (Ed.), *Advances in experimental social psychology* (Vol. 24, pp. 319–359). San Diego, CA: Academic Press.

Harmon-Jones, E., Amodio, D. M., & Harmon-Jones, C. (2009). Action-based model of dissonance: A review, integration, and expansion of conceptions of cognitive conflict. In M. P. Zanna (Ed.), *Advances in experimental social psychology* (Vol. 41, pp. 119–166). London: Academic Press.

Harmon-Jones, E., Gerdjikov, T., & Harmon-Jones, C. (2008). The effect of induced compliance on relative left frontal cortical activity. A test of the action based model of dissonance. *European Journal of Social Psychology, 38*, 35–45.

Harmon-Jones, E., Harmon-Jones, C., & Levy, N. (2015). An action based model of cognitive dissonance processes. *Current Directions in Psychological Science, 24*, 184–189.

Harmon-Jones, E., Harmon-Jones, C., Serra, R., & Gable, P. A. (2014). The effect of commitment on relative left frontal cortical activity: Tests of the action based model of dissonance. *Personality and Social Psychology Bulletin, 37*, 395–408.

Harmon-Jones, C., Schmeichel, B. J., Inzlicht, M., & Harmon-Jones, E. (2011). Trait approach motivation relates to dissonance reduction. *Social Psychological and Personality Science, 2*, 21–78.

Hazan, C., & Diamond, L. M. (2000). The place of attachment in human mating. *Review of General Psychology, 4*, 186–204.

Heimpel, S. A., Elliot, A. J., & Wood, J. V. (2006). Basic personality dispositions, self-esteem, and personal goals: An approach-avoidance analysis. *Journal of Personality, 74*, 1293–1320.

Heine, S. J., Proulx, T., & Vohs, V. (2006). The meaning maintenance model: On the coherence of social motivations. *Personality and Social Psychology Review, 10*, 88–110.

Helzer, E. G., & Dunning, D. (2012). Why and when peer prediction is superior to self-protection: The weight given to future aspiration versus past achievement. *Journal of Personality and Social Psychology, 103*, 38–53.

Higgins, E. T. (1996). Knowledge activation: Accessibility, applicability, and salience. In E. T. Higgins & A. W. Kruglanski (Eds.), *Social psychology: Handbook of basic principles* (pp. 133–168). New York, NY: Guilford Press.

Hill, P. L., & Turiano, N. A. (2014). Purpose in life as a predictor of mortality across adulthood. *Psychological Science, 25*, 1482–1486.

Hofmann, W., Gschwendner, T., Friese, M., Wiers, R. W., & Schmitt, M. (2008). Working memory capacity and self-regulatory behavior: Toward an individual differences perspective on behavior determination by automatic versus controlled processes. *Journal of Personality and Social Psychology, 95*, 962–977.

Holmes, J. G., & Rempel, J. K. (1989). Trust in close relationships. In C. Hendrick (Ed.), *Review of personality and social psychology: Close relationships* (Vol. 10, pp. 187–219). Newbury Park: Sage.

Hoshino-Browne, E., Zanna, A. S., Spencer, S. J., Zanna, M. P., Kitayam, S., & Lackenbauer, S. (2005). On the cultural guises of cognitive dissonance: The case of Easterners and Westerners. *Journal of Personality and Social Psychology, 89*, 294–310.

Huang, J. Y., & Bargh, J. A. (2014). The selfish goal: Autonomously operating motivational structures as the proximate cause of human judgment and behavior. *Behavioral and Brain Sciences, 37*, 121–135.

Ijzerman, H., & Semin, G. R. (2009). The thermometer of social relations: Mapping social proximity on temperature. *Psychological Science, 10*, 1214–1220.

Ireland, M. E., Slatcher, R. B., Eastwick, P. W., Scissors, L. E., Finkel, E. J., & Pennebaker, J. W. (2011). Language style matching predicts relationship initiation and stability. *Psychological Science, 22*, 39–44.

Jaremka, L. M., Bunyan, D. P., Collins, N. L., & Sherman, D. K. (2011). Reducing defensive dissonance: Self-affirmation and risk regulation in response to relationship threats. *Journal of Experimental Social Psychology, 47*, 264–268.

Johnson, D. J., & Rusbult, C. E. (1989). Resisting temptation: Devaluation of alternative partners as a means of maintaining commitment in close relationships. *Journal of Personality and Social Psychology, 57*, 967–980.

Jonas, E., McGregor, I., Klackl, J., Agroskin, D., Fritsche, I., Holbrook, C., Nash, K., Proulx, T., & Quirin, M. (2014). Threat and defense: From anxiety to approach. In J. M. Olson & M. P. Zanna (Eds.), *Advances in experimental social psychology* (Vol. 49, pp. 219–286). San Diego, CA: Elsevier.

Jones, E. E., & Gerard, H. G. (1967). *Fundamentals of social psychology*. New York, NY: John Wiley.

Kalmijn, M. (2003). Shared friendship networks and the life course: An analysis of survey data on married and cohabiting couples. *Social Networks, 25*, 231–245.

Kane, H. S., Mc Call, C., Collins, N. L., & Blascovich, J. (2012). Mere presence is not enough: Responsive support in a virtual world. *Journal of Experimental Social Psychology, 48*, 37–44.

Karney, B. R., & Bradbury, T. N. (1995). The longitudinal course of marital quality and stability: A review of theory, methods, and research. *Psychological Bulletin, 118*, 3–34.

Karney, B. R., & Bradbury, T. N. (1997). Neuroticism, marital interaction, and the trajectory of marital satisfaction. *Journal of Personality and Social Psychology, 72*, 1075–1092.

Karremans, J. C., & Aarts, H. (2007). The role of automaticity in determining the inclination to forgive close others. *Journal of Experimental Social Psychology, 43*, 902–917.

Karrenmans, J. C., Dotsch, R., & Corneille, O. (2011). Romantic relationship status biases memory of faces of attractive opposite-sex others: Evidence from a reverse correlation paradigm. *Cognition, 121*, 422–426.

Karrenmans, J. C., & Verwijmeren, T. (2008). Mimicking attractive opposite-sex others: The role of romantic relationship status. *Personality and Social Psychology Bulletin, 34*, 939–950.

Kawakami, K., Phills, C. E., Steele, J. R., & Dovidio, J. F. (2007). (Close) Distance makes the heart grow fonder: Improving implicit racial attitudes and interracial interactions through approach behaviors. *Journal of Personality and Social Psychology, 92*, 957–971.

Kawakami, K., Steele, J. R., Cifa, C., Phills, C. E., & Dovidio, J. F. (2008). Approaching math increases math = me, math = pleasant. *Journal of Experimental Social Psychology, 44*, 818–825.

Kelley, H. H. (1979). *Personal relationships: Their structures and processes*. Hillsdale, NJ: Erlbaum.

Kelley, H. H., & Thibaut, J. W. (1978). *Interpersonal relations: A theory of interdependence*. New York, NY: Wiley.

Kenrick, D. T., Neuberg, S. L., & White, A. E. (2013). Relationships from an evolutionary life history perspective. In J. A. Simpson & L. Campbell (Eds.), *The Oxford handbook of close relationships* (pp. 13–38). Oxford: Oxford University Press.

Kille, D. R., Forest, A. L., & Wood, J. V. (2013). Tall, dark, and stable: Embodiment motivates mate selection preferences. *Psychological Science, 24*, 112–114.

Knowles, M. L., Green, A., & Weidel, A. (2014). Social rejection biases estimates of interpersonal distance. *Social Psychological and Personality Science, 5*, 158–167.

Knowles, M. L., Lucas, G. M., Molden, D. C., Gardner, W. L., & Dean, K. K. (2010). There is no substitute for belonging: Self-affirmation following social and nonsocial threats. *Personality and Social Psychology Bulletin, 36*, 173–186.

Koranyi, N., Gast, A., & Rothermund, K. (2012). Although quite nice, I was somehow not attracted by that person: Attitudes toward romantic committed opposite sex others are immune to positive evaluative conditioning. *Social Psychological and Personality Science, 4*, 403–410.

Koranyi, N., & Meissner, F. (2015). Handing over the reins: Neutralizing negative attitudes toward dependence in response to reciprocal romantic liking. *Social Psychological and Personality Science, 6*, 685–691.

Koranyi, N., & Rothermund, K. (2012a). Automatic coping mechanisms in committed relationships: Increased interpersonal trust as a response to stress. *Journal of Experimental Social Psychology, 48*, 180–185.

Koranyi, N., & Rothermund, K. (2012b). When the grass on the other side of the fence doesn't matter: Reciprocal romantic interest neutralizes attentional bias toward attractive alternatives. *Journal of Experimental Social Psychology, 48*, 186–191.

Kruglanski, A. W., Shah, J. Y., Fishbach, A., Friedman, R., Chun, W. Y., & Sleeth-Keppler, D. (2002). A theory of goal systems. In M. P. Zanna (Eds.), *Advances in experimental social psychology* (Vol. 34, pp. 331–378). San Diego, CA: Academic Press.

Kunda, Z. (1987). Motivated inference: Self-serving generation and evaluation of causal theories. *Journal of Personality and Social Psychology, 53*, 636–647.

Kunda, Z. (1990). The case for motivated reasoning. *Psychological Bulletin, 108*, 480–498.

Kunda, Z., & Sanitioso, R. (1989). Motivated changes in the self-concept. *Journal of Experimental Social Psychology, 25*, 272–285.

Kupor, D. M., Laurin, K., & Levav, J. (2015). Anticipating divine protection? Reminders of God can increase nonmoral risk taking. *Psychological Science, 26*, 374–384.

Lamarche, V. M., & Murray, S. L. (2014). Selectively myopic? Self-esteem and attentional bias in response to potential relationship threats. *Social Psychology and Personality Science, 5*, 786–795.

Lang, P. J., Bradley, M. M., & Cuthbert, B. N. (1990). Emotion, attention, and startle reflex. *Psychological Review, 97*, 377–395.

Laurin, K., Schumann, K., & Holmes, J. G. (2014). A relationship with God? Connecting with the divine to assuage fears of interpersonal rejection. *Social Psychological and Personality Science, 5*, 777–785.

Le, B., & Agnew, C. R. (2003). Commitment and its theorizes determinants: A meta-analysis of the investment model. *Personal Relationships, 10*, 37–57.

Leary, M. R., & Baumeister, R. F. (2000). The nature and function of self-esteem: Sociometer theory. In M. P. Zanna (Ed.), *Advances in experimental social psychology* (Vol. 32, pp. 2–51). San Diego, CA: Academic Press.

Leary, M. R., Tambor, E. S., Terdal, S. K., & Downs, D. L. (1995). Self-esteem as an interpersonal monitor: The sociometer hypothesis. *Journal of Personality and Social Psychology, 68*, 518–530.

LeBel, E. P., & Campbell, L. (2009). Implicit partner affect, relationship satisfaction, and the prediction of romantic break-up. *Journal of Experimental Social Psychology, 45*, 1291–1294.

Lee, L., Loewenstein, G., Ariely, D., Hong, J., & Young, J. (2008). If I'm not hot, are you hot or not? Physical attractiveness evaluations and dating preferences. *Psychological Science, 19*, 669–677.

Lee, S., Rogge, R. D., & Reis, H. T. (2010). Assessing the seeds of relationship decay: Using implicit evaluations to detect the early stages of disillusionment. *Psychological Science, 21*, 857–864.

Lemay, E. P., & Clark, M. S. (2008). How the head liberates the heart: Projection of communal responsiveness guides relationship promotion. *Journal of Personality and Social Psychology, 94*, 647–671.

Lemay, E. P., Jr., & Clark, M. S. (2015). Motivated cognition in relationships. *Current Opinion in Psychology, 1*, 72–75.

Lemay, E. P., Jr., & Dudley, K. L. (2011). Caution: Fragile! Regulating the security of chronically insecure relationship partners. *Journal of Personality and Social Psychology, 100*, 681–702.

Lemay, E. P., Jr., & Melville, M. C. (2014). Diminishing self-disclosure to maintain security in partners' care. *Journal of Personality and Social Psychology, 106*, 37–57.

Lemay, E. P., Jr., & Neal, A. (2013). The wishful memory of interpersonal responsiveness. *Journal of Personality and Social Psychology, 104*, 653–672.

Lemay, E. P., Jr., & Neal, A. M. (2014). Accurate and biased perceptions of responsive support predict well-being. *Motivation and Emotion, 38*, 270–286.

Li, T., & Fung, H. H. (2012). How negative interactions affect relationship satisfaction: The paradoxical short-term and long-term effects of commitment. *Social Psychological and Personality Science, 4*, 274–281.

Linardatos, L., & Lydon, J. E. (2011). Relationship-specific identification and spontaneous relationship maintenance processes. *Journal of Personality and Social Psychology, 101*, 737–753.

Luchies, L. B., Wieselquist, J., Rusbult, C. E., Kumashiro, M., Eastwick, P. W., Coolsen, M. K., & Finkel, E. J. (2013). Trust and biased memory of transgressions in romantic relationships. *Journal of Personality and Social Psychology, 104*, 673–694.

Lydon, J. E., & Linardatos, L. (2012). Identification: The why of relationship commitment. In L. Campbell, J. Olson, M. P. Zanna, & J. LaGuardia (Eds.), *The science of the couple: The 12th Ontario symposium*. Philadelphia, PA: Psychology Press.

Lydon, J., Meana, M., Sepinwall, D., Richards, N., & Mayman, S. (1999). The commitment calibration hypothesis: When do people devalue attractive alternatives? *Personality and Social Psychology Bulletin, 25*, 152–161.

Lydon, J. E., Menzies-Toman, D., Burton, K., & Bell, C. (2008). If-then contingences and the differential availability of an attractive alternative on relationship maintenance for men and women. *Journal of Personality and Social Psychology, 95*, 50–65.

Lykken, D. T., & Tellegen, A. (1993). Is human mating adventitious or the result of lawful choice? A twin study of mate selection. *Journal of Personality and Social Psychology, 65*, 56–68.

MacDonald, G., Baratta, P. L., & Tzalazidis, R. (2015). Resisting connection following social exclusion: Rejection by an attractive suitor provokes derogation of an unattractive suitor. *Social Psychological and Personality Science, 6*, 766–772.

MacDonald, G., & Jessica, M. (2006). Family approval as a constraint in dependency regulation: Evidence from Australia and Indonesia. *Personal Relationships, 13*, 183–194.

MacDonald, G., & Leary, M. R. (2005). Why does social exclusion hurt? The relationship between social and physical pain. *Psychological Bulletin, 131*, 202–223.

MacGregor, J. C. D., & Holmes, J. G. (2011). Rain on my parade: Perceiving low self-esteem in close others hinders positive self-disclosure. *Social Psychological and Personality Science, 2*, 523–530.

MacLean, P. (1990). *The triune brain in evolution: Role in paleocerebral function*. New York, NY: Plenum.

MacLeod, C., Mathews, A., & Tata, P. (1986). Attentional bias in emotional disorders. *Journal of Abnormal Psychology, 95*, 15–20.

Maner, J. K., & Ackerman, J. M. (2013). Love is a battlefield: Romantic attraction, intrasexual competition, and conflict between the sexes. In J. A. Simpson and L. Campbell (Eds.), *Oxford handbook of close relationships* (pp. 137–160). Oxford: Oxford University Press.

Maner, J. K., DeWall, C. N., Baumeister, R. F., & Schaller, M. (2007). Does social exclusion motivate interpersonal reconnection? Resolving the "porcupine problem." *Journal of Personality and Social Psychology, 92*, 42–55.

Maner, J. K., Gailliot, M. T., & Miller, S. L. (2009). The implicit cognition of relationship maintenance: Inattention to attractive alternatives. *Journal of Experimental Social Psychology, 45*, 174–179.

Maner, J. K., Gailliot, M. T., Rouby, D. A., & Miller, S. L. (2007). I can't take my eyes off you: Attentional adhesion to mates and rivals. *Journal of Personality and Social Psychology, 93*, 389–401.

Maner, J. K., Kenrick, D. T., Becker, V., Delton, A. W., Hofer, B., Wilbur, C. J., & Neuberg, S. L. (2003). Sexually selective cognition: Beauty captures the mind of the beholder. *Journal of Personality and Social Psychology, 85*, 1107–1120.

Maner, J. K., Kenrick, D. T., Becker, D. V., Robertson, T. E., Hofer, B., Neuberg, S. L., Delton, A. W., Butner, J., & Schaller, M. (2005). Functional projection: How fundamental social motives can bias interpersonal perception. *Journal of Personality and Social Psychology, 88*, 63–78.

Maner, J. K., Rouby, D. A., & Gonzaga, G. C. (2008). Automatic inattention to attractive alternatives: The evolved psychology of relationship maintenance. *Evolution and Human Behavior, 29*, 343–349.

Marigold, D., Cavallo, J., Holmes, J. G., & Wood, J. V. (2014). You can't always give what you want: The challenge of providing social support to low self-esteem individuals. *Journal of Personality and Social Psychology, 107*, 56–80.

Martz, J. M., Verette, J., Arriaga, X. B., Slovik, L. F., Cox, C. L., & Rusbult, C. E. (1998). Positive illusion in close relationships. *Personal Relationships, 5*, 159–181.

McCulloch, K. C., Aarts, H., Fujita, K., & Bargh, J. A. (2008). Inhibition in goal systems: A retrieval-induced forgetting account. *Journal of Experimental Social Psychology, 44*, 857–865.

McNulty, J. K. (2010a). Forgiveness increases the likelihood of subsequent partner transgressions in marriage. *Journal of Family Psychology, 24*, 787–790.

McNulty, J. K. (2010b). When positive processes hurt relationships. *Current Directions in Psychological Science, 19*, 167–171.

McNulty, J. K. (2011). The dark side of forgiveness: The tendency to forgive predicts continued psychological and physical aggression in marriage. *Personality and Social Psychology Bulletin, 37*, 770–783.

McNulty, J. K., & Fincham, F. D. (2012). Beyond positive psychology? Toward a contextual view of psychological processes and well-being. *American Psychologist, 67*, 101–110.

McNulty, J. K., & Karney, B. R. (2004). Positive expectations in the early years of marriage: Should couples expect the best or brace for the worst? *Journal of Personality and Social Psychology, 86*, 729–743.

McNulty, J. K., Olson, M. A., Meltzer, A. L., & Shaffer, M. J. (2013). Though they may be unaware, newlyweds implicitly know whether their marriage will be satisfying. *Science, 342*, 1119–1120.

McNulty, J. K., O'Mara, E. M., & Karney B. R. (2008). Benevolent cognitions as a strategy of relationship maintenance: "Don't sweat the small stuff" . . . but it is not all small stuff. *Journal of Personality and Social Psychology, 94*, 631–646.

McNulty, J. K., & Russell, V. M. (2010). When "negative" behaviors are positive: A contextual analysis of the long-term effects of problem-solving behaviors on changes in relationship satisfaction. *Journal of Personality and Social Psychology, 98*, 587–604.

Meier, M. P., Moeller, S. K., Riemer-Peltz, M., & Robinson, M. D. (2012). Sweet taste preferences and experiences predict prosocial inferences, personalities, and behavior. *Journal of Personality and Social Psychology, 102*, 163–174.

Meier, B. P., Schnall, S., Schwarz, N., & Bargh, J. A. (2012). Embodiment in social psychology. *Topics in Cognitive Science, 4*, 1–12.

Mikulincer, M., & Shaver, P. R. (2003). The attachment behavioral system in adulthood: Activation, psychodynamics, and interpersonal processes. In M. Zanna (Ed.), *Advances in experimental social psychology* (Vol. 35, pp. 52–153). New York, NY: Academic Press.

Milardo, R. M. (1982). Friendship networks in developing relationships: Converging and diverging social environments. *Social Psychology Quarterly, 45*, 162–172.

Miles, L. K., Christian, B. M., Masilamani, N., Volpi, L., & Macrae, C. N. (2104). Not so close encounters of the third kind: Visual perspective and imagined social interaction. *Social Psychological and Personality Science, 5*, 558–565.

Miller, P. J. E., Niehuis, S., & Huston, T. L. (2006). Positive illusions in marital relationships: A 13-year longitudinal study. *Personality and Social Psychology Bulletin, 32*, 1579–1594.

Miller, S. L., & Maner, J. K. (2011a). Sick body, vigilant mind: The biological immune system activates the behavioral immune system. *Psychological Science, 22*, 1467–1471.

Miller, S. L., & Maner, J. K. (2011b). Ovulation as a male mating prime: Subtle signs of women's fertility influence men's mating cognition and behavior. *Journal of Personality and Social Psychology, 100*, 295–308.

Miller, S. L., & Maner, J. K. (2012). Overperceiving disease cues: The basic cognition of the behavioral immune system. *Journal of Personality and Social Psychology, 102*, 1198–1213.

Mineka, S., & Sutton, S. K. (1992). Cognitive biases and the emotional disorders. *Psychological Science, 3*, 65–69.

Molden, D. C., Lucas, G. M., Gardner, W. L., Dean, K., & Knowles, M. L. (2009). Motivations for prevention or promotion following social exclusion: Being rejected versus being ignored. *Journal of Personality and Social Psychology, 96*, 415–431.

Mortensen, C. R., Becker, D. V., Ackerman, J. M., Neuberg, S. L., & Kenrick, D. T. (2010). Infection breeds reticence: The effects of disease salience on self-perceptions of personality and behavioral avoidance. *Psychological Science, 21*, 440–447.

Murray, S. L., Aloni, M., Holmes, J. G., Derrick, J. L., Stinson, D. A., & Leder, S. (2009). Fostering partner dependence as trust-insurance: The implicit contingencies of the exchange script in close relationships. *Journal of Personality and Social Psychology, 96*, 324–348.

Murray, S. L., Bellavia, G., Rose, P., & Griffin, D. (2003). Once hurt, twice hurtful: How perceived regard regulates daily marital interaction. *Journal of Personality and Social Psychology, 84*, 126–147.

Murray, S. L., Derrick, J., Leder, S., & Holmes, J. G. (2008). Balancing connectedness and self-protection goals in close relationships: A levels of processing perspective on risk regulation. *Journal of Personality and Social Psychology, 94*, 429–459.

Murray, S. L., Gomillion, S., Holmes, J. G., & Harris, B. L. (2015). Inhibiting self-protection in romantic relationships: Automatic partner attitudes as a resource for low self-esteem people. *Social Psychology and Personality Science, 6*, 173–182.

Murray, S. L., Gomillion, S., Holmes, J. G., Harris, B., & Lamarche, V. (2013). The dynamics of relationship promotion: Controlling the automatic inclination to trust. *Journal of Personality and Social Psychology, 104*, 305–334.

Murray, S. L., Griffin, D. W., Derrick, J., Harris, B., Aloni, M., & Leder, S. (2011). Tempting fate or inviting happiness? Unrealistic idealization prevents the decline of marital satisfaction. *Psychological Science, 22*, 619–626.

Murray, S. L., Griffin, D. W., Rose, P., & Bellavia, G. (2003). Calibrating the sociometer: The relational contingencies of self-esteem. *Journal of Personality and Social Psychology, 85*, 63–84.

Murray, S. L., & Holmes, J. G. (1999). The (mental) ties that bind: Cognitive structures that predict relationship resilience. *Journal of Personality and Social Psychology, 77*, 1228–1244.

Murray, S. L., & Holmes, J. G. (2009). The architecture of interdependent minds: A motivation-management theory of mutual responsiveness. *Psychological Review, 116*, 908–928.

Murray, S. L., & Holmes, J. G. (2011). *Interdependent minds: The dynamics of close relationships*. New York, NY: Guilford Press.

Murray, S. L., Holmes, J. G., Aloni, M., Pinkus, R. T., Derrick, J. L., & Leder, S. (2009). Commitment insurance: Compensating for the autonomy costs of interdependence in close relationships. *Journal of Personality and Social Psychology, 97*, 256–278.

Murray, S. L., Holmes, J. G., & Collins, N. L. (2006). Optimizing assurance: The risk regulation system in relationships. *Psychological Bulletin, 132*, 641–666.

Murray, S. L., Holmes, J. G., Derrick, J. L., Harris, B., Griffin, D. W., & Pinkus, R. T. (2013). Cautious to a fault: Self-protection and the trajectory of marital satisfaction. *Journal of Experimental Social Psychology, 49*, 522–533.

Murray, S. L., Holmes, J. G., Dolderman, D., & Griffin, D. W. (2000). What the motivated mind sees: Comparing friends' perspectives to married partners' views of each other. *Journal of Experimental Social Psychology, 36*, 600–620.

Murray, S. L., Holmes, J. G., & Griffin, D. (1996a). The benefits of positive illusions: Idealization and the construction of satisfaction in close relationships. *Journal of Personality and Social Psychology, 70*, 79–98.

Murray, S. L., Holmes, J. G., & Griffin, D. W. (1996b). The self-fulfilling nature of positive illusions in romantic relationship: Love is not blind, but prescient. *Journal of Personality and Social Psychology, 71*, 1155–1180.

Murray, S. L., Holmes, J. G., & Griffin, D. W. (2000). Self-esteem and the quest for felt security: How perceived regard regulates attachment processes. *Journal of Personality and Social Psychology, 78*, 478–498.

Murray, S. L., Holmes, J. G., Griffin, D. W., Bellavia, G., & Rose, P. (2001). The mismeasure of love: How self-doubt contaminates relationship beliefs. *Personality and Social Psychology Bulletin, 27*, 423–436.

Murray, S. L., Holmes, J. G., Griffin, D. W., & Derrick, J. L. (2015). The equilibrium model of relationship maintenance. *Journal of Personality and Social Psychology, 108*, 93–113.

Murray, S. L., Holmes, J. G., MacDonald, G., & Ellsworth, P. (1998). Through the looking glass darkly? When self-doubts turn into relationship insecurities. *Journal of Personality and Social Psychology, 75*, 1459–1480.

Murray, S. L., Holmes, J. G., & Pinkus, R. T. (2010). A smart unconscious? Procedural origins of automatic partner attitudes in marriage. *Journal of Experimental Social Psychology, 46*, 650–656.

Murray, S. L., Lamarche, V., Gomillion, S., Seery, M. D., & Kondrak, C. (2016). *In defense of commitment: The curative power of violated expectations*. Unpublished manuscript, University at Buffalo, SUNY.

Murray, S. L., Leder, S., McGregor, J. C. D., Holmes, J. G., Pinkus, R. T., & Harris, B. (2009). Becoming irreplaceable: How comparisons to a partner's alternatives differentially affect low and high self-esteem people. *Journal of Experimental Social Psychology, 45*, 1180–1191.

Murray, S. L., Lupien, S. P., & Seery, M. D. (2012). Resilience in the face of romantic rejection: The automatic impulse to trust. *Journal of Experimental Social Psychology, 48*, 845–854.

Murray, S. L., Pinkus, R. T., Holmes, J. G., Harris, B., Gomillion, S., Aloni, M., Derrick, J., & Leder, S. (2011). Signaling when (and when not) to be cautious and self-protective: Impulsive and reflective trust in close relationships. *Journal of Personality and Social Psychology, 101*, 485–502.

References 165

Murray, S.L., Rose, P., Bellavia, G., Holmes, J., & Kusche, A. (2002). When rejection stings: How self-esteem constrains relationship-enhancement processes. *Journal of Personality and Social Psychology, 83*, 556–573.

Murray, S. L., Rose, P., Holmes, J. G., Derrick, J., Podchaski, E., & Bellavia, G. (2005). Putting the partner within reach: A dyadic perspective on felt security in close relationships. *Journal of Personality and Social Psychology, 88*, 327–347.

Newby-Clark, I. R., McGregor, I., & Zanna, M. P. (2002). Thinking and caring about cognitive inconsistency: When and for whom does attitudinal ambivalence feel uncomfortable. *Journal of Personality and Social Psychology, 82*, 157–166.

Nordgren, L. F., van Harreveld, F., & van der Pligt, J. (2006). Ambivalence, discomfort, and motivated information processing. *Journal of Experimental Social Psychology, 42*, 252–258.

Oishi, S., Schiller, J., & Gross, E. B. (2012). Felt understanding and misunderstanding affect the perception of pain, slant, and distance. *Social Psychological and Personality Science, 4*, 259–266.

Olson, M. A., & Fazio, R. H. (2008). Implicit and explicit measures of attitudes: The perspective of the MODE model. In R. E. Petty, R. H. Fazio, & P. Brinol (Eds.), *Attitudes: Insights from the new implicit measures* (pp. 19–63). Mahwah, NJ: Erlbaum.

Orehek, E., & Vazeou-Nieuwenhuis, A. (2013). Sequential and concurrent strategies of multiple goal pursuit. *Review of General Psychology, 17*, 339–349.

Orina, M. M., Collins, W. A., Simpson, J. A., Salvatore, J. E., Haydon, K. C., & Kim, J. S. (2011). Developmental and dyadic perspectives on commitment in adult romantic relationships. *Psychological Science, 22*, 908–915.

Overall, N. C., & Fletcher, G. J. O. (2010). Perceiving regulation from intimate partners: Reflected appraisal and self-regulation processes in relationships. *Personal Relationships, 17*, 433–456.

Overall, N. C., Fletcher, G. J. O., & Simpson, J. A. (2006). Regulation processes in intimate relationships: The role of ideal standards. *Journal of Personality and Social Psychology, 91*, 662–665.

Overall, N., Lemay, E. P., Girme, Y., & Hammond, M. D. (2014). Attachment anxiety and reactions to relationship threat: The benefits and costs of inducing guilt in romantic partners. *Journal of Personality and Social Psychology, 106*, 235–256.

Overall, N. C., & Sibley, C. G. (2008). When accommodation matters: Situational dependency within daily interactions with romantic partners. *Journal of Experimental Social Psychology, 44*, 95–104.

Overall, N. C., & Sibley, C. G. (2009a). Attachment and dependence regulation within daily interactions with romantic partners. *Personal Relationships, 16*, 239–262.

Overall, N. C., & Sibley, C. G. (2009b). When rejection sensitivity matters: Regulating dependence within daily interactions with family and friends. *Personality and Social Psychology Bulletin, 35*, 1057–1070.

Panksepp, J. (1998). *Affective neuroscience: The foundations of human and animal emotions.* New York, NY: Oxford University Press.

Pietrzak, J., Downey, G., & Ayduk, O. (2005). Rejection sensitivity as an interpersonal vulnerability. In M. Baldwin (Ed.), *Interpersonal cognition* (pp. 62–84). New York, NY: Guilford Press.

Pitts, S., Wilson, J. P., & Hugenberg, K. (2014). When one is ostracized, others loom: Social rejection makes other people appear closer. *Social Psychological and Personality Science, 5*, 550–557.

Proulx, T., Inzlicht, M., & Harmon-Jones, E. (2012). Understanding all inconsistency compensation as a palliative response to violated expectations. *Trends in Cognitive Science, 16,* 285–292.

Radel, R., & Clement-Guillotin, D. (2012). Evidence of motivational influences in early visual perception: Hunger modulates conscious access. *Psychological Science, 23,* 232–234.

Randles, D., Proulx, T., & Heine, S. J. (2011). Turn-frogs and careful-sweaters: Non-conscious perception of incongruous word pairings promotes fluid compensation. *Journal of Experimental Social Psychology, 47,* 246–249.

Reis, H. T., Clark, M. S., & Holmes, J. G. (2004). Perceived partner responsiveness as an organizing construct in the study of intimacy and closeness. In D. Mashek & A. P. Aron (Eds.), *Handbook of closeness and intimacy* (pp. 201–225). Mahwah, NJ: Lawrence Erlbaum.

Righetti, F., Finkenauer, C., & Finkel, E. J. (2013). Low self-control promotes the willingness to sacrifice in close relationships. *Psychological Science, 24,* 1533–1540.

Rim, S. Y., Min, K. E., Uleman, J. S., Chartrand, T. L., & Carlston, D. E. (2013). Seeing others through rose-colored glasses: An affiliation goal and positivity bias in implicit trait impressions. *Journal of Experimental Social Psychology, 49,* 1204–1209.

Robinson, K. J., Hoplock, L. B., & Cameron, J. J. (2015). When in doubt, reach out: Touch is a covert but effective mode of soliciting and providing social support. *Social Psychological and Personality Science, 6,* 831–839.

Ross, L., & Nisbett, R. E. (1991). *The person and the situation.* New York, NY: McGraw Hill.

Rueschemeyer, S. A., Lindemann, O., van Elk, M., & Bekkering, H. (2009). Embodied cognition: The interplay between automatic resonance and selection-for-action mechanisms. *European Journal of Social Psychology, 39,* 1180–1187.

Rule, N. O., Rosen, K. S., Slepian, M. L., & Ambady, N. (2011). Mating interest improves women's accuracy in judging male sexual orientation. *Psychological Science, 22,* 881–886.

Rusbult, C. E., & Buunk, B. P. (1993). Commitment processes in close relationships: An interdependence analysis. *Journal of Social and Personal Relationships, 10,* 175–204.

Rusbult, C. E., Martz, J. M., & Agnew, C. R. (1998). The investment model scale: Measuring commitment level, satisfaction level, quality of alternatives, and investment size. *Personal Relationships, 5,* 357–391.

Rusbult, C. E., & Van Lange, P. A. M. (2003). Interdependence, interaction, and relationships. *Annual Review of Psychology, 54,* 351–375.

Rusbult, C. E., Van Lange, P. A. M., Wildschut, T., Yovetich, N. A., & Verette, J. (2000). Perceived superiority in close relationship: Why it exists and persists. *Journal of Personality and Social Psychology, 79,* 521–545.

Rusbult, C. E., Verette, J., Whitney, G. A., Slovik, L. F., & Lipkus, I. (1991). Accommodation processes in close relationship: theory and preliminary research evidence. *Journal of Personality and Social Psychology, 60,* 53–78.

Ryan, R. M., & Deci, E. L. (2000). Self-determination theory and the facilitation of intrinsic motivation, social development, and well-being. *American Psychologist, 55,* 68–78.

Sacco, D. F., Young, S. G., & Hugenberg, K. (2014). Balancing competing motives: Adaptive trade-offs are necessary to satisfy disease avoidance and interpersonal affiliation goals. *Personality and Social Psychology Bulletin, 40,* 1611–1623.

Sadikaj, G., Moskowitz, D. S., & Zuroff, D. C. (2015). Felt security in daily interactions as a mediator of the effect of attachment on relationship satisfaction. *European Journal of Personality, 29,* 187–200.

Schnall, S., Harber, K. D., Stefanucci, J. K., & Proffitt, D. R. (2008). Social support and the perception of geographical slant. *Journal of Experimental Social Psychology, 44*, 1246–1255.

Schneider, I. K., Eerland, A., van Harreveld, F., Rotteveel, M., van der Pligt, J., van der Stoep, N., & Zwaan, R. A. (2013). One way and the other: The bidirectional relationship between ambivalence and body movement. *Psychological Science, 24*, 319–325.

Schoebi, D., Karney, B. R., & Bradbury, T. N. (2012). Stability and change in the first 10 years of marriage. Does commitment confer benefits beyond the effects of satisfaction? *Journal of Personality and Social Psychology, 102*, 729–742.

Schwarz, S., & Singer, M. (2013). Romantic red revisited: Red enhances men's attraction to young, but not menopausal women. *Journal of Experimental Social Psychology, 49*, 161–164.

Scinta, A., & Gable, S. L. (2007). Automatic and self-reported attitudes in romantic relationships. *Personality and Social Psychology Bulletin, 33*, 1008–1022.

Shah, J. Y., Friedman, R., & Kruglanski, A. W. (2002). Forgetting all else: On the antecedents and consequences of goal shielding. *Journal of Personality and Social Psychology, 83*, 1261–1280.

Shah, J. Y., Kruglanski, A. W., & Friedman, R. (2003). Goal systems theory: Integrating the cognitive and motivational aspects of self-regulation. In S. J. Spencer, S. Fein, & M. P. Zanna (Eds.), *Motivated social perception: The Ontario symposium* (Vol. 9, pp. 247–275). Hillsdale, NJ: Lawrence Erlbaum.

Shallcross, S. L., & Simpson, J. A. (2012). Trust and responsiveness in strain-test situations: A dyadic perspective. *Journal of Personality and Social Psychology, 102*, 1031–1044.

Sherman, D. K., & Cohen, G. L. (2006). The psychology of self-defense: Self-affirmation theory. In M. P. Zanna (Ed.), *Advances in experimental social psychology* (Vol. 38, pp. 183–242). San Diego, CA: Academic Press.

Simpson, J. A. (2007). Psychological foundations of trust. *Current Directions in Psychological Science, 16*, 264–268.

Simpson, J. A., Gangestad, S. W., & Lerma, M. (1990). Perception of physical attractiveness: Mechanisms involved in the maintenance of romantic relationships. *Journal of Personality and Social Psychology, 59*, 1192–1201.

Simpson, J. A., Rholes, W. S., & Phillips, D. (1996). Conflict in close relationships: An attachment perspective. *Journal of Personality and Social Psychology, 71*, 899–914.

Slotter, E. B., Finkel, E. J., DeWall, C. N., Lambert, N. M., Pond, R. S., Bodenhausen, G. V., & Fincham, F. D. (2012). Putting the brakes on aggression toward a romantic partner: The inhibitory influence of relationship commitment. *Journal of Personality and Social Psychology, 102*, 291–305.

Slotter, E. B., & Gardner, W. L. (2009). Where do you end and I begin? Evidence for anticipatory, motivated self-other integration between relationship partners. *Journal of Personality and Social Psychology, 96*, 1137–1151.

Slotter, E. B., & Gardner, W. L. (2012). The dangers of dating the "bad boy" (or girl): When does romantic desire encourage us to take on the negative qualities of potential partners? *Journal of Experimental Social Psychology, 48*, 1173–1178.

Smith, E. R., & Semin, R. (2004). Socially situated cognition: Cognition in its social context. In M. P. Zanna (Ed.), *Advances in experimental social psychology* (Vol. 36, pp. 53–117). San Diego, CA: Elsevier.

Smith, E. R., & Semin, G. R. (2007). Situated social cognition. *Current Directions in Psychological Science, 16*, 132–135.

Snyder, M., & Stukas, A. A. (1999). Interpersonal processes: The interplay of cognitive, motivational, and behavioral activities in social interaction. In J. T. Spence (Ed.), *Annual review of psychology* (Vol. 50, pp. 273–303). Thousand Oaks, CA: Annual Reviews.

Steele, C. M. (1988). The psychology of self-affirmation: Sustaining the integrity of the self. In L. Berkowitz (Ed.), *Advances in experimental social psychology* (Vol. 21, pp. 261–302). San Diego, CA: Academic Press.

Stillman, T. F., Lambert, N. M., Fincham, F. D., & Baumeister, R. F. (2011). Meaning as magnetic force: Evidence that meaning in life promotes interpersonal appeal. *Social Psychological and Personality Science, 2*, 13–20.

Stinson, D. A., Cameron, J. J., Wood, J. V., Gaucher, D., & Holmes, J. G. (2009). Deconstructing the reign of error: Interpersonal warmth explains the self-fulfilling prophecy of anticipated acceptance. *Personality and Social Psychology Bulletin, 35*, 1165–1178.

Stinson, D. A., Logel, C., Shepherd, S., & Zanna, M. P. (2011). Rewriting the self-fulfilling prophecy of social rejection: Self-affirmation improves relational security and social behavior up to two months later. *Psychological Science, 22*, 1145–1149.

Swann, W. B., Hixon, J. G., & De La Ronde, C. (1992). Embracing the bitter "truth": Negative self-concepts and marital commitment. *Psychological Science, 3*, 118–121.

Tai, K., Zheng, X., & Narayanan, J. (2011). Touching a teddy bear mitigates negative effects of social exclusion to increase prosocial behavior. *Social Psychological and Personality Science, 2*, 618–626.

Tang, S., Shepherd, S., & Kay, A. C. (2014). Do difficult decisions motivate belief in fate? A test in the context of the 2012 U.S. presidential election. *Psychological Science, 25*, 1046–1048.

Thibaut, J. W., & Kelley, H. H. (1959). *The social psychology of groups*. New York, NY: Wiley.

Tomlinson, J. M., & Aron, A. (2013). The path to closeness: A mediational model for overcoming the risks of increasing closeness. *Journal of Social and Personal Relationships, 30*, 805–812.

Tooby, J., & Cosmides, L. (1996). Friendship and the banker's paradox: Other pathways to the evolution of adaptations for altruism. *Proceedings of the British Academy, 88*, 119–143.

Towles-Schwen, T., & Fazio, R. H. (2006). Automatically activated racial attitudes as predictors of the success of interracial roommate relationships. *Journal of Experimental Social Psychology, 42*, 698–705.

Tritt, S. M., Inzlicht, M., & Harmon-Jones, E. (2012). Toward a biological understanding of mortality salience (and other threat compensation processes). *Social Cognition, 30*, 715–733.

Twenge, J. M., Baumeister, R. F., Tice, D. M., & Stucke, T. S. (2001). If you can't join them, beat them: Effects of social exclusion on aggressive behavior. *Journal of Personality and Social Psychology, 81*, 1058–1069.

Uchino, B., Smith, T. W., & Berg, C. (2014). Spousal relationship quality and cardiovascular risk: Dyadic perceptions of ambivalence are associated with coronary-artery calcification. *Psychological Science, 25*, 1037–1042.

Uysal, A., Lin, H. L., & Bush, A. L. (2012). The reciprocal cycle of self-concealment and trust in romantic relationships. *European Journal of Social Psychology, 42*, 844–851.

Valentine, K. A., Norman, P. L., Penke, L., & Perrett, D. I. (2014). Judging a man by the width of his face: The role of facial ratios and dominance in mate choice at speed-dating events. *Psychological Science, 25*, 806–811.

Van Beest, I., & Williams, K. D. (2011). Why hast though forsaken me? The effect of thinking about God on well-being and prosocial behavior. *Social Psychological and Personality Science, 2*, 379–386.

van Harreveld, F., Rutjens, B. T., Rotteveel, M., Nordgren, L. R., & van der Pligt, J. (2009). Ambivalence and decisional conflict as a cause of psychological discomfort: Feeling tense before jumping off the fence. *Journal of Experimental Social Psychology, 45*, 167–173.

van Harreveld, F., Rutjens, B. T., Schneider, I. K., Nohlen, H. U., & Keskinis, K. (2014). In doubt and disorderly: Ambivalence promotes compensatory perceptions of order. *Journal of Experimental Psychology: General, 143*, 1666–1676.

van Harreveld, F., van der Pligt, J., & de Liver, Y. N. (2009). The agony of ambivalence and ways to resolve it: Introducing the MAID model. *Personality and Social Psychology Review, 13*, 45–61.

van Lange, P. A. M., Rusbult, C. E., Drigotas, S. M., Arriaga, X. B., Witcher, B. S., & Cox, C. L. (1997). Willingness to sacrifice in close relationships. *Journal of Personality and Social Psychology, 72*, 1373–1395.

Van Tongeren, D. R., Green, J. D., Hook, J. N., Davis, D. E., Davis, J. L., & Ramos, M. (2015). Forgiveness increases meaning in life. *Social Psychological and Personality Science, 6*, 47–55.

Vorauer, J. D., Cameron, J. J., Holmes, J. G., & Pearce, D. G. (2003). Invisible overtures: Fears of rejection and the signal amplification bias. *Journal of Personality and Social Psychology, 84*, 793–812.

Vorauer, J. D., & Quesnel, M. (2013). You don't really love me, do you? Negative effects of imagine-other perspective-taking on lower self-esteem individuals' relationship well-being. *Personality and Social Psychology Bulletin, 39*, 1428–1440.

Voss, A., Rothermund, K., & Brandtstädter, J. (2008). Interpreting ambiguous stimuli: Separating perceptual and judgmental biases. *Journal of Experimental Social Psychology, 44*, 1048–1056.

Waller, W. (1938). *The family: A dynamic interpretation*. New York, NY: Condon.

Whitchurch, E. R., Wilson, T. D., & Gilbert, D. T. (2011). He loves me, he loves me not: Uncertainty can increase romantic attraction. *Psychological Science, 22*, 172–175.

Wieselquist, J., Rusbult, C. E., Foster, C. A., & Agnew, C. R. (1999). Commitment, pro-relationship behavior, and trust in close relationships. *Journal of Personality and Social Psychology, 77*, 942–966.

Williams, L. E., & Bargh, J. A. (2008a). Experiencing physical warmth promotes social warmth. *Science, 322*, 606–607.

Williams, L. E., & Bargh, J. A. (2008b). Keeping one's distance: The influence of spatial distance cues on affect and evaluation. *Psychological Science, 19*, 302–308.

Wilson, T. D., & Kraft, D. (1993). Why do I love thee? Effects of repeated introspections about a dating relationship on attitudes toward the relationship. *Personality and Social Psychology Bulletin, 19*, 409–418.

Wilson, T. D., Lindsey, S., & Schooler, J. W. (2000). A dual model of attitudes. *Psychological Review, 107*, 101–126.

Wilson, T. D., & Schooler, J. W. (1991). Thinking too much: Introspection can reduce the quality of preferences and decisions. *Journal of Personality and Social Psychology, 60*, 181–192.

Wood, W., & Neal, D. T. (2007). A new look at habits and the habit–goal interface. *Psychological Review, 14*, 843–863.

Young, S. G., Slepian, M. L., & Sacco, D. F. (2015). Sensitivity to perceived facial trustworthiness is increased by activating self-protection motives. *Social Psychological and Personality Science, 6*, 607–613.

Zanna, M. P., & Cooper J. (1974). Dissonance and the Pill: An attribution approach to studying the arousal properties of dissonance. *Journal of Personality and Social Psychology, 29*, 703–709.

Zajonc, R. B. (1980). Feeling and thinking: Preferences need no inferences. *American Psychologist, 35*, 151–175.

Zayas, V., & Shoda, Y. (2005). Do automatic reactions elicited by thoughts of romantic partner, mother, and self relate to adult romantic attachment? *Personality and Social Psychology Bulletin, 8*, 1011–1025.

Zayas, V., & Shoda, Y. (2015). Love you? Hate you? Maybe it's both: Evidence that significant others trigger bivalent priming. *Social Psychological and Personality Science, 6*, 56–64.

Zheng, X., Fehr, R., Tai, K., Narayanan, J., & Gelfand, M. J. (2015). The unburdening effects of forgiveness: Effects on slant perception and jumping height. *Social Psychological and Personality Science, 6*, 431–438.

AUTHOR INDEX

Balcetis, E. 5–6
Bargh, J. A. 12, 25, 52
Baumeister, R. F. 9, 12, 17, 52
Bowlby, J. 24
Bradbury, T. N. 117–118
Brickman, P. 73
Bullens, L. 66, 67

Cavallo, J. V. 93
Clark, M. S. 116, 117
Cosmides, L. 44

Derrick, J. L. 99
Doyle, D. M. 98
Dunning, D. 5–6

Eibach, R. P. 64–65

Fehr, R. 77
Fessler, D. M. T. 24
Fiske, S. T. 22, 43
Fitzsimons, G. M. 8, 93
Forest, A. L. 86
Frost, Robert 1
Fung, H. H. 79

Gagne, F. M. 117
Gardner, W. L. 33
Gelfand, M. J. 77
Gordon, Julius 1

Harmon-Jones, E. 27
Holbrook, C. 24
Holmes, J. G. 18, 93

Jaremka, L. M. 110

Kane, H. S. 96–97
Karney, B. R. 117–118
Kille, David 16
Knowles, M. L. 91
Koranyi, N. 47
Kunda, Z. 6, 7–8

Leary, M. R. 9, 17, 26
Lemay, E. P. Jr. 116, 117
Li, T. 79
Luchies, L. B. 57
Lydon, J. E. 117
Lykken, D. T. 18, 128

MacDonald, G. 26
MacLean, P. 22
Maner, J. K. 25
McNulty, J. K. 11–12, 125
Mock, S. E. 64–65
Molix, L. 98
Mortensen, C. R. 88, 89
Murray, S. L. 18, 71, 78, 81, 131

Narayanan, J. 77
Nietzsche, Friedrich 1
Nordgren, L. F. 70

Oishi, S. 31
Overall, N. C. 46

Pitts, S. 31

Randles, D. 29
Rothermund, K. 47

Sacco, D. F. 30, 88, 89
Schoebi, D. 117–118
Schooler, J. W. 40
Schulz, Charles M. 1
Shah, J. Y. 8
Shoda, Y. 65, 66
Sibley, C. G. 46
Slepian, M. L. 30

Slotter, E. B. 33
Steele, C. M. 110
Stinson, D. A. 110–111

Tai, K. 77
Tang, S. 27
Tellegen, A. 18, 128
Tooby, J. 44

Van Harreveld, F. 66
Van Tongeren, D. R. 77–78
Voltaire 1

Williams, L. E. 25
Wilson, T. D. 40

Young, S. G. 30

Zayas, V. 65, 66
Zheng, X. 77

SUBJECT INDEX

adaptive problems 10, 14, 21, 22
ambivalence 63, 65, 66–67, 70, 72, 74, 84; *see also* uncertainty
anxiety 29
appreciation 97–98
approach motivation 26, 28–29, 32–33, 67, 92–94
arousal 27, 66; sexual 32, 74
attachment 10, 24, 36; adaptive problems 22; anxious 14, 59, 127–128, 131
attention 5, 6, 7, 150; adaptive problems 10; core goals 11, 12, 14, 21, 134; preoccupation with safety 59; responsive behavior 74–75; risk regulation model 95; value 64
attentiveness 96–97, 104
attitudes: ambivalent 65, 66, 70; automatic 20, 40–43, 53–55, 58, 60n2, 109, 118–122, 123, 140–141, 149; behavior guided by 19–20; interactionist perspective 136; unconscious 12; *see also* automatic evaluative associations
attractive alternatives 76–77, 80, 116
attractiveness 33, 73–74
automatic behavioral inclinations 53, 76, 84n1, 102–103, 149
automatic evaluative associations 12, 19–20; ambivalence 65, 66; Implicit Association Test 60n2; interactionist goal system 140–141; partner goal contagion 109, 118–122, 123; trust 36–37, 39, 40–43, 52, 53–55, 58; *see also* attitudes
availability 95, 96–97, 99, 100
avoidance 92–93

bankers' paradox 44
behavioral intentions 47, 49–50, 51, 52, 56, 58
beliefs 6–7, 36, 44–45, 52, 55–57, 58
belongingness 9–10, 17–21, 37–38, 51, 74, 150; embodiment of goals 22; future scenarios 146, 147, 148, 149; goal balance 88–89, 90, 92, 100; idealization 82; interactionist goal system 138–139; reality constraints 125, 134; relationship context 144–145; risk regulation model 87, 95–96; value 81
"better than alternatives" rule 45
bodily states 63, 69
brain processes 22–23, 26, 28, 108

caregiving relationships 23–24
categorization 6
certainty 27, 63, 64–65; *see also* conviction
closeness 32, 103, 113–114, 118, 129–130; *see also* physical proximity
commitment 3, 4, 11, 44, 70–72; biases 64; cognitive state of 69; escalation of 116–118; expectancy violations 113, 114; "principle of least interest" 38; questioning 78, 95; relationship-specific

identification 115; self-definition 147; threats to 63, 133; value goal progress 79–80, 142
compatibility 3, 4, 9, 125–126, 127–128, 130–134, 144
competence 21–22
consciousness 12
consistency 67
content 9, 125–126
context 125, 144–145
conviction 64, 68–72, 74, 77–81, 83–84; approach motivation 93; compensatory 113–114; constrained by trust 86; cycle of caring and 115; dissonance reduction 112; interactionist goal system 142; lever model 68–69, 72; safety trumped by value 107–108, 109, 115, 123
culture 28, 99

daily diaries 42, 46, 56, 75, 77–78, 79, 104
daily life tasks 18
deception 40, 98
decision making: partner choice 27, 73–74; reversible versus irreversible decisions 67
dependence 36, 37–38, 46–50, 52–53, 58; automatic evaluative associations 53–55; commitment 70–71; divesting 98, 99; interactionist goal system 141–142; low self-esteem 102; minimization of 49–50, 92; parenthood 85; positive attitudes toward 74; reasoned beliefs 56; risk regulation balance 95; risky situations 102–103; situational calibration 51–52; trust 40, 99
diaries 42, 46, 56, 75, 77–78, 79, 104
disease 88–89, 90, 92, 100
dissonance 27–28, 63, 91–92, 150; conviction 69–70, 79, 142; expectancy violations 112; self-affirmation 110
distance 23, 24–25, 50, 95, 97, 99, 121–122
distrust 49–50, 51, 97, 141
divorce 5, 83
doubt 63, 79, 83–84
dynamism 138, 140–143

embeddedness 136, 144–145
embodiment 19, 22, 23–29, 150; embodied cognition 16–17; interactionist goal system 136; safety 20–21, 23–26, 30–32; value 20–21, 26–29, 32–33

"equal match" rule 45
equality 38, 40
equilibrium model of relationship maintenance 78–79
evolutionary theory 10, 22–23, 28, 87
exchange script 48–49
executive resources 41–42
expectancy violations 29, 62–63, 70, 111–114, 123

fairness 45
family relationships 99
fear 25
financial stress 4, 146, 148
forgiveness 6, 40, 44, 57, 76, 118; commitment linked to 80; interactionist goal system 141–142; reality constraints 8; relationship-promotive action 63; research on 77–78; risk regulation model 95
friends 8–9, 10, 23, 24, 62, 138

goals 7–8, 10–14, 17; co-regulation 88; conflicting 13, 87; coordination of 18; embodied 23; future scenarios 145–149; general and relational 30; interactionist goal system 136–145, 150; partner goal contagion 106, 109, 118–122, 123; partner's interference with 75–76, 103–104; reality constraints 14, 124–134; reversal of 102–104, 133–134; risk regulation balance 91–92; satiation of 92; situational affordances 14, 37, 51, 128–129, 130; transactive goal pursuit 104–105, 109, 118; see also safety; value
God, belief in 93–94, 103

habit formation 133
happiness 2, 125
harm 17, 21–22, 23–26, 30–32, 34, 36; see also self-protection
health 84, 88–89
heterosexuality 15n1, 73, 74
hypochondria 100, 101, 130

IAT see Implicit Association Test
iceberg model of trust 39, 52
idealization 81–83, 103
identity: professional 146, 147; relationship-specific identification 115–116, 123; social 98, 99
IF-THEN tendency 44, 52, 78, 131, 133
illusions, positive 81–83, 96, 104

Implicit Association Test (IAT) 41, 42, 54, 61n2, 119
incompatibility 18, 128, 130–132, 133–134, 145
inequality 38, 40, 46
infants 23–24
infatuation 108, 128
inference 5, 6, 7; adaptive problems 10; core goals 12, 14, 21, 134; preoccupation with safety 59; responsive behavior 74–75; value 64
inferiority 48, 51, 52
influence 9, 125–126
ingratitude 97–98, 99
interactionist perspective 2, 136–145, 150
interconnection 137, 138–140
interdependence 10, 17, 37–38, 62, 65; commitment 71; reality constraints 126; transitions 58; trust 36; unexpected costs of 99; value goal progress 72, 115
interests 9, 18, 126–127, 130
interpersonal connections 89, 92, 110, 111
intuition 40

love 1, 8, 33, 108
loyalty 44

marital satisfaction *see* satisfaction
maternal rejection 93
meaning *see* purpose
meaning maintenance 111–112, 150
memory 5, 6, 64, 101; biases 57; working-memory capacity 42, 119–120
men 33, 73–74
mental representations 16–17, 52, 63, 147
mindreading 35–36, 38, 47
misattribution paradigms 70
MODE (Motivation and Opportunity as DEterminants) model 129
motivated cognition 1–2, 5–8, 59, 81, 105, 125
motivation 2–3, 5–7, 39, 117; *see also* goals
mutual dependence 36, 37, 46–50, 51, 53

negative affect 66
newlywed couples: automatic attitudes 41; commitment 71, 78, 117–118; conscious and unconscious attitudes 11–12; lack of trust 99; mutual dependence 48; partner's interference with goals 76; positive illusions 81–83; reversal of goals 133; safety goal pursuit 131–133; self-esteem 104

non-responsiveness 41–42, 76, 129, 143, 146–148; *see also* responsiveness
nurturing behavior 94, 95, 101, 106

optimism 5, 7, 71, 82, 125
order 67, 112
other-oriented motivations 7

pain 25–26
parenthood 21, 58, 64–65, 85, 146
partner choice 27, 73–74, 128
perception 5–6, 20; core goals 11; social 22, 43; value 64
perceptual biases: responsive behavior 74–75; safety 47–48, 49–51, 52, 56–57, 58; situational goal affordances 128; value 64
personal investment 115, 116–117, 123; *see also* commitment
personality 14, 18, 31, 128, 147
physical attractiveness 33, 73–74
physical proximity 23, 24–25, 28–29, 30–32
physical sensations 16–17, 19, 20–21, 33
physical stability 16, 86, 94
positive affect 12
positive illusions 81–83, 96, 104
positivity 42–43
power 38
preferences 3, 6, 7, 9, 18, 126, 128
prevention-orientation 80, 143
"principle of least interest" 38
prioritization 114–115, 129–133, 138, 143–144, 145, 149
promotion-orientation 80, 143
proximity 23, 24–25, 28–29, 30–32
psychological safety 90, 91, 92, 93
purpose 23, 26–29, 32, 66, 67, 71; *see also* value

race 25, 29, 34, 98
reality constraints 8, 13–14, 123, 124–134
reasoned beliefs 36, 44–45, 52, 55–57, 58
rejection 26, 31–32, 35–36, 51–52; automatic attitudes 41, 42, 54, 109, 118–122; maternal 93; reasoned beliefs 56; risk of 38; self-fulfilling prophecies 106
relationship-promotive action 63–64, 68–69, 74, 87, 92
relationship-specific identification 115–116, 123
religion 93–94

Subject Index

resilience 71, 120
resistance 68–69, 72, 74–77, 99, 134n1, 134n2; commitment 79–80; positive illusions 82; promotion-orientation 143; relationship context 144; reversing goals 102; situational 126–127
response conflicts 26–27, 28
responsiveness 10, 17–19, 56–57, 74–75, 100; automatic attitudes 118; conviction 77; future scenario 148–149; interactionist goal system 139; projection of communal 116; promotion-orientation 143; risk regulation model 96; value and 81; *see also* non-responsiveness
reversal of goals 102–104, 133–134
risk: risk taking 93; situational 46, 126–127
risk regulation model 86–87, 90–100, 107–109, 111, 115, 140, 147
romantic infatuation 108, 128

sacrifice 40, 56–57, 64, 81, 118; commitment linked to 80; costs of 74; future scenarios 147, 149; interactionist goal system 140; reasoned beliefs 44–45; relationship-promotive action 63; resistance situations 72, 75, 99; risk regulation model 95
safety 10–11, 12–13, 17, 34, 35–61, 84; automatic attitudes and partner goal contagion 118–122; belongingness goal balance 88–89; conflict with value 85–87, 101, 102, 106; dependence 46–50; desired end-state 37–38; embodiment of 20–21, 23–26, 30–32; expectancy violations 113–114; future scenarios 145–149; general and relational goals 30; goal progress 19–20, 52–53, 140–141; interactionist goal system 136, 138–142, 143–145; preoccupation with 58–60, 106, 129, 145, 146; preparedness for 21–22; reality constraints 14, 124–125, 129–133, 134; risk regulation balance 86, 90–100, 107–109, 111, 140; self-esteem 100–104; self-fulfilling prophecies 105–106; situational calibration 51–52; transactive goal pursuit 104–105, 109, 118; trumped by value 107–123; trust 38–46, 52–58; value trumped by 85–106

same-sex relationships 15n1
satisfaction 12, 99, 125; commitment 117–118; expectancy violations 112, 113–114; positive illusions 81–83; safety goal pursuit 130–133; satisfaction constraints 145
secrets 98, 99
self-affirmation 110–111, 114, 123, 139, 144, 147, 149
self-concept 7, 33, 91
self-disclosure 2, 59, 99, 108, 127–128
self-esteem 2, 14, 18; automatic attitudes 41, 119–122; partner compatibility 127–128, 131; partners of low self-esteem people 105; professional identity 146; relationship-specific identification 115, 116; risk regulation model 87; safety 59–60, 84, 100–104, 105, 129, 145; trust 106n1; value 84, 107, 110, 114, 123, 149
self-fulfilling prophecies 105–106
self-image 5–6
self-interest 18–19, 44–45, 75, 126
self-protection 23–26, 30–32, 34, 110, 118; *see also* safety
self-regulation 103, 119–120, 121, 129, 144
sequential priming tasks 65
sex 4, 33, 81; fantasies 93; sexual arousal 32, 74
situations 8–9, 10, 14, 18, 34, 37; reality constraints 125–126; resistance 72, 74–77, 79–80, 82, 99, 102, 103–104, 134n1, 134n2, 143–144; risk regulation balance 91, 92–93, 94–95; risky 46, 55–56, 102–103, 115, 119–122, 123, 126–127, 134n1, 134n2, 143–144, 149; situational landscape 85–86, 140, 144–145, 146–147, 148, 149
social identity 98, 99
social isolation 25–26
social pain 26
social perception 22, 43
sociometer model 101
stability 16, 17, 86
stigma 98, 99
support 40, 104, 105; lack of 97, 99, 101; low self-esteem 128; relationship-promotive action 63; risk regulation model 95
suspicion 49–50, 51

 Taylor & Francis eBooks

Helping you to choose the right eBooks for your Library

Add Routledge titles to your library's digital collection today. Taylor and Francis ebooks contains over 50,000 titles in the Humanities, Social Sciences, Behavioural Sciences, Built Environment and Law.

Choose from a range of subject packages or create your own!

Benefits for you
» Free MARC records
» COUNTER-compliant usage statistics
» Flexible purchase and pricing options
» All titles DRM-free.

 REQUEST YOUR **FREE** INSTITUTIONAL TRIAL TODAY

Free Trials Available
We offer free trials to qualifying academic, corporate and government customers.

Benefits for your user
» Off-site, anytime access via Athens or referring URL
» Print or copy pages or chapters
» Full content search
» Bookmark, highlight and annotate text
» Access to thousands of pages of quality research at the click of a button.

eCollections – Choose from over 30 subject eCollections, including:

Archaeology	Language Learning
Architecture	Law
Asian Studies	Literature
Business & Management	Media & Communication
Classical Studies	Middle East Studies
Construction	Music
Creative & Media Arts	Philosophy
Criminology & Criminal Justice	Planning
Economics	Politics
Education	Psychology & Mental Health
Energy	Religion
Engineering	Security
English Language & Linguistics	Social Work
Environment & Sustainability	Sociology
Geography	Sport
Health Studies	Theatre & Performance
History	Tourism, Hospitality & Events

For more information, pricing enquiries or to order a free trial, please contact your local sales team:
www.tandfebooks.com/page/sales

 Routledge
Taylor & Francis Group

The home of Routledge books

www.tandfebooks.com

"thinking is for doing" principle 17, 34
touch 32, 108
transgressions 8, 57, 77–78, 80, 116, 118, 133–134, 141–142
transitions 21, 58, 62–63, 117, 140, 144, 145
trust 11, 12–13, 36–37, 38–46, 50–51, 52–58; automatic attitudes 109, 119; betrayal in trust games 93; conviction 80, 86; dependence 47–48; distrust and suspicion 49–50; experience of 60n1; future scenarios 148; iceberg model of 39, 52; interactionist goal system 140–141; newlyweds 99; partner availability and responsiveness 100; preoccupation with safety 59; risk regulation model 94–95, 96; safety distinct from 36; safety goal pursuit 131–132, 134; secrets 98; self-affirmation 110–111; self-esteem 106n1; self-protection 30; situational calibration 51–52; threats to commitment 133

uncertainty 27–28, 29, 63, 66, 123; conviction 68, 69, 114, 142; parents 64–65; partner choice 64, 73–74; romantic infatuation 108; *see also* ambivalence
unconscious processes 12, 26

value 10–11, 12–13, 17, 34, 62–84; automatic attitudes and partner goal contagion 118–122; belongingness goal balance 88–89; commitment 70–72; conflict with safety 85–87, 101, 102, 106; decision deliberation 73–74; decision implementation 74–77; desired end-state 64–67; dissonance 69–70; embodiment of 20–21, 26–29, 32–33; expectancy violations 111–114; future scenarios 145–149; general and relational goals 30; goal progress 19–20, 72–73, 79–80, 142; interactionist goal system 136, 138–140, 142–145; positive illusions 81–83; preparedness for 21–22; reality constraints 14, 124–125, 133–134; risk regulation balance 86, 90–100, 107–109, 111, 115, 140, 147; safety trumped by 107–123; self-affirmation 110–111, 114, 123, 149; self-esteem 102–104; social perception 43; transactive goal pursuit 104–105, 109, 118; trumped by safety 85–106; *see also* conviction
"values traits" rule 44–45
virtual worlds 96–97
visual perception 5–6, 20
vulnerability 38, 46–48, 49, 51, 53; automatic attitudes 118–122; lack of trust 100; preoccupation with safety 58–60, 106; risk regulation balance 95; value prioritization 114–115

warmth 21, 23–24, 32
withdrawal 97
women 33, 73–74, 76–77, 93, 117–118
working-memory capacity 42, 119–120